CRUSADE

CRUSADE

Chronicles of an Unjust War

JAMES CARROLL

METROPOLITAN BOOKS

HENRY HOLT AND COMPANY | NEW YORK

Metropolitan Books
Henry Holt and Company, LLC
Publishers since 1866
115 West 18th Street
New York, New York 10011

Metropolitan Books™ is a registered
trademark of Henry Holt and Company, LLC.

Library of Congress Cataloging-in-Publication Data

Carroll, James, 1943–
    Crusade : chronicles of an unjust war / James Carroll.—1st ed.
    p. cm.
    ISBN 0-8050-7703-0
    1. Iraq War, 2003.   2. War on Terrorism, 2001–   I. Title.

DS79.76.C365 2004
956.7044'3—dc22   2004044988

Henry Holt books are available for special promotions and
premiums. For details contact: Director, Special Markets.

First Edition 2004
Designed by Victoria Hartman
Printed in the United States of America
1   3   5   7   9   10   8   6   4   2

For William Sloane Coffin Jr.

In dark times will there also be singing?
Yes. There will also be singing about the dark times.

—*Bertolt Brecht*

CONTENTS

PART THREE · AS TO WAR

INTRODUCTION

At the turn of the millennium, the world was braced for terrible things. Most "rational" worries were tied to an anticipated computer glitch, the Y2K problem, and even the most scientifically oriented of people seemed temporarily at the mercy of powerful mythic forces. Imagined hobgoblins leaped from hard drives directly into nightmares. Airlines canceled flights scheduled for the first day of the new year, citing fears that the computers for the traffic control system would not work. The calendar as such had not previously been a source of dread, but all at once, time itself held a new danger. As the year 2000 approached, I bought bottled water and extra cans of tuna fish. I even withdrew a large amount of cash from the bank. Friends mocked me, then admitted to having done similar things. There were no dances-of-death or outbreaks of flagellant cults, but a millennial fever worthy of medieval superstition infected the most secular of cultures. Of course, the mystical date came and went, the computers did fine, airplanes flew, and the world went back to normal.

Then came September 11, 2001, the millennial catastrophe—just a little late. Airplanes fell from the sky, thousands died, and an entirely new kind of horror gripped the human imagination. Time, too, played its role, but time as warped by television, which created a global simultaneity, turning the whole human race into a witness, as the awful events were endlessly replayed, as if those bodies leaping from the Twin Towers would never hit the ground. Nightmare in broad daylight. New York's World Trade Center collapsed not just onto the surrounding streets but into the hearts of every person with access to CNN. Hundreds of millions of people instinctively reached out to those they loved, grateful to be alive. Death had shown itself in a new way. But if a vast throng experienced the terrible events of 9-11 as one, only one man, the president of the United States, bore a unique responsibility for finding a way to respond to them.

George W. Bush plumbed the deepest place in himself, looking for a simple expression of what the assaults of September 11 required. It was his role to lead the nation, and the very world. The president, at a moment of crisis, defines the communal response. A few days after the assault, George W. Bush did this. Speaking spontaneously, without the aid of advisers or speechwriters, he put a word on the new American purpose that both shaped it and gave it meaning. "This crusade," he said, "this war on terrorism."

Crusade. I remember a momentary feeling of vertigo at the president's use of that word, the outrageous ineptitude of it. The vertigo lifted, and what I felt then was fear, sensing not ineptitude but exactitude. My thoughts went to the elusive Osama bin Laden, how pleased he must have been, Bush already reading from his script. I am a Roman Catholic with a feeling for history, and strong regrets, therefore, over what went wrong in my own tradition once the Crusades were launched. Contrary to schoolboy romances, Hollywood fantasies, and the nostalgia of royalty, the Crusades were a set of world-historic crimes. I hear the word with a third ear, alert to its dangers. Bush's use of *crusade*, as it were, conscripted my complete attention, and from that instant on I found myself an unwilling witness to the slow-motion wreck of American values that has occurred over the past three years. I had long been a writer of slice-of-life essays. My subject had been the passing scene, but once George Bush launched his crusade, it became my only subject. Week after week, despite myself, I wrote, in my column in the *Boston Globe*, of almost nothing else. This is the record of what I witnessed, and I offer it here to mark the most extraordinary shift in American meaning and purpose of which I am aware.

Memory fades, and the past gets forever twisted up in arguments of the present. But a close reading of what actually happened as Bush and his circle used the moment of postmillennial crisis in an attempt to transform politics and culture can make plain why that transformation must not be brought to completion. How Bush used a crime to justify a war. How he deflected one failure—to capture bin Laden—into another—bringing "order" to Afghanistan. How he declared victory in Iraq, as a slow, grinding defeat was just beginning. How the airy ambitions of a neoconservative clique were thwarted by a combination of primitive fervor, tribal factionalism, and the simple stubbornness of human beings who refuse to be told what to think and feel. How the expectation that other nations, including once firm allies, would have no choice but to obey an imperial Washington proved to be illusion. How the wars of the Middle East went from bad to worse. How George W. Bush proved to be the ultimate proliferator. How he lied to us. How he betrayed, above all, the young men and women whom he so carelessly sent into harm's way. On September 11, 1990, as it happened, George W. Bush's father had declared a "new world order." Eleven years to the day later, the son set out on his crusade to make that order his. Destruction followed upon destruction, and this is its chronicle.

•   •   •

For George W. Bush, *crusade* was an offhand reference. But all the more powerfully for that, it was an accidental probing of unintended but nevertheless real meaning. That the president used the word inadvertently suggests how it expressed his exact truth, an unmasking of his most deeply felt purpose. *Crusade*, he said. Later, his embarrassed aides suggested that he had meant to use the word only as a synonym for *struggle*, but Bush's own syntax belied that. He *defined crusade* as *war*. Even offhandedly, he had said exactly what he meant.

Osama bin Laden was already understood to be trying to spark a "clash of civilizations" that would set the West against the whole House of Islam. After 9-11, agitated voices on all sides insisted that no such clash was inevitable. But *crusade* was a match for *jihad*, and such words threatened nothing less than apocalyptic conflict between irreconcilable cultures. Indeed, the president's reference flashed through the Arab news media. Its resonance went deeper, even, than the embarrassed aides expected—and not only among Muslims. After all, the word refers to a long series of military campaigns, which, taken together, were the defining event in the shaping of what we call Western civilization. A coherent set of political, economic, social, and even mythological traditions of the Eurasian continent, from the British Isles to the far side of Arabia, grew out of the transformations wrought by the Crusades. And it is far from incidental still, both that those campaigns were conducted by Christians against Muslims, and that they, too, were attached to the irrationalities of millennial fever.

If the American president was the person carrying the main burden of shaping a response to the catastrophe of September 11, his predecessor in such a grave role, nearly a thousand years earlier, was the Catholic pope. Seeking to overcome the century-long dislocations of a postmillennial Christendom, he rallied both its leaders and commoners with a rousing call to holy war. Muslims were the infidel people who had taken the Holy Land hundreds of years before. Now, that occupation was defined as an intolerable blasphemy. The Holy Land must be redeemed. Within months of the pope's call, a hundred thousand people had "taken the cross" to reclaim the Holy Land for Christ. As a proportion of population of Europe, a comparable movement today would involve more than a million people, dropping everything to go to war.

In the name of Jesus, and certain of God's blessing, crusaders launched what might be called "shock and awe" attacks—laying siege, first, to the Asia Minor city of Nicaea, where they used catapults to hurl the severed heads of Muslim defenders over fortified walls. In Jerusalem they savagely slaughtered Muslims and Jews alike—practically the whole city. Eventually, Latin crusaders would turn on Eastern Christians, and then on Christian heretics, as blood-lust outran the initial "holy" impulse. That trail of violence scars the earth and human memory even to this day—especially in the places where the crusaders wreaked their havoc. And the mental map of the Crusades, with Jerusalem at the center of the earth, still defines world politics. But the main point, in relation to Bush's instinctive response to 9-11, is that those religious invasions and wars of long ago established a cohesive Western identity precisely in opposition to Islam, an opposition that survives to this day.

With the Crusades, the violent theology of the killer God came into its own. To save the world, in this understanding, God willed the violent death of God's only beloved son. Here is the relevance of that mental map, for the crusaders were going to war to rescue the site of the salvific death of Jesus, and they displayed their devotion to the cross on which Jesus died by wearing it on their breasts. When Bush's remark was translated into Arabic for broadcast throughout the Middle East, the word *crusade* was rendered as *war of the cross*.

Before the Crusades, Christian theology had given central emphasis to the resurrection of Jesus, and to the idea of incarnation itself, but with the war of the cross, the bloody crucifixion began to dominate the Latin Christian imagination. A theology narrowly focused on the brutal death of Jesus reinforced the primitive notion that violence can be a sacred act. The cult of martyrdom, even to the point of suicidal valor, was institutionalized in the Crusades, and it is not incidental to the events of 9-11 that a culture of sacred self-destruction took equally firm hold among Muslims. The suicide-murderers of the World Trade Center, like the suicide-bombers from the West Bank and Gaza, exploit a perverse link between the willingness to die for a cause and the willingness to kill for it. Crusaders, thinking of heaven, honored that link, too.

Here is the deeper significance of Bush's inadvertent reference to the Crusades: instead of being a last recourse or a necessary evil, violence was established then as the perfectly appropriate, even chivalrous, first response to what is wrong in the world. George W.

Bush is a Christian for whom this particular theology lives. While he identified Jesus as his "favorite political philosopher" when running for president in 2000, the Jesus of this evangelical president is not the "turn-the-other-cheek" one. Bush's savior is the Jesus whose cross is wielded as a sword. George W. Bush, having cheerfully accepted responsibility for the executions of 152 death-row inmates in Texas, had already shown himself to be entirely at home with divinely sanctioned violence. After 9-11, no wonder it defined his deepest urge.

But sacred violence, once unleashed in 1096, as in 2001, had a momentum of its own. The urgent purpose of war against the "enemy outside"—what some today call the "clash of civilizations"—led quickly to the discovery of an "enemy inside." The crusaders, en route from northwestern Europe to attack the infidel far away, first fell upon, as they said, "the infidel near at hand." Jews. For the first time in Europe, large numbers of Jews were murdered for being Jews. A crucifixion-obsessed theology saw God as willing the death of Jesus, but in the bifurcated evangelical imagination, Jews could be blamed for it, and the offense the crusaders took was mortal.

The same dynamic—war against an enemy outside leading to war against an enemy inside—can be seen at work today. It is a more complex dynamic now, with immigrant Muslims, and people of Arabic descent, coming under heavy pressure in the West. In Europe, Muslims are routinely demonized. In America, they are "profiled," even to the point of being deprived of basic rights. But at the same time, once again, Jews are targeted. The broad resurgence of anti-semitism, and the tendency to scapegoat Israel as the primary source of the new discord, reflect an old tidal pull. This is true notwithstanding the harsh fact that Ariel Sharon's government took up the Bush "dead-or-alive" credo with enthusiasm and used the "war on terrorism" to fuel self-defeating overreactions to Palestinian provocations. But some of Israel's critics fall into the old pattern of measuring Jews against standards to which no one else is held, not even our president. That the war on terrorism is the context within which violence in Israel and Jerusalem has intensified should be no surprise. It wasn't "Israel" then, but conflict over Jerusalem played exactly such a flashpoint role a thousand years ago.

The Crusades proved to have other destructive dynamics as well. The medieval war against Islam, having also targeted Europe's Jews, soon enough became a war against all forms of cultural and religious dissent, a war against heresy. As it hadn't been in hundreds of years, doctrine now became rigidly defined in the Latin West, and those who did not affirm dominant interpretations—Cathars, Albigensians, Eastern Orthodox—were attacked. Doctrinal uniformity, too, could be enforced with sacred violence. When the U.S. attorney general defines criticism of the administration in wartime as treason, or when Congress enacts legislation that justifies the erosion of civil liberties with appeals to patriotism, they are enacting a Crusades script.

All of this is implicit in the word that President Bush first used, that came to him as naturally as a baseball reference, to define the war on terrorism. That such a dark, seething religious history of sacred violence remains largely unspoken in our world does not defuse it as an explosive force in the human unconscious. In the world of Islam, of course, its meaning could not be more explicit, or closer to consciousness. The full historical and cultural significance of *crusade* is instantly obvious, which is why a howl of protest from the Middle East drove Bush into instant verbal retreat. Yet the very inadvertence of his use of *crusade* is the revelation: Americans do not know what fire they are playing with. Osama bin Laden, however, knows all too well, and in his periodic pronouncements, he uses the word *crusade* to this day, as a flamethrower.

Religious war is the danger here, and it is a graver one than Americans think. Despite our much vaunted separation of church and state, America has always had a quasi-religious understanding of itself, reflected in the messianism of Puritan founder John Winthrop, the Deist optimism of Thomas Jefferson, the embrace of redemptive suffering that marked Abraham Lincoln, and, for that matter, the conviction of Eisenhower's secretary of state, John Foster Dulles, that communism had to be opposed on a global scale if only because of its atheism. But never before has America been brought deeper into a dynamite-wired holy of holies than in our president's war on terrorism. Despite the post-Iraq toning down of Washington's rhetoric of empire, and the rejection of further crusader references—although Secretary of State Colin Powell used the word in March 2004—Bush's war openly remains a cosmic battle between nothing less than the transcendent forces of good and evil. Such a battle is necessarily unlimited and open-ended, and so justifies radical actions—the abandonment, for example, of established notions of civic justice at home and of traditional alliances abroad.

A cosmic moral-religious battle justifies, equally, risks of world-historic proportioned disaster, since the ultimate outcome of such a conflict is to be measured not by actual consequences on this earth but by the earth-transcending will of God. Our war on terrorism, before it is anything else, is thus an *imagined* conflict, taking place primarily in a mythic realm beyond history.

In waging such a "war," the enemy is to be engaged everywhere and nowhere, not just because the actual nihilists who threaten the social order are faceless and deracinated, but because each fanatical suicide-bomber is only an instance of the transcendent enemy—and so the other face of us. Each terrorist is, in effect, a sacrament of the larger reality, which is "terrorism." Instead of perceiving unconnected centers of inhuman violence—tribal warlords, mafia chieftains, nationalist fighters, xenophobic Luddites—President Bush projects the grandest and most interlocking strategies of conspiracy, belief, and organization. By the canonization of the war on terrorism, petty nihilists are elevated to the status of world-historic warriors, exactly the fate they might have wished for. This is why the conflict readily bleeds from one locus to another—Afghanistan now, Iraq then, Iran or some other land of evil soon—and why, for that matter, the targeted enemies are entirely interchangeable—here Osama bin Laden, there Saddam Hussein, here the leader of Iran, there of North Korea. They are all essentially one enemy—one "axis"—despite their differences from each other, or even hatred of each other.

George W. Bush has taken on, as he pridefully declares, Evil itself. (In 2004, shapers of the "Bush Doctrine" David Frum and Richard Perle published a book titled *An End to Evil*.) Bush does this with no awareness of the association between his project and larger, mythic forces, but future historians may well look back on America's panic-stricken global campaign in the context of millennial fever. It happened a thousand years ago, and it is happening now. The idea of the millennium seems to stimulate an apocalyptic imagination, a sense that end-time is dawning, an epoch when some final battle between good and evil is destined to be undertaken. (And one sign of that end-time in the evangelical imagination is the elimination—through conversion or sacred violence—of the infidel, an expectation that unconsciously plays its part in the hatred of Muslims, in fresh hostility toward Jews, and even in the Christian right's anxious support of Israel, as a prelude to Jewish conversion.) One needn't attribute the kooky extremes of this intuition to Bush to recognize in his rhetoric signs of a cosmic concern that transcends geopolitics and national security.

The Crusades, too, were a manifestation of end-time millennialism. When crusaders slaughtered the infidel, and forced conversion on Jews, they thought they were ushering in the new age. Robert Jay Lifton shows how this phenomenon manifests itself now, with Islamist and American apocalyptic visions in fierce competition, both aimed at "purification and renewal." In his book *Superpower Syndrome*, Lifton observes, "We are experiencing what could be called an apocalyptic face-off between Islamist forces, overtly visionary in their willingness to kill and die for their religion, and American forces claiming to be restrained and reasonable but no less visionary in their projection of a cleansing war-making and military power."

Hard-boiled men and women who may not share Bush's fervent spirituality can nonetheless support his purpose because, undergirding the new ideology, there *is* an authentic global crisis that requires an urgent response. New technologies are now making it possible for small groups of nihilists, or even single individuals, to wreak havoc on a scale unprecedented in history. This is the ultimate "asymmetric threat." The attacks of 9-11, amplified by the murderous echo of the anthrax mailer, the as yet unapprehended psychopath who sent deadly letters to journalists and government officials in the weeks after 9-11, put that new condition on display for all the world to see. Innovations in physics, biology, chemistry, and information technology—and soon, possibly, in nanotechnology and genetic engineering—have had the unforeseen effect of threatening to put in a few hands the destructive power that, in former times, could be exercised only by sizable armies. The millennialist Adolf Hitler was a crackpot nonentity until he had the German nation behind him, and promises of a thousand-year Reich helped him do it. Today's Hitler needs no nation, no party, no army. A pound of anthrax will do. A suitcase nuke. Even a cleverly manipulated computer virus. Such power in the hands of any one person amounts to a new sphere of existence on the earth, to a "new metaphysics," as the journalist Lance Morrow put it in his book *Evil*, that "transforms both the political and personal dynamics of evil."

This is the *real* condition to which the Bush administration is responding. The problem is actual, if not yet fully present. The danger *is* transcendent—after all, the 9-11 attackers, using far more modest means, created a televised version of a mini-apocalypse—but the Bush administration is taking steps that, instead of meeting the danger, make it far worse. The impulse that has driven this administration's global policies is defined, at its simplest, by the determination that no hostile power will be allowed to have so-called weapons of mass destruction. Leaders of "rogue regimes," so the Bush reading goes, by definition lust after such weapons, and so "regime change" has become the dominant purpose of American power, whether by means of "preventive war," as in Afghanistan and Iraq, or by other forms of coercion. Even as the difficulties of Iraq have undercut glib American assertions of imperial sway, it remains likely that Washington will permit neither Iran nor even North Korea, which evidently has a head start on the process, nor any number of other unfriendly states to develop active and usable nuclear arsenals. It is nukes, above all, that roil the sleep of the White House, with the recurrent dream of 9-11 as the mildest hint of what would come if such an act went nuclear.

So, to put the best face on the Bush agenda (leaving aside questions of oil, global market control, and economic or military hegemony), a humane project of antiproliferation can be seen at its core. Yet a nation that was trying to *promote* the proliferation of weapons of mass destruction, especially nuclear weapons, would behave precisely as the Bush administration has behaved over the past three years. The Pentagon's chest-thumping concept of "full spectrum dominance" itself motivates other nations to seek sources of countervailing power, and when the United States actually goes to war to impose its widely disputed notion of order on some states, but not others, nations—friendly as well as unfriendly—find themselves with an urgent reason to acquire some means of deterring such intervention.

On December 19, 2003, the Bush administration claimed a victory for its "counterproliferation" belligerency in announcing that Libya had agreed to dismantle its weapons of mass destruction, but Libyan leader Moammar Khadafy's decision actually put the lie to the Bush approach. Following revelations of its complicity in the terror bombing of Pan Am Flight 103 in 1988, Libya had been subject to years of coercive diplomacy, sanctions, and isolation. These U.N.-centered pressures, firmly advanced by the Clinton administration, finally worked. Preventive war and regime change were simply not necessary to stem Khadafy's aggression. And not incidentally, with Libya's new cooperation, it was confirmed that a steady supporter of its abandoned nuclear project had been Pakistan, which the Bush administration counts as an ally, proving that proliferators do not fall into the good-versus-evil categories favored in Washington. And in counterpoint to the December announcement of Libya's compliance, it was announced on the same day that Japan would spend billions of dollars on a U.S.-sponsored ballistic missile shield. Another "victory" for the Bush administration. But this first major exporting of "Stars Wars" abroad amounted to an unprecedented escalation both of Japanese military expenditures and of the arms race in Asia.

It will inevitably prompt countermeasures from North Korea, China, and Russia. Those will, in turn, spark the further militarization of Japan, as defense leads to offense, an upward spiraling that is likely to increase the dangers of nuclear war. Here on earth and in the heavens could be found the real meaning of the Bush approach to the problem of proliferation.

The odd and tragic thing is that the world before Bush was actually nearing consensus on how to manage the problem of the proliferation of weapons of mass destruction, and had begun to put in place promising structures designed to prevent such spread. Centrally embodied in the Nuclear Nonproliferation Treaty of 1968, which had successfully and amazingly kept the number of nuclear powers, actual as well as admitted, relatively low, that consensus gave primacy to treaty obligations, international cooperation, and a serious commitment by existing nuclear powers to move toward ultimate nuclear abolition. All of that has been trashed by Bush. "International law?" he smirked in December 2003. "I better call my lawyer."

Now indications are that nations all over the globe—Japan, Saudi Arabia, Argentina, Brazil, Australia—have begun reevaluating their rejections of nukes, and some are positively rushing to acquire them. Iran and North Korea are likely to be only the tip of this radioactive iceberg. Nuclear-armed Pakistan and India are a grim forecast of the future on every continent. And the Bush administration—by declaring its own nuclear arsenal permanent, by threatening nuclear first strikes against other nations, by "warehousing" treaty-defused warheads instead of destroying them, by developing a new line of "usable" nukes, by moving to weaponize the "high frontier" of outer space, by doing little to help Russia get rid of its rotting nuclear stockpile, by embracing "preventive war"—is enabling this trend instead of discouraging it. How can this be?

The problem has its roots in a long-term American forgetfulness, going back to the acid fog in which the United States ended World War II. There was never a complete moral reckoning with the harsh momentum of that conflict's denouement—how American leaders embraced a strategy of terror bombing, slaughtering whole urban populations, and how, finally, they ushered in the atomic age with the attacks on Hiroshima and Nagasaki. Scholars have debated those questions, but politicians have avoided them, and most citizens have pretended they aren't really questions at all. America's enduring assumptions about its own moral supremacy, its own altruism, its own exceptionalism, have hardly been punctured by consideration of the possibility that we, too, are capable of grave mistakes, terrible crimes. Such awareness, drawn from a fuller reckoning with days gone by— with August 6 and 9, 1945, above all—would inhibit America's present claim to moral grandeur, which is simultaneously a claim, of course, to economic and political grandiosity. The indispensable nation must dispense with what went before.

"The past is never dead," William Faulkner said. "It isn't even past." How Americans remember their country's use of terror bombing affects how they think of terrorism; how they remember the first use of nuclear weapons has profound relevance for how the United States behaves in relation to nuclear weapons today. If the long American embrace of nuclear "mutual assured destruction" is unexamined; if the Pentagon's treaty-violating rejection of the ideal of eventual nuclear abolition is unquestioned—then the Bush administration's embrace of nukes as normal, usable weapons will not seem offensive.

Memory is a political act. Forgetfulness is the handmaiden of tyranny. The Bush administration is fully committed to maintaining what the historian Marc Trachtenberg calls our "nuclear amnesia" even as the administration seeks to impose a unilateral structure of control on the world. As it pursues a world-threatening campaign against *other* peoples' weapons of mass destruction, that is, the Bush administration refuses to confront the moral meaning of America's own weapons of mass destruction, not to mention their viral character, as other nations seek smaller versions of the American arsenal, if only to deter Bush's next "preventive" war. The United States' own arsenal, in other words, remains the primordial cause of the WMD plague.

"Memory," the novelist Paul Auster has written, "is the space in which a thing happens for the second time." This collection of writings against Bush's war, a detailed and contemporaneous chronicle of that war, intends to be a book of memory. No one wants the terrible events that came after the rising of the sun on September 11, 2001, to happen for a second time *except* in the realm of remembrance, leading to understanding and commitment. All the ways George Bush exploited those events, betraying the memory of those who died in them, must be lifted up and examined again, so that the outrageousness of his political purpose can be felt in its fullness. Exactly how the war on terrorism unfolded; how it bled into the wars against Afghanistan, then Iraq; how American fears were exacerbated by administration alarms; how civil rights were undermined, treaties broken, alliances abandoned, coarseness embraced—none of this should be forgotten.

Given how they have been so dramatically unfulfilled, Washington's initial hubristic impulses toward a new imperial dominance should not be forgotten. That the first purpose of the war—Osama "dead or alive"—changed when al Qaeda proved elusive should not be forgotten. That the early justification for the war against Iraq—Saddam's weapons of mass destruction—changed when they proved nonexistent should not be forgotten. That in former times the U.S. government behaved as if facts mattered, as if evidence informed policy, should not be forgotten. That Afghanistan and Iraq are in shambles, with thousands dead and hundreds of thousands at risk from disease, disorder, and despair, should not be forgotten. That a now disdainful world gave itself in unbridled love to America on 9-11 should not be forgotten.

We remember the past, even the recent past embodied in this chronicle, to motivate resistance in the present. We remember the past, especially as in this chronicle of Bush's "crusade," so that the future can be different.

PART ONE

ONWARD CHRISTIAN

1

HOLY WAR

We're at war," President George W. Bush said in Sarasota, Florida, on the morning of September 11, 2001. He said the words aloud, but he was speaking, in effect, to himself, as he first watched the television replay of the World Trade Center towers being hit by jet airliners. A primal response. Instant. And shaping. After watching the replay, the president began to move. His handlers told him he was himself a prime target of that war, and so Bush allowed himself to be shuttled from Florida to an air force base in Louisiana, and then to the supersecure headquarters of the Strategic Air Command in Nebraska. Soon enough, the president's main emotion on this day would turn to shame, when he realized how this rush to a safe hole contrasted with the ordinary heroism of thousands in New York, Washington, and in the skies over Pennsylvania. When Bush finally emerged to address the American public, transforming his humiliation into rage, he formally defined the attacks on the World Trade Center and the Pentagon as "acts of war." To other nations he said, "Either you are with us, or you are with the terrorists." At the wounded Pentagon, the president told a somber gathering of military officials that he wanted Osama bin Laden "dead or alive."

On September 14, the president started the day at a prayer service at the National Cathedral in Washington. The ritual was defined as ecumenical, with a Muslim presence, but the overwhelmingly Christian iconography of the cathedral—television cameras lingered on an especially literal rendition of the crucifixion—conveyed another impression entirely. The service was an expression of national grief, but it seemed equally an epiphany of martial will. As simply as that, images of Christian religion were starkly joined to America's new purpose.

From the cathedral, Bush went straight to the World Trade Center site in New York. Standing atop the rubble, before a spread of American flags, the president declared, "The people who knocked these buildings down will hear from all of us soon." On that same day, the U.S. Senate voted 98–0 and the House of Representatives voted 420–1 (with California's Barbara Lee the lone dissenter) to give President Bush unlimited authority to use force against America's enemies as he saw fit. National polls put the percentage of Americans in favor of "a major military campaign" at 90 percent. No one said whom the campaign should be waged against. In three days, the Bush war was begun, blessed by religion, affirmed by pundits, and authorized by Congress, although the war was yet to be defined.

Law Not War

September 15, 2001

How we love our country! For days now, we Americans, while mourning and shuddering, have felt the accumulating weight of our patriotic devotion. We are joined in the shocking recognition of what a rare and precious treasure is the United States of America.

Our nation's sudden vulnerability makes us shrug off, just as suddenly, the habit of taking for granted its nobility. We see it in the throat-choking empty place of the New York skyline, and in the gaping wound of the building beside Arlington Cemetery. We see it in the grimy faces of the resolute rescue workers, and in the implication that doomed airline passengers fought back against hijackers. We see it in the splendid diversity of our features, our accents, our beliefs, our responses even. Never has the national motto seemed more true: out of many, one.

But so far our main expression of this intense patriotism has been oddly in tension with its inner meaning, for the thing we treasure above all about America at this moment is the way it measures its hope by principles of democracy, tolerance, law, respect for the other, and even social compassion. Our supreme patriotic gesture in this crisis has been a nearly universal call for war, and indeed the growing sentiment for war, fueled by the rhetoric of our highest leaders, may soon be embodied in a formal congressional declaration of war. Before we go much farther, we should think carefully about why we are heading down this path, and where it is likely to lead. Do the rhetoric of war and the actions it already sets in motion really serve the urgent purpose of stopping terrorism? And is the launching of war really the only way to demonstrate our love for America?

Before going any farther, let me state the obvious. The nearly worldwide consensus that the terrorist attacks on New York and Washington must be met with force is entirely correct. The network of suicidal mass murderers, however large and wherever hidden, must be eliminated. But force can be exercised decisively and overwhelmingly in another context than that of "war." One of the great advances in civilization occurred when human beings found a way to channel necessary violence away from "war" and toward a new, counterbalancing context embodied in the idea of "law." The distinction may seem too fine to be relevant in the aftermath of this catastrophe, but it is after catastrophe that the distinction matters most. The difference between "war" and "law" is not the use of force. The United States of America, with its world allies, should be embarked not on a war but on an unprecedented, swift, sure, and massive campaign of law enforcement. As the term *law enforcement* implies, the proper use of force would be of the essence of this campaign.

Why does this distinction matter? Four reasons:

- War, by definition, is an activity undertaken against a political or social entity, while the terrorist network responsible for this catastrophe, from all reports, is a coalition of individuals, perhaps a large one. Law enforcement, by definition, is an activity undertaken against just such individuals or networks. By clothing our response to the terrorist acts in the rhetoric of war, we make it far more likely that members of groups associated by extrinsic factors with the perpetrators (Arabs, Muslims, Afghans, Pakistanis, etc.) will suffer terrible consequences, from being bombed in Kabul to being discriminated against in Boston. Furthermore, the rhetoric of war, as it falls on the ears of such people (a billion Muslims), makes it all the more likely that they will only see America as their enemy.
- War, by definition, is relatively imprecise. Steps can be taken to limit "collateral damage," but the method of war, in fact, is to bring pressure to bear against a hostile power structure by inflicting suffering on the society of which it is part. History shows that once wars begin, violence becomes general. As President Bush threatened, no distinctions are made. In law enforcement, by contrast, distinctions remain of the essence. Law enforcement submits to disciplines that are jettisoned in war. Do we really have the right to jettison such disciplines now?
- War, similarly, is less concerned with procedure than with result; or, more plainly, in war the ends justify the means. In law enforcement, the end remains embodied in the means, which is why procedures are so scrupulously observed in criminal justice activity. To respond to a terrorist's grievous violation of the social order with further violations of that order means the terrorist has won.

- War inevitably generates its own momentum, which has a way of inhumanely overwhelming the humane purposes for which the war is begun in the first place. In the death-ground of combat violence, self-criticism can seem like fatal self-doubt, and so the savage momentum of war is rarely recognized as such until too late. The rule of unintended consequences universally applies in war. Law enforcement, on the other hand, with its system of checks and balances between police and courts, is inevitably self-critical. The moral link between act and consequence is far more likely to be protected.

What does "winning" a war against terrorism mean? How has hatred of America become a source of meaning for vast numbers whose poverty already amounts to a state of war? Must a massive campaign of unleashed violence become America's new source of meaning, too? The World Trade Center was a symbol of the social, economic, and political hope Americans treasure, a hope embodied above all in law. To win the struggle against terrorism means inspiring that same hope in the hearts of all who do not have it. How we respond to this catastrophe will define our patriotism, shape the century, and memorialize our beloved dead.

The Pentagon Mourning

September 18, 2001

On January 22, 1943, the day I was born, the new War Department headquarters in Arlington formally opened. That the Pentagon and I share this anniversary came to seem a defining symbol of my life when, as the son of an air force officer who spent most of his career working in what insiders call "the Building," I became intimately attached to the Pentagon. Erected on a site formerly known as Hell's Bottom, the Pentagon replaced Washington's original airport, Hoover Field, which, to make room for the massive new structure, was moved downriver and renamed National Airport. That detail of a lost history seems ghostly now, a week after a hijacked airplane retraced an ancient approach to make its deadly landing, killing many and plunging the rest of us in grief for the dead, and grief, even, for the Building.

It is not too much to say that, as a child going there after school to meet my father, I fell in love with his monumental place of work. Indeed, it became a kind of living monument to my love for him. Its corridors were a playground; its retail concourse a first shopping mall. Its uniformed men and women were my first idols. In those innocent days, no security guard hindered my explorations, although once or twice I was whistled down for sliding in my stocking feet on the broad ramps. As an invisible boy free to wander through hedges of battle flags and portraits of heroes hung on walls the color of robins' eggs, I knew I could get lost in the maze, but I never did. And anyway, Dad would always find me.

And then, as a young man opposed to the war in Vietnam, it is not too much to say that I hated the Pentagon for a time, knowing too little. The antiwar demonstrations that took place there were, for me and many others, rites of passage into a different sort of patriotism. Yet unlike most of my fellow protesters, I was never able to see the Pentagon as simply evil, "the charnel house," as some called it. Later I would understand that resistance to the escalations of Vietnam was going on as much inside the Building as outside—including objections by my father of which I knew nothing at the time. The war came between me and my father, a chasm we never bridged. So it is not surprising that, for many years afterward, I cultivated a careful indifference to the place.

Then, a few years ago, writing an article for the *New Yorker*, I spent some days rediscovering the Building and its complexities: the article was called "War Inside the Pentagon." Interviewing one senior official, I felt a sudden chill on my neck and realized I was in my father's old office, the exact room forty years later. In the corridor after that interview I was ambushed by feeling for the first dream I'd had of America. The dignity with which the Building stood guard over Washington from its position between the river and the cemetery had made it seem the very tabernacle of our nation's virtue. In my young, untested mind the place had seemed holy.

Despite my decades-long disavowal of the god it worships, what I discovered last Tuesday, with so many others, is that the Pentagon forever occupies a cherished place in my heart. In my case, it is indeed as if the Building and I are twins, each carrying like marks of the moral complexity inherent in human life. The Pentagon was home to heroes of the struggle against Nazism and Stalinism, and to critics of the Vietnam War from within. Yet the Pentagon is shadowed by the dark history of our era, too. Vietnam, after all, remains a festering scar. Perhaps nothing defines the shadow better than the fact that the man who oversaw the Building's construction, Brigadier General Leslie Groves, promptly moved on to oversee a next massive project—the Manhattan Project—which set in motion consequences that still spark the nightmares of the globe. The Manhattan Project's very name resonates this week of the Manhattan attacks in ways we could never have imagined.

President Bush has defined the nation's struggle as between good and evil, understandably. The murders of a week ago were nothing if not diabolical. Yet there is wisdom to be claimed from the life span of the Pentagon, for in these decades assumptions of absolute American virtue have been stripped from us, the way life strips every person of youth. At a certain point, we stop looking for our dads. We know that when moral complexity yields to a Manichaean vision dividing the world between angels and devils, it is human beings who get caught in the middle. As we grieve for the people who died at the Pentagon, let us also honor them by carrying our struggle forward not only with the courage for which the Building stands, but with the humility that its history requires of us.

This Crusade, This War

September 24, 2001

When President Bush used the term *crusade* last week, his spokes-
people quickly disavowed it, and with good reason. But far from being a long-ago history that we can blithely abjure, the Crusades
created a state of consciousness that still shapes the mind of the
West, and if Americans don't know that, many Muslims do. We
should take the president's inadvertent remark as an occasion to
think about that.

Scholars count seven or eight Crusades as having taken place in
the two-hundred-year period between 1096 and 1291. They were
wars waged against Islam for control of what Christians called the
Holy Land, but they also involved fierce conflict between Latins and
Orthodox, and ultimately within Latin Christendom itself. It is not
only that the savagery of these wars remains unforgotten in vast
stretches of the world today, but also that the lines they drew remain
contested borders even now—as the Balkans wars of the 1990s reveal. There are at least four key pillars of the Western mind that the
Crusades put in place.

- The Crusades were the first time that violence was defined by
the church as a sacred act. "God wills it!" was the battle cry
with which Pope Urban II launched the First Crusade in 1095.
Anyone "taking the cross" to fight the infidel was offered indulgences, and, if killed, assured a place in heaven. The energy for
war came from the conviction that, as President Bush put it in
his address to Congress, "God is not neutral." Crusaders go to
war certain of God's blessing.
- The crusading mind divides the world between Us and Them.
Indeed, the Crusades were a deliberate effort to get Europe's

princes to stop making war against each other in favor of war against an enemy outside, and it worked. The Crusades established a binding ideological consensus among Christians that led ultimately to unifying structures of politics and culture. Indeed, Europe did not become "Europe" until it defined itself against Islam, and that negation remains embedded in the West's self-understanding today.

- But a mobilization against an enemy outside inevitably led to a paranoid fear of enemies within. Anyone not participating in the new consensus was instantly in danger. The war against Islam abroad became a war against dissent at home. That is why "schismatics," or Orthodox Christians, and Albigensian heretics were soon targets of Crusades, too.

- But the ultimate enemy within, of course, was the Jew. The movement from the religious anti-Judaism of the early church toward the lethal antisemitism of modernity took its most decisive turn with the First Crusade, which was the occasion, in the Rhineland in the spring of 1096, of the first large-scale pogrom in Europe's history. Church leaders repudiated violence against Jews in subsequent Crusades, but without ever repudiating the underlying theological assumptions that made it inevitable. Leaders today decry a generalized hatred of Muslims, but the character of their war against terrorism may make it inevitable.

Here are the questions this history puts to us:

- Can we respond to this crisis without once more dividing the world between "us and them"? Is it wise, for example, for America to insist on a global choosing of sides, what Islam can hear as the same old call to arms? Can we not more subtly enlist the support of those caught in the middle, like Pakistan's Pervez Musharraf or other Arab leaders, without igniting their populations against them?

- Must we define this conflict in the cosmic—and self-justifying—language of good versus evil? As is true of every human conflict, this one is morally ambiguous. There was no ambiguity about the evil of the September 11 assaults, but they arose out of a complicated set of prior conditions, some of which involve our own moral culpability. America must act in this crisis with the full knowledge of its own capacity for deadly mistakes and evil acts. America must not define dissent as disloyalty.

- Is war our only possible response to this crisis? In addition to bringing terrorists to justice, wouldn't we do well right now to initiate a massive, simultaneous effort to address the ultimate source of terrorism—the radical impoverishment of millions of people, especially in the Arab world, especially in the West Bank and Gaza? Can more come from America than cruise missiles and MTV?

The only way "this crusade, this war on terrorism," in the president's phrase, will not be a replay of past crimes and tragedies is if we repudiate not just the word *crusade* but the mind of the crusader. We can start by acknowledging, above all, that when humans go to war, God in no way wills it.

Gandhi's Birthday

October 2, 2001

When Italian prime minister Silvio Berlusconi, a self-appointed spokesman for the West, asserted last week the "superiority of our civilization," one wonders what Mahatma Gandhi would have made of it. The question arises because today is Gandhi's birthday. What is to be learned from a consideration of the present crisis in the light of the Indian national leader's life and teaching?

Mohandas Karamchand Gandhi was born in India to a family of the merchant class in 1869. As a young man, he studied law in London and set out to practice in Durban, South Africa. His twenty years in South Africa were shaped by the struggle against that country's racist structures. In his memoir, Gandhi gives the date of his conversion to nonviolent political resistance at a protest meeting in Johannesburg: the year was 1906, and the day was September 11.

Returning to India, Gandhi became part of the Home Rule movement, which, over the decades, developed into a full-fledged independence movement of which he became the main leader. Following strategies of noncooperation and civil disobedience, the movement grew. One of its great climaxes, in 1930, was the March to the Sea, where thousands gathered to make their own salt as a protest against a government tax on salt. Time in British prisons, rigorous public fasts, an extreme asceticism, and the discovery in his own Hindu religious tradition of spiritual resources that undergirded the great political struggle—these were marks of Gandhi's life. He opposed not only British colonialism but also the Indian caste system; not only the raj but also the oppressions of India's own petty tyrants. His followers bestowed on him the honorific "Mahatma," or "Great Soul." In 1947 the independence of India was achieved, but the conflict was not over. Muslim and Hindu factions were set against each other, a split that would lead to the establishment of two separate countries, Pakistan and India. Gandhi opposed the split. In early 1948, he undertook a public fast for the ideal of Muslim-Hindu amity. Within days, he was assassinated by an extremist from his own Hindu tradition.

Gandhian pacifism is admired in the abstract today, but in practice it is widely dismissed as too idealistic, and even as morally irresponsible. Gandhian pacifism is misunderstood as a refusal to resist evil or oppose violence, when, in fact, it spawned some of the most powerful acts of resistance of the twentieth century. Indeed Gandhian nonviolence proved to be an unstoppable force that led to political transformations around the globe, from the United States

(Martin Luther King Jr.), to Ireland (John Hume), to the Philippines
(Corazon Aquino), to the Soviet Union (Lech Walesa). The movement that recognized Gandhi as a founding hero was the greatest
moral event of the century and, equally, one of the most politically
effective.

To observe Gandhi's birthday today, in the light of heightened
dangers from terrorism, the prospect of conflict between the West
and Islam, and the particular nightmare represented by nuclear
weapons on the subcontinent, is to recall how very much was unfinished when Gandhi died. After all, a terrorist murdered Gandhi,
Gandhi's hope for Hindu peace with Islam failed, and his successors
embarked on India's own nuclear weapons program. But none of
that removes the great insight that Gandhi brought to the world
(and that I recall with help from the authors John S. Dunne, Martin
Green, Sissela Bok, Taylor Branch, and Jonathan Schell). Beginning
with a sentimental embrace of "love," as found in Tolstoy's reading
of Jesus, and moving to an appreciation, in Thoreau, of civil disobedience, Gandhi invented a new notion of a nonviolent but coercive
resistance. Conceived by a figure who crossed over from one culture
to another and back, his idea is innately respectful of religious and
cultural differences—unlike, say, Berlusconi's. Quite simply, Gandhi
relied on what he called *satyagraha*, or truth-force. The truth will set
you free. Gandhi's lifelong strategy was to bring about moments of
epiphany when wide populations might come to decisive political
and moral recognitions. Acts of resistance that lay bare the real character of evil, Gandhi taught, will lead to broad rejection of that evil.
The history of the movements named above suggests that this is
anything but the platitudinous meekness derided by those who prefer war.

The events of September 11 were the dead opposite of *satyagraha*, but they were a world-historic moment of truth, a profound
laying bare of the evil of global terrorism. More than that, the savage
assault against thousands of innocent civilians amounted to an
epiphany in which the real meaning of anticivilian violence could be
seen with rare clarity. At last, war against civilians, the main mode of

war for half a century, is seen for what it is. The American response must enshrine both of these epiphanies—by resisting terrorism, but without an indiscriminate war. Mahatma Gandhi's faith in the power of truth, and in the readiness of human beings to change when faced with truth, has never been a more vivid image of hope.

Religion: Problem or Solution?

October 9, 2001

Politicians and commentators are going to great lengths to affirm the religion of Muslims, rejecting the terrorists' claim that the heinous crime of September 11 was an act of Islamic devotion. That is as it should be. Islam is a noble religion that emphasizes "surrender" to God and compassionate love for the neighbor. It is a source of meaning for millions, and, as the commentary insists, all but the smallest fraction of those millions reject violence and the savagery of terrorists. Islamic religious leaders have been forthright in condemning the murderous assaults against America. But something is lost in the well-intentioned assertion that Islam is a pure religion entirely unrelated to evil acts committed in its name. With so much violence being inflicted in the name of God by religionists of various kinds around the globe, an old question presents itself, and not just about Islam: is religion the solution, or is it the problem? Or is it both?

Britain's prime minister Tony Blair said last week that the terrorist attacks were no more a reflection of true Islam than the Crusades were of the Gospels. Fair enough. But the comparison is instructive. Latin Christians would like to be able to say that the rampaging fanatics who, to cite only one instance, assaulted Jerusalem in 1099 were acting in ways that had nothing to do with Christian belief or practice, but in fact—and this is what makes the Crusades so chilling—that holy war was integrally tied to theology (violence of God), liturgy (the sign of the cross), and authority (Crusader popes). Today, we like to think of religion as one of those purely positive aspects of life, and we are quick to dismiss negative acts or attitudes spawned by religion as not "really" religious. The Vatican does this in asserting that the Catholic Church is entirely sinless, which means the crimes of the church (Crusades, Inquisition, etc.) were committed by "sinful members," never by the church "as such." Religion is good. If religion prompts bad behavior, it is not "real" religion.

But this way of thinking lets religion off the hook. It means we can deplore the "sins" of sinful members without asking hard questions about where those sins came from. To stay with the Christian example, were the endless acts of Christian antisemitism aberrations, or were they tied somehow to anti-Jewish texts in the New Testament, or to the fundamental way Christianity defined itself over against Judaism, and so on? If antisemitism was an aberration, an apology for acts of "sinful members" is enough. If antisemitism grew out of core beliefs and practices, apology is not enough. Core beliefs and practices would have to change. If crimes committed in the name of religion can be easily separated from religion "as such," a full understanding of those crimes, and a way to resist them at the source, may elude us.

Obviously, I am talking here about all religions. It is misleading and unproductive to think of religion as purely good. Religion, like everything of the human condition, is ambiguous—partly good and partly bad; part solution, part problem. Religion has enabled major improvements in human life and still supports some of the world's greatest works for good. But religion also easily confuses the object of its worship—God—with itself, often prompting human beings to make absolute claims that lead inevitably to absolute disaster. Feelings of religious superiority can and do lead to ranking by race, nationality, gender, and class. Religion can make unholy alliances with commerce and with conquest, as happened throughout the era of European imperialism. The univocal claims of monotheists can lead to contempt for human beings who do not share them, and the open-endedness of polytheism can undermine the distinctions essential to thought. And the certainty that often accompanies the phenomenon of "true belief" seems always to result in a cruel rooting out of what—or who—might threaten it. The religious impulse to die for the faith slides all too quickly into the impulse to kill for it.

There is no crime of which Muslims acting as Muslims have been accused that Christians, to cite only one other religion, do not also stand accused by history. To be religious is, first, to be repentant. The danger of a "clash of civilizations," or even of a new holy war between the remnants of a Christian West and "the Islamic World," will be far less if we all understand that we are alike as human beings. Our noblest impulses come inevitably intertwined with opposite inclinations that betray them. We religious humans must constantly submit to the judgment of history, practicing self-criticism, always seeking the reform that will draw us closer to our best ideals. Certainly Islam is engaged in such a reckoning today. But this task belongs to all religious people—the only way to honor God and love our neighbor as ourselves.

2

AFGHANISTAN

Shortly after 9-11, Deputy Secretary of Defense Paul D. Wolfowitz said that the American aim was to "end" states that sponsored terrorism. In the case of al Qaeda, the question of "sponsorship" is complex, since the group began in the 1980s as a U.S.-supported force resisting the Soviet occupation of Afghanistan. Fiercely Islamic, al Qaeda allied itself with the religiously fascist Taliban in its wars against rival factions inside Afghanistan. When President Bush asked Taliban leaders to "turn over" bin Laden after 9-11, it was far from clear that they had the power to do such a thing. Taliban requests for evidence tying al Qaeda to the terrorist attacks were swatted away.

On October 7, 2001, the United States began the bombing of Afghanistan. Starting with Germany and Japan in World War II, continuing in Southeast Asia, in the first Gulf War, and, in the 1990s, in the Balkans, Pentagon faith in pain inflicted from the air proved absolute. Now, strategic bombing would again appear as the primary American method of achieving foreign policy goals. The air strikes, including Vietnam-style carpet bombing by B-52s, were not selectively focused on al Qaeda targets. Perhaps only because it *could* be targeted, the Taliban had replaced al Qaeda as the main American enemy. Two months later, Operation Enduring Freedom had successfully ended the Taliban regime. The United States suffered few casualties. The Pentagon makes a point of not counting "enemy" casualties, but reliable sources suggest that about four thousand Taliban fighters were killed, and about an equal number of Afghan civilians died as a result of the U.S. campaign. Almost no al Qaeda leaders were known to be captured or killed at the time. The war did nothing to combat al Qaeda cells outside Afghanistan, although the September 11 attacks seem to have been organized in Hamburg, Germany, and Florida, as well as in Afghanistan. On the contrary, it reinforced the al Qaeda image of jihad, with the United States behaving just as Osama bin Laden would have predicted—and would have wanted.

Bin Laden escaped. Of seven thousand or so Taliban and some low-level al Qaeda fighters taken prisoner, more than six hundred were transferred to U.S. custody. The Bush administration asserted that Geneva POW protocols did not apply to them, although when Americans were taken prisoner by Taliban fighters, Washington demanded—and got—observance of Geneva Convention standards. More than two years later, approximately six hundred detainees from forty countries were still being held at Camp Delta in Guantánamo Bay, Cuba, in violation of international law and American tradition. By war's end, a secret network of U.S. military prisons had been established across the world.

Operation Enduring Freedom's one positive accomplishment was the "ending" of the repressive Taliban regime, as if the purpose of Bush's war had been the liberation of Afghan women—and even that would be called into question within the year. But, in truth, as events have since shown, no one was truly liberated by the Afghan war. With the escape of bin Laden, the American appetite for revenge was not satisfied. This war would not be enough.

But What Changed?

October 16, 2001

America was changed forever by the catastrophe of September 11—
so they say. But what kind of change? As the U.S. response at home
and abroad unfolds, concerns mount about forces set in motion.
Change can obviously be very much for the worse. Escalated violence, eroded civil liberties, undercut economy, the mortal clash of
religions and cultures, nukes in Pakistan, a war in Afghanistan—we
have become connoisseurs of the dangers that may lie ahead. But
don't we owe it to the gravity of this moment, not to mention those
who died, to imagine quite explicitly what change *for the better*
might mean? What if the catastrophe of September 11 resulted,
over the long term, in recognitions and initiatives that made America—and the world—a far better place? My simple purpose here is
to invite a movement away from the present context which necessarily remains clouded with threats and questions.

Instead, cast your mind forward fifty years or so. When human
beings look back at September 11, 2001, from that place in midcen-
tury, here is what I hope they will see:

- A turning point at which regionalisms of every kind gave way
  in primacy to a widely shared vision of one world. The understandable urge of "first-world" people to pursue self-interest
  without regard for the earth's other inhabitants was recognized
  as a self-defeating illusion. Political structures of governance
  dating to the eighteenth century gave way to governance that
  reflected what twenty-first-century technologies had done to
  global awareness. This shift made of the earth not one, univocal, and therefore totalitarian community but a community of
  communities, with full respect for regional and cultural differ-

ences. "God bless America" remained a slogan, but within "God bless the world."

- A turning point at which the main mode of resolving world conflict shifted away from the culture of war and toward the culture of law. The decisive change occurred when Osama bin Laden and his lieutenants were arrested by a force acting, with restraint, in the name of law. He was not summarily executed while still in fatigues, but was brought to trial in a newly invigorated International Criminal Court where the case against him and his network was laid out. He was given a chance to mount a defense, and did. His patently false appeals to fellow Muslims mostly went unheeded. He and his lieutenants were found guilty and were imprisoned for the rest of their lives. This breakthrough exercise of international law *itself* changed the way humans respond even to savage provocation.

- A turning point at which the radical poverty of millions was recognized as an urgent moral question and a political disaster that had to be addressed by politics on a world scale. Hunger as an inevitable breeder of violence finally came to be defined as *itself* a form of violence. Adjustments were made in the way democratic capitalism understood itself, with markets no longer acting as sole arbiters of the flow of money and resources. Information technologies made possible a revolution in education that led in turn to the spread of democracy, tolerance, and, especially, the equality of women. Capitalism found its human face.

- A turning point at which power based on a massive threat aimed at civilians was seen for what it was—not only among terrorists but among the nations still hoarding arsenals of nuclear weapons long after cold-war justifications were gone. Terrorism was understood as the poor man's nuke. In addition to combating terrorism, nuclear states turned against their own deterrence theory because it, too, was based on readiness to commit mass murder. Washington began by renouncing first use of nuclear weapons, unilaterally destroying warheads, recommitting itself to arms-reduction treaties, and reaffirming the ultimate aim of nuclear abolition. The National Missile Defense quietly fell off the American agenda. Terrorism was defeated when the "balance of terror" was dismantled.

As of today such changes seem like impossible dreams, but are they? Isn't the present crisis a revelation, ultimately, of the ground zero that awaits the human race if we continue to define our sense of possibility in narrow terms? "Realism" is no longer realistic.

There is no redeeming the anguish of September 11, as if such loss can be turned into gain. But there is a way to make what happened that day even worse—if, in our responses to it, we do not drastically change the way we live on this planet, beginning with how we respond to those who hate us. Last month, W. H. Auden's great poem "September 1, 1939" flashed across the Internet, and I think I know why. Because of its simplest, truest, most difficult line, a line which prompted conflict in Auden himself as events unfolded after he wrote it. But his line, after September 11, 2001, seemed never simpler, never truer, never more difficult: "We must love one another or die."

The Bombing Reconsidered

November 6, 2001

When I first laid eyes on a B-52 bomber in the mid-1950s, I was struck by the motto of the Strategic Air Command emblazoned on the fuselage: "Peace Is Our Profession." Such words on a fearsome warplane were a consolation, and I wanted to believe them. Even as a boy, though, I was instinctively attuned to the moral complexity of bombing, and I wasn't that surprised when, during Vietnam, that motto was revealed to be a big lie. The profession of those planes was to wreak havoc, period. Last week, B-52s were sent into action over Afghanistan, a first exercise in carpet bombing. The unleashing of this crude ghost-plane, which drops imprecise ordnance from forty thousand feet, is a chilling harbinger. Whatever the broad justifications of the U.S.-led war against terrorism, the way in which that war spirals around an increasingly brutal bombing campaign cries out to be reconsidered.

What are the purposes and effects of bombing? That straightforward question has hardly ever been answered truthfully by our government. The air war in Afghanistan is being conducted behind a veil of secrecy—but a veil of secrecy shielding Americans, not the Afghans on whom the bombs explode. Our government insists that civilians are not being targeted, and that Taliban claims of large numbers of civilian casualties are propaganda. But however much we long to be consoled by a distinction between military and civilian targets, carpet bombing notwithstanding, the history of bombing suggests that this distinction itself is a lie. *A History of Bombing* is the title of a book by the Swedish writer Sven Lindqvist, and his findings are instructive.

One of the first countries to be bombed from the air, ironically, was Afghanistan, during British imperial adventurism in 1919. After World War I, the British air staff declared it would impose civilian-protecting limits on bombing, but an internal memo defined that declaration as having been made "to preserve appearances" because "the truth [is] that air warfare has made such restriction obsolete and impossible." Thus the dilemma presented itself at the very onset of the age of bombing. In 1940, the British definition of a *military target* was extended to include industrial centers and the homes of industrial workers—which meant city centers could be hit. American strategists resisted such blatant targeting of civilians for a time, but by the end of World War II, the United States blithely engaged in mass firebombing of entire Japanese cities, especially Tokyo.

Even then, lip service was paid to the consoling distinction between military and civilian, as if it were still being observed. It is stunning to recall, with Lindqvist, that when Harry Truman announced to the world that America had used the atomic bomb, he defined its target as having been "an important Japanese army base." The atomic bomb was dropped on the "base," he said, because "we wished in the first attack to avoid as much as possible the killing of civilians." At least 95 percent of the one hundred thousand killed immediately at that "base," also known as Hiroshima, were civilians, as Truman surely knew. But he also knew the importance of "preserving appearances."

The U.S. lies about bombing in Vietnam, where dead civilians were routinely added to the military body count, are well known. After the revelations of the immorality of that war, Americans had a right to assume that carpet bombing by B-52s was a thing of the past. During the Gulf War of 1991, with the advent of "smart" bombs and laser-guided missiles, "ethical" bombing that spared civilians seemed to have arrived, but those claims, too, turned out to be false. And the B-52 operated there as well. The NATO air war against Serbia in 1999, despite great claims for its "humanitarian" purpose, was distinguished by a strategy that kept bombers flying high enough to protect pilots, but too high to protect Kosovar civilians on the ground either from bomb imprecision or from assaults by Serbian killers. History suggests that war managers have never told the truth about the real purposes and effects of their bombing campaigns.

And now? Last week the moral bankruptcy of bombing was on display when Secretary of Defense Donald Rumsfeld refused to rule out American use of nuclear weapons in this war. We should be clear what this means: the United States is prepared, under some circumstance, to cross the nuclear threshold into the realm of massive civilian death—what, to protect civilian life? How does the motto "Peace Is Our Profession" translate into Arabic? These contradictions suggest that a kind of moral blindness has accompanied the phenomenon of bombing from the start. Indeed, moral blindness is necessary for it, blocking our view, for example, of the way U.S.

bombing, at the very least, is creating conditions of humanitarian catastrophe this winter. I believe that Osama bin Laden is counting on such blindness, and that with our bombing, we have not disappointed him.

Why I Love This Country

November 14, 2001

"Good!" he said, as I took my seat. He was a large man about thirty years old, with the self-assured carriage of, say, a former football player. He had the window seat, and I was on the aisle. We were near the front of the cabin. This was about a month after the World Trade Center catastrophe. Our American Airlines flight was taking us from Charlotte, North Carolina, to San Francisco.

"Good?" I asked.

"Yes, good," he answered, and he made a point to look me over, apparently approving of my six-foot frame. He tossed his head back toward the rest of the cabin. "Nobody gets by us."

And just like that I was initiated into the new American consciousness. There was absolutely no doubt that this man was prepared to defend himself and his fellow passengers, and his expectation that I would gallantly join him was complete. I said, with necessary self-deprecation, "Nobody gets by *you*," and we both laughed. But, of course, I was on the aisle.

Beginning with a lecture in New York City on September 25, I have been traveling all across America, speaking at universities, taking part in interfaith conversations at churches and synagogues, and joining discussions on the national emergency. I have intimately experienced the ways in which Americans are responding to this crisis, from students to retired folks; from antiwar activists at a Quaker college to Wall Street brokers who lost colleagues and offices in the attack; to the travel professionals whose nobility consists in just showing up for work. I have been deeply moved by what I have seen.

One early morning flight was bringing me home to Boston from Toronto. At cruising altitude, the flight attendant was distributing coffee and bran muffins. The man in the row ahead of me looked at the muffin and said, "Where's the hot breakfast?" The flight attendant replied, "We are serving muffins this morning, sir."

"But you always serve a hot breakfast on this flight."

"In the new situation, sir, it's muffins."

"How much money can that save the airline?" the man asked.

"Not much," the flight attendant replied. And then she fixed the man with a cold stare. "The savings is in the salary of one less flight attendant needed to serve you. For you it's a muffin, sir. For my friend, it's a lost job."

"Oh," the man said sheepishly. His gracelessness was nothing beside the flight attendant's dignity. Another time, I happened through Chicago's O'Hare International Airport as a man with a bag full of knives passed through security, belatedly setting off alarms that shut down the airport. The day I arrived in Tacoma, Washington, so far from the traumatized East Coast, a nearby suspension bridge was identified as a potential terrorist target. State police were posted. At a bus station in a small town in Vermont, I felt far away from the threat, only to read the next day that two suspects seized at the Canadian border had caught their bus at that same station. The anxiety is universal. You observe it in the faces of passengers waiting in the terminals, as they stare at the CNN airport news scrawls, which only warn and threaten. You sense it in the ease with which strangers speak to one another. You see it in the quickened pace with which people walk, wanting to get home. You feel it yourself.

The polls suggest an American population that, in its anxiety, is uncritically united behind the president at war, and the omnipresent flags could indicate a resurgence of unthinking nationalism. But what I have seen in a dozen different venues is a people plunged into introspection, complex moral reflection entirely unlike the glib sloganeering of pundits. My work has qualified me to raise questions about the sources of religious hatred, which inevitably lead to questions about one's own tradition, national as well as religious. In one group after another, I have, for example, seen people grappling with Islam, but instead of denigration, what I have witnessed is the shame we non-Muslims feel at our profound ignorance of such an important world phenomenon. In other words, Americans are rejecting advice to see this crisis simplistically, as originating elsewhere. There is no contradiction between a passionate feeling of patriotism and the recognition that American assumptions have been woefully flawed. People are flying the flag and asking hard questions of themselves at the same time.

We speak of "the greatest generation," those who defeated Nazism by going to war. The next generation had its war, too. That generation's greatness consisted in the tragic choice to accept defeat because the war was wrong. America is being tested again. For now the instinctive urge for revenge has trumped the restrained wisdom of authentic self-defense, but I believe the American people— "Good!"—will not let the government pursue this wildly imprudent war for long.

This War Is Not Just

November 21, 2001

In recent days, sage editorial writers, religious leaders, politicians, liberal pundits, and admired columnists have joined in the Rumsfeld-Rice chorus praising the American war in Afghanistan as "just." The Taliban are described as all but defeated. The "noose" around Osama bin Laden grows ever tighter, they say. Afghans are seen rejoicing in the streets, and the women among them are liberated. All because the United States turned the full force of its firepower loose on the evil enemy. Anyone still refusing to sign on to this campaign is increasingly regarded as unpatriotic. Next, we will be called "kooks."

Not so fast. The broad American consensus that Bush's war is "just" represents a shallow assessment of that war, a shallowness that results from three things.

- First, ignorance. The U.S. government has revealed very little of what has happened in the war zone. Journalists impeded by restricted access and blind patriotism have uncovered even less. How many of those outside the military establishment who have blithely deemed this war "just" know what it actually involves? It is clear that a massive bombardment has been occurring throughout Afghanistan, but to what effect? And against whom? Is the focus on the readily targeted Taliban, in fact, allowing a far more elusive al Qaeda to slip away? The crucial judgment about a war's "proportionality," central to any conclusion about its being "just," simply cannot be made on the basis of information available at present. And how is this war "just" if the so far unprovoked war it is bleeding into—against Iraq—is unjust?

- Second, narrow context. The celebrated results that have so far followed from the American war—collapse of the Taliban, liberation of women—are welcome indeed, but they are relatively peripheral outcomes, unrelated to the stated American war aim of defeating terrorism. And these outcomes pale in significance when the conflict is seen in the context of a larger question: does this intervention break, or at least impede, the cycle of violence in which terrorism is only the latest turn? Or, by affirming the inevitability of violence, does this war prepare the ground for the next one? By unleashing such massive firepower, do we make potential enemies even more likely to try to match it with the very weapons of mass destruction we so dread? Alas, the answer is clear. This "overwhelming" exercise of

American power has been a crude reinforcement of the worst impulse of human history; but this is the nuclear age, and that impulse simply must be checked. This old-style American war is unwise in the extreme, and if other nations—Pakistan, India, Israel, Russia—begin to play according to the rules of "dead or alive," will this American model still seem "just"?

• Third, wrongly defined use of force. This war is not "just" because it was not necessary. It may be the only kind of force the behemoth Pentagon knows to exercise, but that doesn't make it "just" either. The terrorist attacks of September 11 could have been defined not as acts of war but as crimes. That was the first mistake, one critics like me flagged as it was happening. As among the most savage crimes in history, the terrorist acts should have been met with a swift, forceful response far more targeted than the present war has been. Police action, not war. The criminals, not an impoverished nation, should be on the receiving end of the punishment. Instead, a massive war against a substitute enemy leaves the sprawling criminal network intact—perhaps in Afghanistan, certainly in major cities elsewhere. Meanwhile, because of the war, the rule of law at home is being undermined. Because of the war-driven pressure to be "united," the shocking incompetence of U.S. domestic security agencies goes unchallenged.

Early in the war, the highest U.S. officials, including the president and vice president, encouraged the idea that the anthrax attacks were originating with the bin Laden network. The understandable paranoia that consequently gripped the public imagination—an enemy that could shut down Congress!—was a crucial aspect of what led both press and politicians to accept the idea that a massive war against an evil enemy would be both necessary and moral. Now, the operating assumption is that the anthrax cases, unrelated to bin Laden, are domestic crimes, not acts of war. But for a crucial moment, they effectively played the role in this war that the Gulf of

Tonkin "assault" played in the Vietnam War, as sources of a war hysteria that "united" the nation around a mistake. In such a context, the more doubt is labeled disloyal, the more it grows. The more this war is deemed "just," the more it seems wrong.

The Way the War Ends

December 18, 2001

"The way the war ended could be more important than the way it began," wrote Thomas C. Schelling in his classic work *Arms and Influence.* "The last word might be more important than the first strike." The truth of this observation was certainly clear in the way World War I ended, with an enemy-punishing treaty that guaranteed a future war. World War II ended with the Allies squandering their moral edge by unleashing savage air assaults against cities, especially Hiroshima and Nagasaki. The end of that war was the beginning of nuclear terror.

The end of the Gulf War in 1991 was a different story. Although now widely derided as a failure of nerve, the decision by George H. W. Bush and General Colin L. Powell to halt the massacre of Iraq's defanged army was a humane act. Leaving the demonized Saddam Hussein in power in preference to destabilizing chaos was an exercise in hardheaded realism. The "last word" of that war, however, was the sanctions regime that, over a decade, has brutally punished Iraq's civilian population without, apparently, deterring Hussein's further mischief. If there was a portent in the elder Bush's war, it wasn't in the end but in the beginning. The date on which he gave his defining "New World Order" speech before Congress—"the rule of law supplants the rule of the jungle"—was September 11, 1990.

Eleven years later, the question is: how will the American war against the Taliban, Osama bin Laden, and al Qaeda end? Whether one's judgment about this war is approving or dissenting, it seems obvious that one of its effects has been to establish a broad climate of "overwhelming force" reprisal for terrorist assaults—what in a bygone age was called "overkill." As a result, the political weather has changed drastically in the Middle East, probably in Russia's war in Chechnya, and, with the terrorist attack in India last week, in the Kashmir dispute. And clouds are gathering elsewhere. The spirit of "dead or alive," with its new American imprimatur, threatens to escalate violence to previously uncontemplated levels in every situation of conflict. Minimal bonds of reciprocity, which formerly committed antagonists to negotiations, diplomacy, and multilateralism, have broken down—and the U.S. decision to abrogate the ABM Treaty last week only underscores this wartime phenomenon. In ending the war in Afghanistan, what can America do to urgently restore the norms of restraint and the ties of international solidarity that our strategy, even if justified as a response to the savage homeland attack of September 11, has undercut?

In ending this war, four things might be considered:

- Encourage the surrender of al Qaeda fighters, including Osama bin Laden himself, by affirming that they will be treated according to principles of international law. Eschew Afghani tribal warfare methods and Northern Alliance threats to kill not only the fighters but villagers who help them, since coercion is ubiquitous in the desperate endgame.
- Abandon the self-demeaning rhetoric of "dead or alive," and announce a decided preference for "alive"—precisely to bring bin Laden and his cohort to trial. Public adjudication of the crimes of September 11 will bring the criminals to justice, but even more important, proper trials will undercut the nihilist appeal of such heinous acts in the minds of potential terrorists.
- Move promptly to the United Nations as the organizing authority not only for the immediate rescue of refugees and repair of Afghanistan, but for the resolution of war-related

questions such as status of prisoners and culpability of Taliban leaders. The United Nations, not a swaggering United States, should be the center of international opposition to terrorism. The implicit new rule of this war, that states can operate in unbridled isolation against terrorists, must be repealed before it is played out in Israel, India, Russia.

• Affirm that the war in Afghanistan will not be carried forward to Iraq, North Korea, or anywhere else. The fabric of restraint must be repaired, and with it the idea that in conflict situations military force comes as a last resort, not a first reaction. Faith in violence as a solution must once more be demythologized. Let the campaign against terrorism be carried forward now as law enforcement, not war. Emphasis must be on focused pursuit of potential terrorists and protection of civilian populations.

The "just war" debate over the means used in the "just cause" of stopping terror, in a distinction of the historian Howard Zinn's, will properly continue, but there need be no debate over how we proceed now. In concluding this war, America must have in mind the variation on the old moral precept: if the end doesn't justify the means, nothing does.

3

WAR AT HOME

On October 19, 2001, as the American bombing of Afghanistan was moving into gear, letters containing potentially lethal amounts of anthrax were received at CBS News in New York, and at Senate offices in Washington. A postal worker in New Jersey was infected. Postal services were massively disrupted. Senate offices were closed. In little more than two weeks, anthrax sent through the mail killed four people and infected at least thirteen others. Though casualties were limited, this was the first use of an officially designated "weapon of mass destruction"—atomic tests aside—in North America. The accompanying letters, with crude threats against Israel, were intended to be taken as linked to the 9-11 terror attacks, and FBI officials promptly said they probably were.

Within seven days of the first reports of anthrax, the Congress had passed the USA Patriot Act, and on October 26, the president signed it into law. Almost unread, and hardly debated in Congress, the act expanded the government's powers to wiretap, detain, and punish suspects, and it widened government authority to summarily deport noncitizens. U.S. representative Barney Frank asked, "Who decided that to defend democracy, we had to degrade it?"

Attorney General John Ashcroft announced a major reorganization of the Justice Department and the FBI to focus on counterterrorism.

Acknowledging that more than a thousand people had been detained inside the United States and, as of November, more than six hundred remained in custody, Ashcroft insisted that the threat of terrorism required the government to keep its suspicions about the detained secret. When questioned about this and other Justice Department antiterrorism tactics by members of the Senate Judiciary Committee on December 6, 2001, the attorney general effectively defined criticism of his department as treason. "Your tactics aid terrorists," he told the senators, "for they erode our national unity and diminish our resolve. They give ammunition to America's enemies, and pause to America's friends."

Meanwhile, the FBI and the Justice Department were unable to develop significant leads in the anthrax case. Eventually, officials acknowledged that there was no evidence tying the anthrax murderer to the 9-11 attacks or to al Qaeda, but by then an anthrax-induced panic had already had the effect of stifling qualms about American responses to terrorism at home and abroad. All evidence, as it turned out, suggested that the anthrax culprit was American, probably a disgruntled former associate of the Defense Department's own bioterrorism research efforts. This still-unknown killer had one thing in common with Osama bin Laden, however: he remained at large.

Robert Kennedy and John Ashcroft

November 20, 2001

Today in Washington, President Bush will honor Robert Kennedy by naming the Justice Department building for him. By any measure, this is an extraordinary public event, but it has a poignant personal meaning for me. It was the summer of 1961. I was a college student employed as a summer intern at the FBI. In those days, the northeast half of the Justice Department building was given over to the bureau, and J. Edgar Hoover's office was in the corner opposite Kennedy's. Those of us on the bureau side knew that Hoover hated the young attorney general, which made little sense because both men seemed devoted to the same causes: the campaigns against communism and organized crime. One day, we interns were summoned to the departmental auditorium on the Justice side of the building. The attorney general was going to address the department's college-student employees, inviting us to sign up with the New Frontier after graduation.

I have a vivid memory of Kennedy at that podium—his tousled hair, his shirtsleeves, his palm slapping the wood for emphasis—but what remains with me as the source of a life-changing epiphany is the content of his speech. Instead of the expected diatribe against communism or crime, the attorney general spoke feelingly about civil rights. He identified the end of racial segregation as the most important challenge facing America—and the Justice Department. It was shocking to us, especially to those of us from the FBI side, since the bureau was almost entirely white—and we knew it was Hoover's intention to keep it that way. In 1961, the civil rights movement was still generally regarded by whites as threatening, perhaps subversive. For Kennedy to identify with the movement, and to bring its agenda into the heart of government, represented a transformation in the making—personal as well as political. I returned to the other side of the Justice Department building that day changed. The word *justice* would never fall on my ear in the same way again.

Robert Kennedy is precious in the American memory because he embodied the possibility of personal and political transformation. The arc of his own life was the story of such change, but so was his impact on government. The summer of 1961—the summit at Vienna, the Berlin crisis—was the apex of confrontation between the United States and the Soviet Union. Military men dominated

American responses, with some advocating "preventive war." Robert Kennedy played a crucial role in helping his brother transform hard-nosed confrontation into a spirit of negotiation, especially during the Cuban Missile Crisis. The Kennedys' tilt away from war at that crucial moment would define the future. The president's death thirty-eight years ago this Thursday would further Robert Kennedy's personal transformation and would prepare the nation to recognize its own need for new ways of understanding itself.

By the time Robert Kennedy launched his own campaign for president in 1968, his transformation was complete. The disenfranchised recognized this son of privilege as their own tribune. Blue-collar workers, whom many liberals disdained, saw him as an advocate. Those who had viscerally turned away from the war in Vietnam found in his embrace of peace a reason to turn back to politics. Traditional distinctions between right and left seemed not to apply among those who responded to him, and that phenomenon was the most promising aspect of the change he represented. The coincidence of Robert Kennedy's assassination on the heels of the assassination of Martin Luther King Jr. could seem like no coincidence at the time. Their deaths together sealed forever the meaning of American political hope—and for many Americans the names Bobby and Martin continue to resonate as anthems of an unfinished campaign.

That is why the naming of the Justice Department building for Robert Kennedy is a good thing. But there is, also, a contradiction in today's observance. As attorneys general go, John Ashcroft is a total repudiation of what Robert Kennedy came to stand for, and the Bush administration's approach to law enforcement in a time of national emergency evokes the memory of J. Edgar Hoover far more readily than that of his young nemesis. The assault on civil liberties in the name of "homeland security," especially the open contempt for noncitizens and the president's order establishing military tribunals, represent not only grave threats to justice but signals of surrender to terrorists aiming to undermine democracy. And the unbridled war in Afghanistan, however "successful," reverses the very progress embodied in Robert Kennedy's own journey from fierce cold warrior to advocate of negotiation and peace. On these several scores, one imagines Robert Kennedy interrupting today's ceremony to stand and say a word—his palm slapping the podium—of dissent.

Advent in a Time of Terror

December 4, 2001

I had just come in from attending Saturday evening Mass to mark the Christian observance of the start of Advent when the TV news broadcast the first bulletins of the terror attacks in Jerusalem. Like many others, I called friends at once to be sure their relatives were safe. Only a month ago, I had strolled the pedestrian mall that had just been turned into the latest scene of carnage. "They killed Jerusalem," one of my Israeli friends told another. The grief and anger of all who love Jerusalem came rushing in.

The refrain from the Advent hymn—"O come, O come, Emmanuel to rescue captive Israel . . ."—echoed in my mind through the next hours and day as the terrible story unfolded, culminating in the news of the even deadlier attack in Haifa. "Israel" of the hymn deferred suddenly to the Israel of actuality, a people held, if not captive, gravely at risk by suicide recruits—those pathetic young men convinced by the radical absolutism of their cause to put their own existence at the service of murder. Pathetic and profoundly dangerous.

As has been true so often, I am left wondering what I can do about this terrible ratcheting of violence, and as usual, of course, the answer is, nothing much. But the violence afflicting the world does not occur in a vacuum. Indeed, the rising levels of mayhem require all of us to discern in our own attitudes whatever might implicate us in the climate of hate, despite our first sense of ourselves as innocent.

What is our relation, for example, to the underlying question of religious absolutism, which fuels the winding of the terrorist gyre? I ask the question as a Christian and realize at once that the Advent season offers a clue.

Advent is a time of longing and expectation, when the Christian imagination is fired by all that is lacking in the human condition, by "the overwhelmingly 'not-yet' actuality of history itself," as the Catholic theologian David Tracy put it. Emmanuel, the hoped-for Messiah, will fulfill the promise of life, reveal the mysteries of existence—"establish the reign of God." Most Christian preaching nowadays locates the arrival of the Messiah at Christmas, and, indeed, Advent is taken mainly as prelude to the annual feast of the Incarnation. But emphasizing December 25 as the sole fulfillment of Christian hope is a mistake, one with implications for the tragic question posed by religion-based violence.

Advent is better understood as expressing the Christian longing not for the first coming of the Messiah, the birth of Jesus, but for the second, at the end of time. This seems like an arcane point, but it is crucial. The ancient Christian creed affirms that the life, death, and resurrection of Jesus was a partial fulfillment of God's plan, but salvation and redemption—"grace"—will be fully established only with the Second Coming of Christ. This means that Christians who claim to already be in full possession of the truth, or who understand the manifestations tied to the historical Jesus of Nazareth as the complete and finished revelation of God—such Christians have abandoned a key element of traditional faith, one that properly keeps Christianity from being a religion of radical absolutism. Here is how the Catholic theologian Gregory Baum put it: "Since divine redemption is not finished in Jesus, except by way of anticipation, the Church is not the unique vehicle of grace: room remains in world history for other ways of grace, for many religions, and in particular for the other biblical faith, for Judaism."

The Second Coming of Christ is rarely the subject of Christian sermons, perhaps because, as the absolute future, it inevitably relativizes present Christian truth claims. We Christians have grown fond of our exclusive universalism—one true church, one way to God. But events this year—this week—are showing us, too, how dangerous is all such religious absolutism. Islam and Judaism take the weight of this problem in their own ways. For us Christians, the antidote to religious absolutism is belief in the Second Coming, which openly defines truth here and now as perceptible only "through a glass darkly," in St. Paul's phrase. Christians, Muslims, Jews, people of other religions, and people of no religion—peace among us presumes a mutual honoring of the various dark lenses through which we see our different aspects of the truth. For those of us who are Christians, this respect for the other is a special calling in this season, when we long not for a narrowly defined celebration of our triumph but for the very fulfillment of history, for all people, the true advent of peace on earth.

The Unjustice Department

December 11, 2001

As the American war in Afghanistan shifts focus from the nearly concluded campaign against the Taliban to the properly narrower pursuit of Osama bin Laden, concerns in America are shifting, too. Many who have enthusiastically supported the Bush administration's response to the September catastrophe are now giving voice to serious doubts about the government's conduct and intentions, especially at home. Most objections are centered on policies of the Justice Department, with questions being raised about the status of hundreds of people who have been detained; about the dangers of government intrusion between attorneys and clients; about a climate that reduces constitutional principles to "niceties" to be sacrificed in a time of emergency.

A further question arose when the primacy of the government's antiterrorist emphasis suddenly took second place to the old Republican purpose of protecting gun owners' rights. In the context of all that has been jettisoned in the name of catching evildoers, past and future, it seemed anomalous when the Justice Department prevented its own FBI from determining if any of its terrorism suspects had purchased guns. The Justice Department spokesperson explained last week that this decision was made after the department determined that the law mandating the collection of such information did not allow it to be used in the identification of particular persons, even in the terrorism investigation. Such high-level government concern for individual rights might be edifying were it not so exceptional, and it seemed more than coincidence that the main beneficiaries of this one legal scruple, in addition to possible terrorists, would be the administration's political core.

Attorney General John Ashcroft has done little to dispel such uneasiness, and much to fuel it. Last week, for example, he deflected the rising tide of questions and criticisms by denouncing them as tactics that "give aid to the terrorists." It is always a signal moment when those entrusted with the protection of the U.S. Constitution define the activity that created the Constitution, and that the Constitution exists to create—the free exchange of ideas—as treason. This has happened before. One of the reasons the Vietnam War lasted so long was that Lyndon Johnson, and then Richard Nixon, succeeded in just such manipulation: criticism aids the enemy; therefore criticism is muted and marginalized. The effect of this strategy during Vietnam was that a war that should have ended in 1968, when the people voted against it, ended in 1975. And in Ashcroft's exploitation of this cynical ploy, he wasn't even talking of the war effort in Afghanistan, of which there has been so little criticism. He was speaking of questions aimed at policies that immediately affect life in America.

For these reasons, it might seem that Ashcroft was going overboard in evoking such an idea, but, for his administration's purposes, he is right to try to silence the voices of dissent before they gather.

Rising uneasiness about the handling of home-front questions could lead to a break in the patriotic consensus of support for policies abroad—especially the war as it threatens to expand to Iraq. Indeed with the defeat of the Taliban, it has already become evident that President Bush's oversimplified view that divided Afghanistan and other places between "us and them" never applied. Our Northern Alliance and Pakistani allies, it turns out, reject our simplifications about the Taliban, with some supporting the escape of fighters and others apparently prepared even to allow its fugitive leader to "live in dignity." Osama bin Laden belongs in the crosshairs of fierce American reaction, but as the dust settles from this first phase of the war, it remains unclear how the others got there. As war damage is toted up, that question will become powerful.

President Bush's establishment of military tribunals has drawn the hottest fire, but here, too, it is impossible to confine the issue to a domestic concern, without implications for a broader judgment about the war itself. Military tribunals are derided by critics on constitutional grounds, but the tribunals point to the larger problem of this entire enterprise. As an unregulated exercise of power, requiring little in the way of persuasive evidence, compelling testimony, regard for procedure, the possibility of appeal, or respect for complexity, these tribunals will institutionalize the administration's self-justifying moralism. The tribunals will legitimate the Bush preference of assertion over argument, diktat over advocacy. At the outset of this crisis, the leaders of Afghanistan asked to see America's evidence tying bin Laden to the crimes of September 11, a request which Bush mischaracterized as an obstinate call for negotiations. He swatted it away, making Taliban hostility inevitable.

Whether the Bush administration can continue to treat proper demands for accountability as a cause of war abroad and as treason at home remains to be seen. But already the grave question arises: is our government exploiting this emergency for its own narrow purposes?

Red Christmas

December 25, 2001

Today marks the birthday of Jesus of Nazareth, and also the tenth anniversary of the birth of the United States of America as the world's only superpower. On December 25, 1991, the flag of the Union of Soviet Socialist Republics was lowered from the Kremlin for the last time. The USSR officially ceased to exist. A month later, in his State of the Union speech, President George H. W. Bush declared that America had "won the cold war."

That the unparalleled contemporary political event occurred on the date of the epochal religious holiday might seem to be a coincidence of no particular significance, yet the juxtaposition can illuminate the meaning both of America's new preeminence and of the complex challenge posed by the simple nativity story.

Obviously, the anniversary of the birth of Jesus—the feast of the Incarnation—is reverently observed by Christians around the world, but the particular form the observance has taken in the United States is laden with political, cultural, and economic implications. All that we mean by *Christmas*—frantic shopping, gift giving, Santa Claus, decorations, evergreens, seasonal music, friendly greetings, family reunions, even the hope for a certain kind of weather—has become intertwined with the core of American identity. This is the subject of *Christmas Unwrapped: Consumerism, Christ, and Culture* (edited by Richard Horsley and James Tracy), a new book which inspires my meditation.

The holiday celebration in the United States is unlike any other country's—except where the American style is being consciously imitated. Adopting the particularities of this observance is one of the ways immigrants take on an American identity. Of course, America is not a merely "Christian" country, but the cultural centrality of Christmas is made clear in the way it stimulated the elevation of Hanukkah, a formerly minor holiday among Jews, and the invention of Kwanza, a holiday embraced by blacks who failed to recognize themselves in the "white" Christmas.

In fact, the song of that name, which serves as the preeminent American Christmas anthem, offers the clue. The scholar Kathleen M. Sands observes that when Bing Crosby yearns for a white Christmas "just like the ones we used to know," he is actually evoking a sentimental past that never was. Nostalgia becomes, in Sands's acute definition, "a forgetfulness that poses as memory." The Irving Berlin song was first performed by Crosby in *Holiday Inn*, an early World War II movie, and then reprised in the 1954 film *White Christmas*. In both cases, "Christmas is represented not only as a consoling memory for soldiers at war, but also as an emblem of American-ness itself, the home for which they were fighting." As hinted at by the appearance of the second movie as the cold war was frighteningly under way, Christmas by then, as Sands writes, "took on an even greater significance. For it now heralded in effect a new economy of 'grace,' abundance, interpersonal love, and individual freedom—an economy understood to contrast dramatically with the Communist economy of 'work,' sustenance, socialist citizenship, and state control." Seen in this way, the American Christmas is a celebration of all that helped us "win" the cold war. The lowering of the Red flag in Moscow is a confirmation of the moral, cultural, and economic supremacy of the American way. Thus Christmas, on this ten-year anniversary, is more American than ever.

In the dominant Christian memory, the nativity narratives set Jesus against the Jewish people. It is Jews who make no room at the inn, and a Jewish king who tries to kill the child, while gentiles travel from afar to worship him. This anti-Jewish reading of the Gospel undergirds the traditional assumption that the "Good News" is addressed to Christians and, by extension, Christian America. But what if the opposition posited by this story is not between Jesus and Judaism, but between Jesus and Rome, an oppressive imperial power? "The newly born Messiah of Israel, laid in a feeding trough,"

Horsley writes, "was the very opposite of a symbol of power that determined people's lives. He represented the hopes and aspirations of a subject people to be free from the exploitative imperial system that controlled their lives." The essential meaning of the nativity story, that is, is more political than religious. Instead of confirming an existing power structure, with its economic and cultural assumptions, the coming of this child defies every misuse of unchallenged dominance.

America is not the Soviet Union, nor is it ancient Rome. Our liberal democracy offers hope to the world. But our new status as the only surviving "superpower" carries a temptation to triumphalism that is increasingly dangerous. The story of the Jewish child set against that first "imperium" should make us ask whether this observance of his birth itself inadvertently manifests the imperium we are becoming.

New Year's Resolutions

January 1, 2002

You will lose five pounds. You will fix the broken window. You will clean the basement. You will do your exercise five days a week instead of two. You will visit the cemetery where Mom and Dad are buried. You will call your brothers and sisters. You will encourage your children. You will be a better spouse.

You will read Proust all the way through to the end. You will meditate every day. You will spend less time at your desk. You will get to the symphony before Seiji Ozawa departs. You will learn to appreciate the music young people listen to, or learn at least to hear it as music. You will resume piano lessons. You will sing in the shower. You will get that theater subscription. You will go to French movies. You will work on your French.

You will never use a cell phone in a public place. You will stay out of the passing lane except to pass. You will slow down, yield in rotaries. You will get the car serviced on schedule. You will take public transportation. You will walk more. You will make the connection between oil and politics, between politics and the economy. You will be aware of the underpaid workers who make your clothes.

You will answer your mail more thoughtfully. You will accept invitations, learn to say yes. You will work on the book you were born to write. You will believe it possible to surpass yourself, while letting go of vain ambition. You will remember what it was that once made you presume yourself a poet. You will reread Rilke. And you *will* read Proust through to the end.

You will remember the September dead, while carrying the heroes in your heart. You will regard flight attendants, pilots, and airport security people with absolute respect. You will cling to your revived patriotism, even as you listen for the voices of those for whom American privilege is an impossible dream. You will question your part in that privilege. You will understand the questioning as the greatest privilege. You will doubt the answers if they come with armed escorts, being more suspicious than ever of violence. You will sharpen your argument against war, even now. You will not let advocates of war pigeonhole you as well meaning but impractical. You will make the case for diplomacy and against belligerence, based not on pacifist moralism but on superior prospects for real and lasting success. You will show how bombing is inevitably disproportionate, how missile defense is self-defeating, and how force projection does not protect. You will not be surprised when those who disagree get personal, letting that be their problem. You will insist that the time for war is past. You will insist again.

You will speak up. You will express yourself even when you are not sure. You will dare to be wrong, then dare to admit it. You will call your long-estranged friend and propose coffee. At the café, you will pick up the tab. You will let your friend pick up the tab if your friend offers. You will laugh at yourself. You will say, if your friend agrees, that life is too short for bad feelings. Or even if your friend does not agree.

Now and then, you will call your own death to mind. You will make choices in its light. You will choose to believe in an afterlife without needing to define it. You will pray without expecting an answer. You will resign from your position as self-appointed manager of the universe. You will forgive yourself for being human. You will forgive yourself for the thought that being human requires forgiveness. You will allow the Holy One to be beyond imagining, even while you sense the presence of the Holy One in the sweetness of life, the kindness of strangers, the loyalty of those who love you. You will admit the fact of evil, its possible grip on you, without letting go of hope, passion, wide-eyed expectation. You will treat each day as a beginning. You will show up. You will be fully alive in the short term, letting the long run take care of itself. You will give what you can. You will receive.

You will pay attention to what matters most. You will lose five pounds. You will fix the window. You will clean the basement. You will be kind to yourself, a first kindness to others. For starters, you will not be surprised when you fail to keep these resolutions, especially the one about Proust. Except this: You will be good to your family. You will encourage your children. You will love your spouse.

PART TWO

SOLDIERS MARCHING

4

DEAD OR ALIVE

On December 13, 2001, a suicide-terrorist attack on the Parliament of India resulted in fourteen deaths and a major crisis between India and Pakistan. The unyielding American example of "dead or alive" set precedents for leaders of both nations, and threats quickly escalated. The Indian prime minister ordered evacuations of villages near disputed territories. Shelling began. Missiles and troops from both nations were mobilized and moved to the border between them. Nuclear exchange seemed possible.

On that same day, in Washington, President Bush announced that the United States would no longer consider itself bound by the Anti-Ballistic Missile Treaty with Russia, which had been in force since 1972. "As the events of September 11 made all too clear," he said in the Rose Garden of the White House, "the greatest threats to both our countries come not from each other or other big powers in the world, but from terrorists who strike without warning or rogue states that seek weapons of mass destruction." Yet Russia, and also China, opposed this move, and it was widely seen as yet another blow against the treaty regime—the complex of international agreements—that had brought some semblance of stability to the nuclear age.

Three weeks later, on January 8, 2002, the Pentagon produced its

Nuclear Posture Review, which substituted nuclear arms storage for reduction, outlined plans for U.S. resumption of nuclear testing, and broke with a long-established taboo by proposing the construction of "usable" nuclear weapons—a new generation of bunker-busting "mininukes." The review also explicitly anticipated the possible American use of nuclear weapons in future conflicts between Arabs and Israelis, China and Taiwan, North Korea and South Korea—or between Iraq and one of its neighbors.

It was in this context that tension mounted throughout January 2002 between India and Pakistan. A renewed American embrace of nuclear terror as a source of power is also the context in which to view the now famous "Axis of Evil" warning issued by President Bush in his State of the Union message on January 29, 2002. Though the president's solemnly stated purpose was to thwart "proliferation," his policies were its most fervent sponsors. If India and Pakistan felt freer to use their nuclear arsenals as sources of intimidation and threat, and if Iran, Iraq, North Korea, and other states sought or threatened to develop such arsenals (or other weapons of mass destruction) either for the power to intimidate or to deter threats, it was in part because such dead-or-alive tactics had been newly legitimized by the United States.

U.S. Moves Fuel Bellicosity Elsewhere

January 14, 2002

"If we have to go to war," said India's top military leader last week, "jolly good." And then he added, as if mournfully, "If we don't, we will still manage."

Once, Americans could hear such belligerent talk, and view two nations like India and Pakistan on the bloody cusp of major war, with a certain superior, if alarmed, detachment. But no more. U.S. secretary of state Colin L. Powell will be traveling to the region this week to press the increasingly hawkish leaders of both New Delhi and Islamabad to trust in diplomacy and mutual compromise as a way of resolving their differences, even over Kashmir. America wants Pakistan to rein in the extremist elements that have launched terrorist attacks against India, and America wants India to give Pakistan more leeway to do just that.

Pakistan's leader, General Pervez Musharraf, showed signs of cooperating this past weekend, but India responded that it wants deeds, not words. Thus Powell faces a major obstacle as he tries to defuse the most dangerous confrontation since the end of the cold war. Powell's problem? The harsh and reckless new rules India is playing by, alas, were written in Washington.

In fact, the threat-heavy script being read by India's prime minister, Atal Behari Vajpayee, eerily echoes the script from which George W. Bush has been reading for months. Vajpayee is telling Musharraf that he regards unchecked terrorist operations conducted from Pakistan against India as justification for a full-scale Indian attack—on Pakistan. Musharraf has been presented with a version of Bush's "us-or-them" ultimatum, but now Musharraf, having announced his intention to crack down on anti-Indian extremists in Pakistan, says there are limits to how far he can go in meeting such demands. For example, he seems to have rejected in principle the Indian demand to hand over culprits responsible for the December 13 suicide attack on India's Parliament, effectively asserting Pakistan's sovereign right to pursue justice on its own terms. Now the world waits to see, in effect, if New Delhi's next step will duplicate Washington's.

In this column, I have repeatedly invited readers to contemplate the shape of a world in which America's hypermartial response to terrorism became the new template for the exercise of power. It is no longer a hypothetical prospect. Even before we have accomplished the single most important war aim—"decapitating al

Qaeda"—our war has transformed the meaning of conflict else-where and has forced other nations, in imitating us, to previously unimagined levels of bellicosity. And not only on the subcontinent. The American mode of "dead or alive," robustly adopted since Octo-ber by Israel's Ariel Sharon, has already led to a disastrous break-down in the Middle East and promises nothing but further catastrophe. Palestinian terrorists feel licensed to escalate anticivil-ian outrages, and certainly will. And when Washington then urges restraint on Israel, why should Israelis not laugh bitterly?

Because a unilateral war formed the core of America's response to 9-11, the greatest moral shift to have occurred among nations in the twentieth century—the fragile but precious idea of institution-alized international mutuality—has been undercut. Nations owe each other minimal levels of cooperation, respect, and even defer-ence. Admittedly, this idea was already battered, especially by Amer-ica's post-cold-war contempt for the United Nations. But with the American declaration that it will pursue terrorists in any way it pleases, accountable to no one, no matter the consequences to oth-ers, the dream of the world as a community of peoples, each worthy of respect, is dead. Now the world is the scene onto which one na-tion presumes to project its power, leaving to others only the deci-sion whether to bow before that power or risk being bombed.

And here's the joke: this crude strategy of swaggering power does not work. It does not lead to the accomplishment of minimal Amer-ican purposes. This inconvenient fact is becoming embarrassingly evident as the war in Afghanistan winds down. A collection of des-peradoes has been brought to the U.S. detention center in Cuba, but there is no reason to believe that the al Qaeda elite are among them. And if Osama bin Laden has, in fact, escaped, despite the bombing and its perhaps thousands of dead Afghan civilians, will we still be satisfied that this was the proper way to respond to September 11?

And if India and Pakistan now go to war? Will America even then find it possible to entertain a second thought about the momentum we set going? Or are such reconsiderations unworthy of the Wild West Texas our nation has become? Drunken cowboys—and you can be drunk on power—don't give a damn for consequences. Or, as India's top military man put it the other day, "When two wild bulls decide to fight in a jungle, they carry on regardless."

The Axis to Fear

February 5, 2002

The defeat of Hitler, coming only weeks after the death of Franklin D. Roosevelt, marked the end of one era and the beginning of another, when the Soviet Union went immediately from being America's indispensable partner to being America's nemesis. Roosevelt's inclination to pursue cooperation with Moscow was replaced by Truman's apparent hunger for confrontation. On April 23, 1945, the new president met in Washington with Soviet foreign minister V. M. Molotov. The Russian had requested the meeting hoping to avoid "differences of interpretation and possible complications" that would not have arisen "if Roosevelt lived."

But Molotov was met with what the historian Daniel Yergin calls "a stern lecture" from Truman. "I have never been talked to like that in my life," protested Molotov. To which Truman answered, "Carry out your agreements and you won't get talked to like that." This at the moment when the bloodied Red Army, carrying out its ultimate agreement, was closing in on Berlin. In his classic work *Shattered Peace*, Yergin comments, "A stern lecture by the President of the United States to the Foreign Minister of the Soviet Union was hardly the cause of the Cold War. Yet that exchange did symbolize the beginning of the postwar divergence that led to confrontation."

A few weeks later, at the organizing meeting of the United Nations in San Francisco, the American delegation escalated the confrontation with the Soviets, prompting the journalist Walter

Lippmann to sound an alarm. The U.S.-Soviet face-off, he wrote, "is not inherent in the nature of things but is due to inexperience and emotional instability in our own delegation. . . . This should never have happened. It would never have happened, I feel sure, if President Roosevelt were still alive, and it will lead to great trouble."

These incidents are often recalled in the context of the question whether the cold war was necessary. But my interest is simpler. Truman's enforcers were convinced that the Soviets would yield before such pressure. After all, the United States of America stood alone as an unchallenged superpower, the only nation to come out of World War II intact, far stronger than it had ever been. The devastated Soviet Union would have no choice, in Yergin's words, except "to accept a subsidiary role in the postwar world."

Sound familiar? The new American position of absolute preeminence was on full display in President Bush's State of the Union speech last week. Washington bluntly dictates its will on everything from the international treaties it chooses to abrogate or ignore, to monetary policy, to the next battlegrounds for the war on terrorism. When President Bush declared his readiness to attack the "Axis of Evil," it mattered less that there is no such axis among the three named states than that, in the face of such bluster, they now have a reason to create one. The Manichaeism of the evangelical president requires an "evil" against which America can be "good." Oh, and by the way, that cosmic contest, once declared, justifies the largest military buildup since the first Reagan administration.

Against what enemy? Not terrorists. The impotence of American chest-thumping is revealed in nothing more pointedly than the embarrassing—and rarely noted—fact that the triumphant war against the Taliban led to the apprehension of neither Osama bin Laden nor the anthrax attacker. The war against terrorism requires far subtler responses than the Pentagon sledgehammer. Adding weight to the hammerhead, at the cost of billions, will not make us safer from anthrax psychopaths or suicidal fanatics. But it may lead to something worse.

When Walter Lippmann warned of trouble in 1945, he could not have imagined with what efficiency the Soviet Union would respond to the arrogant ultimatum it received from Washington. Moscow rejected any notion of subsidiarity. Its quick—and in America, almost entirely unforeseen—development of its own nuclear arsenal revealed Truman's initial swagger for what it was: the brutishness of a puerile fool. And today? It seems inconceivable that any state power will emerge to challenge American dominance, but we would likewise have to be fools to assume our sway is permanent.

Yes, we are the most powerful nation in the history of the planet. Yet we are terrified. Out of fears driven by one kind of threat, based on the capacity of anarchic individuals to cause mass suffering, we are creating an overwhelming response to an entirely other kind of threat, one existing only in the imaginations of Pentagon planners—and of contract-happy defense contractors. The coming military buildup, irrelevant to terrorism, may lead instead to the creation of a monster that can indeed oppose us. It happened before. "Inexperience and emotional instability," together with the puerile thrill of power, rampant moralism, and supreme arrogance—there is an axis to fear.

Bush the Radical

February 19, 2002

George W. Bush is widely regarded as the avatar of a conservative restoration, but he is the opposite. This presidency marks a radical overthrow of traditional American values and policies. Civil liberties are obviously at issue in the new regime of homeland security, but the most drastic shift involves American attitudes toward war.

For a generation, the massive U.S. arsenal has been managed with the purpose of *not being used*. With the exceptions of the first Gulf War, and the NATO air war against Serbia, this purpose was achieved. It was rooted in the post-Vietnam assumption that war is a last resort, to be avoided if possible. And it was confirmed when the terrifying conflict with the Soviet Union ended nonviolently, a victory for the policies of deterrence and containment that finally enabled the Soviet peoples themselves to take back their governments. Something called the "peace process" moved from the idealistic fringe to the heart of the exercise of American power.

Now, a radically different assumption is undergirding American purpose, a repudiation of the experience of the last fifty-five years. With putative battlefields around the globe, war is all at once being defined as the essence of who we are, and nothing makes this clearer than the new Pentagon budget.

For the next fiscal year, the Bush administration proposes to spend nearly $400 billion on defense. Last week, in testimony before the House Budget Committee, Lawrence J. Korb of the Council on Foreign Relations and a member of Business Leaders for Sensible Priorities, put this figure in perspective. It represents a 30 percent increase over last year; a level 15 percent more than what the cold war required; the biggest budget jump since Vietnam. If this budget is approved, America's military spending will exceed the total defense outlays "of the next 15 countries in the world combined." This year's "increase of $48 billion alone is more than the total military budgets of every nation in the world."

This budget request, Korb observed, surpasses any budget that Donald Rumsfeld sent to Congress when he served as secretary of defense during the height of the cold war. But doesn't Rumsfeld's war on terrorism require such urgent increases? No. As Korb notes, the war in Afghanistan has cost about $6 billion, and the budget for next year allocates $10 billion for the ongoing conflict against terrorism—both figures falling far short of the new increases, which, Korb argues, will push the budget total to $580 billion by 2007.

The proposal funds programs and equipment that will play no role in any conceivable war against stateless terrorists: high-tech aircraft, submarines, tanks, the missile defense system. Fulfilling just these commitments will cost more than $100 billion. All of which amounts, in Korb's view, to "throwing . . . money at the Pentagon and refusing to make choices." Korb's is a lonely voice in this debate, and, incidentally, not one raised from the left. He served as assistant secretary of defense under Ronald Reagan.

Here are the questions raised by the Bush administration's proposed military budget:

- Who benefits? Alas, the old answer, in the era of Enron, suggests itself with a new edge. Of dubious security value, these unprecedented expenditures will enrich resuscitated defense contractors and reelect politicians they fund. Compared to this nexus of corporate-political corruption, Enron is benign.
- Aware that the preparation for war has its own momentum, are we setting loose forces we cannot control? Has the shoot-first-ask-questions-later mode of the war on terrorism led to a new recklessness in relation to anticipated wars against states that alone justify such a budget?
- Knowing what the effect on our enemies of such a massive new arsenal will be, what will be its effect on us, just having it? The moral question: when America could have used its unprecedented power to lead the world away from war, what will it reveal about our national character that we did the opposite?
- If this budget is adopted, will it mean that we Americans responded to our traumatic season of vulnerability with a radical new military posture because it seemed to salve a wound? World violence more likely, the long-term economic health of our own country undermined—and for what? To feel better?

These questions boil down to questions about our president. In proposing such a wildly disproportionate defense budget, is George

W. Bush deluded, or is he cynical? Is he consciously exploiting the nation's moment of uncritical patriotism, or is he himself ontologically uncritical? And which would be worse?

In wrapping himself in the flag, while putting the interests of defense contractors ahead of the nation's, is President Bush betraying what the flag stands for? And while this radical change is being implemented in Washington, why aren't conservatives asking such questions?

America as Sparta

March 12, 2002

When did Athens become Sparta? When did America redefine itself so profoundly around war? Events of this winter had already prompted the question, but then two days ago the *New York Times* published the stunning news of the Pentagon's Nuclear Posture Review. Reversing a longtime trend away from nuclear dependence, our government is openly projecting an American military strategy based on usable nukes, with unprecedented potential for first use against nonnuclear states, for development of new nuclear weapons, and even for a resumption of nuclear testing. This is a move from Mutual Assured Destruction, as the *Times* put it, to Unilateral Assured Destruction—our enemy's. Washington is thinking the unthinkable.

How did this happen? In less than half a year we have reinvented ourselves as the most belligerent people on earth. Why? The conventional answers are that the terror assaults of September required this response, and that an evil axis poses a deadly threat. But a deeper answer, perhaps, is that the September blow to the American psyche set in motion a reaction of grief, anger, and fear never before felt so powerfully. The war on terrorism can seem to purge such emotions. The savage face embodied in the new nuclear posture can seem a perfect expression of the wound we suffered, whether it makes future suffering less likely or more.

But the ease with which we have commissioned another generation of young people to wreak havoc in our defense, as we imagine it, and the blithe spirit with which we are now rolling the nuclear dice cry out for other explanations. What notes in the American character might account for this amazing shift? Here are four that occur to me.

- *American time.* Uniquely among nations, we define ourselves by the future, not the past. This is the source of our optimism, key to our greatness. But it also means we waste little effort on self-criticism, the lessons of history. Thus we are permanently innocent and quick to see those who oppose us as evil. If we behave with good intentions, it is enough. That our good intentions have often gone awry in the past is forgotten.
- *American money.* Valuing entrepreneurial creativity, we trust our companies, another key to our greatness. But companies have an unexamined bias toward war. Weapons manufacture has been an economic engine for half a century, a source of prosperity. And then, once weapons exist, pressure to use them is eventually irresistible, setting off a new round of development and manufacture. The only check on this cycle is politics, but now politicians are entirely subservient to the companies that pay them with "contributions." The war economy, reeling after détente with Moscow, has just reinvigorated itself.
- *American selfhood.* We are never more ourselves than when going it alone, from the "rugged individual" to the Texas Ranger. Despite the communal character of our best work (science, technology), our congenital skepticism toward international collectivity (e.g., the U.N.) undercuts the cross-border law enforcement (e.g., the International Criminal Court) that alone can combat terrorism effectively. Unilateral warfare feels normal to us because we conduct it on our own terms, accountable to no one—like real Americans.

- *American exemption.* Because the September attacks were the first massive violence suffered in the continental United States since the Civil War, they left us uncertain and afraid. But elsewhere in the world, the devastations of war are all too common. To us they remain abstract. September memories, in fact, underscore how the horrors of modern warfare have never touched the cities of America. That is the only reason we can reinvent American force projection around robot strikes, strategic bombing, and even usable nuclear weapons. All of this represents a failure of the American imagination to grasp the real effect on real people of such assaults. What if the *New York Times* published an individual obituary of every person killed by U.S. forces?

In each of these instances, the source of the greatness of the American character proves to have a dark side, and its forces are unleashed by overwhelming grief, anger, and fear. Darkness indeed. But the great insight of tragic literature—what Athens gave to the world—is that grief, anger, and fear can lead, in the mystery of human freedom, not to revenge but to wisdom. What is wisdom in our present circumstance except another way to think of war? Beware the war on terrorism, and beware the Nuclear Posture Review! Beware the Bush administration's exploitation of our grief, anger, and fear. We must urgently reconsider the course we have set out upon this year before it leads us into a dead end of our own making.

Then survivors will ask: when did America become Sparta? And the answer will come: it was now.

Pakistan versus India

May 28, 2002

The shock of headlines leaves us unable to distinguish between the merely awful and a world-historic threat. The Catholic Church's priest sex-abuse crisis and even the war on terrorism will be mere footnotes to the present age if the conflict between India and Pakistan moves from border skirmishing to general war. As the prospect of such escalation grows more likely by the day, here are several points deserving of renewed emphasis:

- There has never been a shooting war between two nuclear powers. And war, by definition, carries its own irrational momentum. The possibility of new Hiroshimas on the subcontinent is real, perhaps imminent.
- From within the dispute between India and Pakistan, issues of national sovereignty and religious identity seem worth the risk even of nuclear war, but from outside there is no conceivable justification of that risk. This is the position of the United States and other nations.
- But that contradiction adheres in every situation of war. From within a dispute, drastic action is always justified. From outside it, compromise, negotiation, and restraint are always seen as preferable to violence. The India-Pakistan war, in other words, is a revelation of the futility of war as such. Therefore it is not enough for the United States and other nations to urge restraint on New Delhi and Islamabad.
- The escalation of this conflict has not occurred in a vacuum. Two things have made it possible: a broad international climate of moral approbation in favor of war, and widespread indifference to the threat still posed by nuclear weapons. The real and

immediate prospect of a nuclear war must generate changes on both these fronts.

There was a time when the populations of nations got out ahead of their governments on the urgent question of nuclear war. From the "ban the bomb" movement of the 1950s to the "nuclear freeze" movement of the 1980s; from student activists to aging peaceniks; from the scientists of Pugwash to the mothers of Women's Action for Nuclear Disarmament; from antinuclear organizations of physicians and lawyers to those of businesspeople and bishops—the voices of ordinary citizens have been raised in the past to tremendous effect on this question. Indeed, it may be that the arms race itself was reversed by those voices, once governments were forced to hear them.

Where are such voices today? Or, to ask the question another way, what happened to the tradition of "resistance"? During the height of the cold war, many human beings across the globe discovered that the only way to live humanly in the nuclear age was in active opposition to the coming prospect of the nuclear nightmare. After 1990, the danger seemed to abate, and the resistance evaporated. The same broad population that once regarded the risk of nuclear war as an urgent public problem accepted the myth that nuclear war would never happen. In America, this led to indifference even as government officials abandoned nuclear-limiting treaties (Test Ban, ABM), proposed new nuclear weapons programs (bunker-busting nukes, weaponization of space), and reiterated the dogma that American power rests on its permanent nuclear arsenal. Hardly anyone seemed to notice as these trends in the United States reinforced the determination of other nations to wield such power. Hardly anyone seemed to notice, even more concretely, when the moral capacity of the United States to object to nuclear testing by India and Pakistan was undercut by the U.S. Senate's just-prior rejection of the Comprehensive Test Ban Treaty.

The context within which India and Pakistan have moved to the brink of nuclear war has thus been defined not only by the irresponsibility of other governments but by the detachment of citizens everywhere who no longer see the prevention of such war as involving them. And now? Are we really to watch the unfolding of the crisis along the border of India and Pakistan as if it is the Catholic bishops, say, in contest with the press? As if it is the FBI in blame-game competition with the CIA?

We owe it to the "fate of the earth," in Jonathan Schell's great phrase, to do far more than that. We must, first, think the unthinkable again, imagining what the world after even a limited nuclear war will be like. And we must face the question that such a possible future already puts to every one of us: what are you doing to try to prevent this disaster?

The only way to live humanly—still—is in resistance to war. The prevention of war, in the nuclear age, must be a central purpose of every person's life. Scientists, physicians, lawyers, bishops, mothers, fathers, students, businesspeople, writers—where are you? We must remember what we learned already but forgot; what the leaders of India and Pakistan are showing us again: if we human beings leave this problem to our governments, we are doomed.

5

JERUSALEM

Within weeks of the 9-11 attacks in New York and Washington, a Palestinian attack on a Jerusalem restaurant killed Israeli tourism minister Rehavam Zeevi. The assassination of a government official was taken as a major escalation of the terror campaign. Zeevi was targeted probably because he had voiced support for the idea of "transfer" of Palestinians from disputed territories. When suspected assassins were tracked to Palestinian leader Yasir Arafat's headquarters in Ramallah—their presence there an emblem of Arafat's duplicity—Israeli tanks and soldiers surrounded the compound. Israel's prime minister, Ariel Sharon, took the fresh Palestinian provocation, in combination with Washington's new "dead-or-alive" absolutism, as the occasion to define Israel's campaign as the front line of the war on terrorism. The "overwhelming force" standard set in Washington would be used to justify ever harsher Israeli tactics, including home demolitions, generalized punishment, extrajudicial assassinations, and a sealing off of the West Bank and Gaza that would choke the Palestinian economy, leading to widespread joblessness among young Palestinian men—a prime recruiting pool for terrorism—and to grave levels of malnourishment among Palestinian children.

Eventually, that sealing off would lead to a "security barrier," a vast fortified wall-and-fence that effectively appropriated disputed territory. Referring to the peace agreement struck between Israel and the Palestinians in 1993, Sharon said in early December 2001, "Oslo is long gone." A majority of Israelis continued to believe in the tenets of Oslo—two states, compromise over Jerusalem, the withdrawal of most Jewish settlements from disputed territory, a firm Palestinian commitment to Israeli security—but that majority, feeling under siege, also accepted Sharon's tough response to Palestinian assaults.

In Ramallah, Arafat became a virtual prisoner. Israel would no longer treat him as a negotiating partner. Hamas and Islamic Jihad renewed their campaigns to destroy the state of Israel. The nihilist tactic of suicide-murder was accepted as legitimate by many Palestinians and by many of their supporters. Throughout the Arab world, the belief that the attacks on the World Trade Center and the Pentagon were the work of Jews spread widely, and openly anti-Semitic rhetoric became a feature of much Islamic preaching. In Europe, complaints about Israel morphed into slurs on Jews, while "anti-Zionism" fueled anti-Americanism.

A Bush administration spokesman placed part of the blame for the increased tensions on the Clinton administration's Middle East peace initiatives, characterized as attempting to "shoot the moon." Contrasting Bush policies toward the Middle East—no serious peace efforts, no criticism, even, of ongoing settlements in the West Bank—would be decisively influenced by neoconservative Washington allies of Likud, Israel's right-wing ruling party. Proponents of the Bush hard line would welcome Sharon's. The cooperation between the two leaders was symbolized, on April 18, 2002, when Bush called Sharon a "man of peace."

Muslims, Jews, Christians, and Peace

October 23, 2001

I am writing this en route to a long-scheduled interfaith conference at the Shalom Hartman Institute in Jerusalem. For a quarter of a century, the institute has been a center of interreligious reconciliation, bringing Jews, Christians, and, more recently, Muslims together for frank exchange on the most difficult questions. The center is presided over by Rabbi David Hartman, and his prophetic work has obviously never been more important. As the Catholic theologian Hans Küng has famously put it: "No peace among the nations without peace among the religions. No peace among the religions without dialogue between the religions. No dialogue between the religions without investigations of the foundations of the religions."

Take, for example, the title of the conference session at which I am to present: "Correcting our memories and traditions—confronting the passions of religious fundamentalism." If all goes well, by the time you read this I will have joined Muslims and Jews in considering the questions of how, as the conference program puts it, we "correct our traditions" when they show themselves to be inhuman—and how basic change in religious affirmation can be made "without undermining the authority" of tradition itself.

I bring to this inquiry the experience of a Christian aware of the challenge posed to the Christian conscience by the history of church antisemitism. Momentous as that challenge has been—a nearly two-thousand-year-long arc of Christian contempt for Jews, without which the Holocaust would not have happened—it is only one thread of the religious problem that makes the future of Israelis and Palestinians so uncertain, and that makes the world such a newly dangerous place. The "clash of civilizations" between the West and Islam, after all, not only may loom ahead but defines much of what lies behind as well. With such a gulf of understanding separating the apparent majority of Muslims and the successors of a Christian West, what chance is there, first, to avoid the wider conflict now, and, second, to achieve a mutuality of full respect? The most intense, local version of that question, shifting away from Europe and a remnant Christendom, is: what hope can there be for peace between Israel and Palestinians? These already difficult questions are compounded, of course, when the faces contending parties show to one another are contorted by the "passions of religious fundamentalism."

Anticipating these discussions, I have no illusions about their difficulty. Political and economic realities are daunting enough without religious miscomprehension. Yet the history of the relatively narrow Jewish-Christian dialogue suggests the real possibility of major progress with Islam—for two reasons. First, the antagonism between Christianity and Judaism has been intrinsic to the relationship in a way that antagonisms with Islam are not. It wasn't just that the church "superseded" Judaism, as Islam sees itself as superseding Christianity and Judaism, but that the church defined itself in positive terms against the negative of Jews and Jewish religion. *This* ontological structure of mind is reflected in Christian Scriptures (New versus Old), in Christology (Jesus the New Temple), in theology (Jews as degraded witnesses). These are hints of the foundational Christian traditions that cried out to be corrected after recognitions tied to the Holocaust. This is a level of needed correction that goes far deeper than any correction required by tensions either between Islam and Judaism or between Islam and Christianity.

The second reason for expectations of progress with Islam is the fact that even this deep level of needed correction in Christian attitudes toward Judaism is being addressed. There is hope for relations with Islam, that is, in the progress Jews and Christians have made with each other. The church increasingly sees what must be corrected in its beliefs and attitudes, and despite the fact that such change can seem to undermine the authority of the tradition, earnest attempts at accomplishing those corrections are under way. Such reform proceeds, admittedly, in fits and starts, but correction of anti-Jewish bigotry has been a mark, especially, of the post-Holocaust Roman Catholic Church. If the most ingrained of inhuman religious prejudice can be uprooted, so can other religiously justified bigotries and barbarities—from male supremacy, to ethnic chauvinism, to the idolatry of nationalism, to the complacency of the affluent who mistake their excess for a divine blessing, to the rage of the dispossessed who can see suicidal violence as sacred.

We take the contemporary phenomenon of Jewish-Christian reconciliation almost for granted, but not so long ago, such progress would have been unthinkable. Alas, this progress results from awareness growing out of the most savage crime in history, which suggests what is at stake in the present crisis. In working for religious reconciliation before a larger explosion of inhuman violence, we build on the reconciliation that inhuman violence already made mandatory. A tragic past between Christians and Jews opened to a new future. That future can include Islam, too. Therefore, this Christian returns to Jerusalem, even now, in hope.

The Palestinian and the Israeli

October 30, 2001

I arrive as a dinner guest at the home in Arab Jerusalem of a professor at Al Quds University, a member of a prominent Palestinian family. Upon my arrival, my host and his five-year-old daughter dance in the living room, each with a forefinger in the air, a dance of welcome. Other guests include a second Al Quds professor, also Palestinian, and two Israeli intellectuals. We sit with wine and make small talk. Mark Twain's portrait of Jerusalem comes up, and then we are discussing Tom Sawyer's feeling of being caught between two worlds.

The dinner is delayed because the final guest has not arrived. Our host and his wife exchange a worried glance. Then the telephone rings. It is the missing guest, calling from Bethlehem not many miles away. After hanging up, our host explains that she won't be coming. Israeli tanks are in the town, and one is firing just outside her house. She is sorry. She sends her greetings.

No more Mark Twain. Our hosts usher us to a gracious table, but the anguish of the war across the hills has taken the place of the missing guest. The new cycle of violence began turning the other day when Israeli cabinet minister Rehavam Zeevi was assassinated by a Palestinian terrorist. Zeevi had been on the far extreme of Israeli politics, an advocate of "transfer" of all Arabs out of Israel, a formula for total war. But no cabinet minister had ever been murdered by a Palestinian before, and at the state funeral the Zeevi family's rage had seemed to become Israel's. The terrorist had killed him, no doubt, hoping to spark reprisals that would make progress toward a negotiated peace even less likely. The reprisals are under way. Dozens of people have been killed.

At the table, we raise our glasses, each one making a point to touch the glass of every other. But then, inevitably, as food is passed, the painful subject dominates. Our host's Al Quds colleague passionately reiterates the story of Palestinian dispossession. One of the Israelis, a former U.N. official, fervently replies with the story of a Jew's return to his homeland. But whose homeland? Each recapitulates the tragedy of the two narratives. The Jew is himself a Holocaust survivor, but the real edge of his story comes from a people's nearly two thousand years of praying "Next year in Jerusalem." The Palestinian is himself the son of the forcibly exiled, living in the city of his birth on a visitor's visa. Each refers to his own history as proof. Two worlds indeed.

Hurt and fury fill the room. I have never heard the contradictory truths so vividly stated, stories that could seem to cancel each other out. Indeed "canceling" has come to dominate both Israeli politics and Palestinian strategy. Only months ago, parties on both sides were able to hear the validity of the other's claims, but now many on each side are saying that only one or the other can be victorious. It seems impolite to ask: and what is victory?

Even at this desperate moment, it is clear that more important than any abstract talk of "rights" is the twin reality of two peoples side by side in the same place, equally resolved to stay. "Transfer" is a deadly fantasy for either side. Also clear is that majorities on both sides have embraced that twin reality, and still assume the consequent necessity of compromise. For now, uncompromising fringe minorities have taken control. Arafat is at the mercy of killers whom he has sponsored in the past and keeps alive in the present. The Sharon government, with this crude assault, is enacting a script written by the terrorists themselves. Is there more security for Israel in sparking the rage of Palestinian boys who can now be recruited as suicide-bombers?

Unleashed violence has been justified in the past in a thousand ways, but when killing enemies must take second place to winning over larger populations within which enemies thrive, such violence is manifestly obsolete. The invasion of Bethlehem proves that, and so does the bombing of Afghanistan. The meaning of victory has been redefined, but the "dead-or-alive" warriors haven't heard. They do not see how irrelevant their heavy weapons are in the new conflict that faces us all.

At the end of the dinner party, our gracious hosts make it possible for us to depart wishing each other well, antagonists included, and that alone seems a small sign of hope. Back at my hotel, I stand at the window looking out at the hills beyond which war rages. I offer a prayer for the guest who could not come, for this city, my country, the world. I am safe in my room yet afraid.

Lost Children of the Conflict

March 19, 2002

"O ruined piece of nature. This great world shall so wear out to naught." This line, spoken by Gloucester in *King Lear*, refers to individual mortality, but the frightful destiny of the great world can also be glimpsed in the affairs of nations. The conflict between the Israelis and the Palestinians is disturbing for numerous reasons—not least of which is the fact that the old Arab determination to fully annihilate the state of Israel seems to have regained currency among Palestinians. That might be counted as Arafat's single success, yet it is surely a measure, also, of Sharon's failure—and of the failure of the Bush policy of "dead or alive," which licensed Sharon's fatal escalation.

But now, with the Israeli Defense Force and the suicidal killers of the Palestinian militias locked in a conflict neither can withdraw from, one sees an instance of the most terrifying scenario that can be imagined. This is the way the very earth could move to self-destruction—two forces in conflict that, even as it unfolds, is understood by both as leading inevitably to mutual doom, yet neither party can stop. The complete irrationality of violence has never been more clearly on display than in the Middle East this year, yet the grip of violence on the minds of Israeli and Palestinian leaders could not be stronger. In America, meanwhile, we tell ourselves that our robust war on terrorism has gone well, yet the Israeli experience suggests how efficiently amoral terrorists are recruited out of the ruined pieces of nature that fall from "overwhelming force." Israel's dilemma is a foretaste of America's: *this great nation shall so wear out to naught.*

Where is the hope? Today, at the Dag Hammerskjold Plaza at the United Nations in New York, more than a thousand coffins will be laid out in rows. They will be covered with flags—blue-and-white flags of the state of Israel and red-green-black-and-white flags of the Palestinian Authority. The coffins represent each of the persons killed in the eighteen months of warfare, a display which refuses to treat the casualty numbers as an abstraction. Each of the dead was a person with a name, a history, a hope; each was a person with a family. Each was someone's child. And each will be represented on the plaza today.

Remarkably enough, it is parents of the Israeli and Palestinian dead who have arranged today's display of coffins—a reaction of grief and heartbreak that has led not to a cry for revenge but to a plea for peace. The Parents' Circle is a cross-conflict group consisting of 190 Israelis and 140 Palestinians who have the overriding experience in common of having lost a child to the violence. And by seeing the violence through the lens of that loss, they see it differently. Suddenly, birth and youth and generational hope enter the picture to balance the dread mortality of the old. By insisting on the fact that the lives of children are overwhelmingly what is at stake in this war, the Parents' Circle is demanding an alternative to the despair of violence.

Not only that. By reminding us that these dead began as beloved children, and are still mourned as such, the Parents' Circle puts the fate of children squarely before the decision makers—not only as a responsibility but as an opportunity. "Every new child who comes into the world carries within himself or herself the promise of a bright future," Boston's Dr. Jane Schaller, president of the International Pediatric Association, told a major gathering in Israel last month. "No child is born with discrimination in his or her mind, hatred in his or her heart, or rocks in his or her hands. These are acquired conditions." They are not innate. They are not necessary. They are not inevitable. The future can be different from the past.

In the midst of an unending war, what does it take to see that? In the case of the Parents' Circle, it took the shattering of personal hope to create the possibility of political hope. These Israelis and Palestinians, working together, have erected billboards across the battle zones of Israel, the West Bank, and Gaza, saying simply, "Better the pains of peace than the agonies of war—Yitzhak Rabin." Having lost children of their own, these parents see better than anyone else how war brings the great world to naught. All those coffins. Yet still, they call for another way. "When people who have made the ultimate sacrifice can commit themselves, out of profound loss and grief, to reconciliation and peace," one of their American supporters told me, "those of us who care about the region have no right to lose hope."

The Disappearing Border

May 1, 2002

The mystery, as Ariel Sharon meets President Bush in Washington today, is why supporters of Israel do not regard Sharon more skeptically. In the past, Sharon has done more to shame the Jewish state than any other leader, and his current term in office is an unparalleled disaster—obviously so for Palestinians, but even more so for Israelis. Why not hold Sharon to the most basic test of governance: does he improve the safety of his own citizens, or does he undercut it? Ask the question with his long career in mind.

In the early 1970s, Sharon was a leading force behind the "creation of facts," the salting of the West Bank and Gaza with Jewish settlements. That unchecked movement is the ground of the present conflict. The "facts" of Israeli settlements on the disputed land were originally seen by a small minority of Jews as a righteous claim to biblical territory, while most Israelis saw the settlements, especially those distant from Jerusalem, as cards to be traded away in a final negotiation. Land for peace. But with the encouragement of Sharon and others, the claim of the fringe minority strengthened over the years, and the "facts" hardened. The settlements are populated now by more than two hundred thousand people, and Sharon declared only last week that he will not preside over the removal of even one of them. What began mainly as a ploy aimed toward resolution has become, under Sharon, the greatest obstacle to resolution. What began as a fringe movement in Israel has shifted, under Sharon, to the political center.

To Palestinians, meanwhile, the settlements, especially those constructed after the Oslo agreement, are proof that Israel cannot be trusted. Situated strategically on tops of hills, and lavish in comparison to nearby Palestinian communities, the settlements are stark manifestations of inequality and sources therefore of Palestinian rage. The settlement access roads are further "facts" that undercut Palestinian territorial claims. These complaints are well known.

What is less often remarked upon is the single most drastic consequence for the state of Israel resulting from the Sharon-led settlement movement. If there has been one word to define the hope of Israel's Jews, that word is *security*. The fundamental responsibility of the government of Israel has been to guarantee security to its citizens. And the first rule of modern statecraft is that such security begins with clearly defined, and agreed upon, national borders. It was at the Treaty of Westphalia in 1648, ending a decades-long religious war in the heart of Europe, that the principle of absolutely defined political boundaries was enshrined as the main structure of peace. The Congress of Vienna in 1815 reinstitutionalized this impulse, and so did the Treaty of Versailles in 1919. No peace without clear borders, ratified by states on either side of them.

In a pattern of breathtaking self-destruction, Israeli governments, again and again, have deliberately blurred the eastern border of the state, effectively dissolving it. That, at bottom, is what Sharon and his settlements have made of Israel—a nation with no clearly defined border. The result? Radical insecurity no matter what Palestinians do. Even nations that are friendly, like, say, the United States and Canada, depend on clearly demarcated, agreed-upon borders. The maintenance and protection of those borders are the first duty of government. Doubly so if the neighbor is a potential enemy.

Yet no Israeli government can maintain or protect the border between the West Bank and Israel because it simply does not exist. There are, to be sure, military checkpoints along the vestigial Green Line, the borders of 1967, but the real line between the territories now and "Israel" is necessarily porous and ambiguous exactly because so many Jewish enclaves are located amid so many Palestinian towns and camps. That many Jewish settlers have valued that ambiguity because it has enabled them to claim more and more Palestinian land only makes their plight ironic.

The Jewish enclaves, surrounded by a hostile populace, are entirely vulnerable to terrorist assaults. Equally, the Israeli Defense Force is incapable of "securing" such ill-defined territory, which partly explains why, in its frustration, the IDF struck out so inhumanely in recent weeks. The Israeli incursions into the West Bank have been irrational and counterproductive exactly because the presence there of Israeli settlements is irrational and counterproductive. When Israeli military leaders complain that settlements are indefensible, as they did again only last week, they are really decrying the lack of a border to defend. And, at bottom, a simple border is what Israeli advocates of the problematic "separation" long for, but there can be no agreed border when the line is broken by territories in dispute. The border-blurring settlements have been bad for the Palestinians, but—obliterating Jewish security—they have been worse for Israel.

And who is the architect of this teetering house of cards? Ariel Sharon, Israel's self-proclaimed defender. Yet if he were Israel's sworn enemy, how could he have done the Jewish state more damage?

Suicide-Murder

June 25, 2002

Suicide was once seen as an intensely personal act. Then, with the mid-twentieth-century deaths of numerous artists and writers (between, say, Virginia Woolf in 1941 and Anne Sexton in 1974), suicide came to be taken as an aesthetic statement, a subject of literary and philosophical debate. The Vietnam War saw the protesting self-immolations of Buddhist monks in Saigon and then of American pacifists (like Alice Herz, Norman Morrison, and Roger LaPorte in 1965). Such suicides, whatever else one made of them, were powerful political statements. (Former defense secretary Robert McNamara reports being particularly troubled by Morrison's death, which occurred at the Pentagon.) During the 1990s an epidemic of teen suicides, nowhere more than in Boston, was taken as a signal of youthful jeopardy, and the broader society has worked hard to respond. The act of self-killing so violates the life instinct that it demands attention, whether the context is personal and private, or public and political. Suicide is one human act that cannot be ignored.

Then last year suicide emerged with new potency as a form of mass murder, with fanatics turning their own deaths into weapons. History had seen this before, as, for example, with kamikaze pilots, but by bringing such acts out of the narrowly defined realm of combat into mundane settings of urban life, targeting civilians at random, this form of suicide-murder seemed new. And now, in Israel, self-proclaimed martyrs for Palestine have transformed the Al Aqsa Intifada into a major Middle East war by making their bodies into bombs. The horrors in Jerusalem and other Israeli cities evoke more than repugnance at the perpetrators and their cynical sponsors; more than sympathy for the victims. A kind of social radioactivity leaks out of each suicide-murder explosion, and we all live within its zone of contamination. The fallout is spiritual.

Like every suicide, these acts compel attention—but not just attention to motive or to the circumstances that produce them, as if compassion for the plight of Palestinians can properly follow from these awful deeds. Suicide-murderers contradict every legitimate Palestinian aspiration. Their glorious martial justifications are lies. They are enemies of their own people, because Palestinians, too, are human beings with as much to lose as anyone if the ethos of the suicide-bombers finds an honored place in the twenty-first-century imagination. Suicide-murderers have brought the human race to a threshold, and if we cross it, all that humans value most is lost. That applies across the otherwise determinative boundaries of nation, race, class, culture—and the Green Line, the pre-1967 border that separates Israel from the West Bank. The intensely fragile character of human life on earth is at stake.

Think of yourself at the wheel of your car, hurtling down the highway at sixty miles an hour. You are surrounded by other drivers, strangers, all doing the same. Only one thing enables this mortal dance of traffic—which is your trust in the other drivers, and theirs in you. This entirely unspoken bond among total strangers is infinitely precious, yet we take it completely for granted. On the road, everyone trusts everyone else with nothing less than life itself. The precondition of this trust is the assumption that the instinct for life is universal, and that it is nearly absolute. Almost nothing is worth the taking of a life—one's own or anyone else's. We trust each other to believe that.

This trust is the real target of the suicide-bombers, and the radioactivity that spreads out, unseen, from their explosions is already making us ill. We are a deeply unsettled people, with numerous sources of anxiety lately—from the scandals of religion and the economy to a general homesickness for a simpler, slower world. But the joint fracturing of two primal taboos—against suicide and murder—cuts our social order to the quick. Last September, this perversion was spectacularly loosed upon New York and Washington, but the outrageously mundane regularity with which it now falls upon Israel has unbalanced something in the world's turning. The flywheel of civilization is off.

Alas, the usefulness of the suicide-murder tactic as an odds-evener for the relatively powerless has become shockingly clear. Hence the grotesque cheering among so many Palestinians, which is itself a warning. The possibility that suicide-murder will therefore emerge as a major strategy of world conflict, driven by armies of the self-deluded and their cynical sponsors, already sets in motion not the literal fear of being blown up in a Boston café, say, but the deeper fear that strangers are not to be trusted after all. We see what the first phase of this fear has done to our airports. If suicide-murder is not firmly repudiated by all humans, imagine what it will do to our highways.

6

AFRAID

In his six years as governor of Texas, George W. Bush presided over the executions of 152 people. This profligate willingness to put human beings to death sets him apart and perhaps foreshadowed the "bring 'em on" callousness of his war making. But in the United States, devotion to the death penalty is widespread. Majorities of citizens favor it in polls, and at elections politicians who oppose state-sponsored killing lose. In the 2004 presidential campaign, every major Democrat challenging Bush was in favor of the death penalty—including some who had once opposed it, but now reserved it for heinous crimes like terrorism.

Yet the American death penalty is a serious obstacle to a fully effective war on terrorism. This is so because, among industrialized countries, capital punishment is increasingly regarded as barbaric. No member of the European Union allows it. Thus, the allies, whose cooperation in tracking and arresting terrorists is crucial, will cooperate with American law enforcement only up to a point. Germany has refused to extradite terrorist suspects to the United States, and, as the writer Samantha Powers and others point out, London has put Washington on notice that if British soldiers capture Osama bin Laden, he will not be handed over to American authorities without assurances that the death penalty will be waived.

Why does the United States stand nearly alone on this question? Is it a matter of revenge? Or is something else at work? In primitive cultures, rituals of human sacrifice were intended to appease hostile gods. Does the bloodthirstiness implied in state-sponsored killing, and embodied so manifestly in George Bush, indicate such deep-seated, irrational fearfulness? Capital punishment, at bottom, is human sacrifice. And human sacrifice is nothing but the desperate effort by terrified people to ward off unimaginable and transcendent threats. But what exactly are we threatened with? What are we afraid of?

In the Bunker

March 5, 2002

My father was a senior Pentagon official during the Cuban Missile Crisis in the autumn of 1962. My family lived at Bolling Air Force Base in Washington on a street known as "Generals' Row." Our neighbors were the top officers of the air force, and during the heat of the showdown with the Soviets my father and his colleagues did not come home for days on end. When I later asked my mother what that had been like for her and the other wives left behind at Bolling, she told me that they had a way of knowing if the outbreak of war was imminent, and that it never was.

"How did you know?" I asked. She answered that she and the other generals' wives had organized themselves into shifts. At every hour, one of them would drive to the remote corner of the air base where helicopters were positioned, to see if the rotor-aircraft were still there. The women knew that those helicopters were poised to ferry the top Pentagon officials out of Washington to the secure command bunker in the Blue Ridge Mountains from which the war would be fought. As long as the helicopters were still on the flight line, the wives knew their husbands were still in Washington. The helicopters never left. My mother told this story with a curl of pride, that her Joe had been one of those to coolly manage the crisis so that the underground command bunker had never been necessary.

I thought of this story when news surfaced last week of the Bush administration's "shadow government"—the force of up to a hundred senior officials who have been living in cold-war-era bunkers since September 11, the "National Emergency Management Team." As the *Boston Globe*'s Glen Johnson put it, "Osama bin Laden has done what Nikita Khrushchev, Mao Zedong, and Fidel Castro never could: drive the United States government underground."

To recall the Kennedy administration's handling of the Cuban Missile Crisis, especially in light of recently published transcripts, is to have an example of steady, firm resolve. Compared to Kennedy under that ferocious pressure, other presidents do not come off so well, from Lyndon Johnson's erratic obsessiveness at one end of Vietnam to Richard Nixon's bizarre emotional collapse at the other. ("The nuclear bomb," he said to Henry Kissinger, as we learned last week, "does that bother you?")

George W. Bush's frantic, ad hoc war on terrorism can seem to be yet another manifestation of presidential unsteadiness. Indeed, an air of low-grade panic has been a mark of Bush's responses since the very day the World Trade Center and the Pentagon were attacked. Since then the president's careless rhetoric and puerile bluster have appalled allies, mobilized new enemies, and turned the U.S. State Department into a damage control center. The vice president's status as the man-in-hiding has become a national joke. The Defense Department initiated, then dropped, a Soviet-style office of strategic disinformation. Meanwhile, the ongoing deployment of U.S. troops—the Philippines? Yemen? the former Soviet republic of Georgia?—has seemed anything but prudent. And the scattershot air campaign against Afghanistan was a "success" only because of a sleight of hand substitution of the Taliban for al Qaeda as our mortal enemy. Osama bin Laden? Now the administration says he was never that important. Or maybe he's in the caves that are being bombed today as targets in the renewed air war. Cross your fingers and—what?—hope he dies?

In the context of such unsteadiness, the revelation of U.S. officials ordered into mothballed bunkers might reinforce the image of a callow, frightened president who, after all, spent the first day of this crisis on the run. But is something else at work here? Odd how all of these Bush-sponsored manifestations of a nation under siege shore up the state of emergency on which this government has come to depend for its exercise of power. If officials are in bunkers for the first time in the nation's history, how dare anyone raise questions about the policies those officials pursue? Last week, congressional Democrats finally wondered aloud about the war on terrorism. They raised pathetically timid questions, long overdue, yet Republicans slapped them down as offering comfort to our faceless enemies. And the cowed Democrats backed off.

What did my mother see when she drove to that corner of Bolling Air Force Base? She saw evidence of a government that understood the relationship between the appearance of mature judgment and the actual exercise of it. When a nation's leaders flail about, indulging their fears and insecurities, desperately taking cover against bad things that might happen, they make those bad things all the more likely. By contrast, those stress-tested women of Generals' Row had good reasons to feel confident. We their children, with the helicopters gone, have none.

America the Fearful

May 21, 2002

The more powerful the United States of America becomes, the more frightened we are. Why is that? An undercurrent of hysteria has coursed through the talk out of Washington over the last week as, first, critics demanded to know if government officials had ignored advance warnings of the terrorist attacks of last September, and as, second, those same officials—in response?—issued a new warning of coming attacks that might be even worse. The new warning is sharp enough to generate fear, but too vague to enable any defensive preparation. In airports, citizens sheepishly submit to screening measures which are administered with such incompetence, still, that they can only enhance uneasiness—prompting the question: is that the point? Meanwhile, the FBI admits it has no clue about the anthrax attacks, American soldiers remain on the hunt in Afghanistan, Pentagon war planners are getting ready for Iraq, and even Cuba is said to be readying biological weapons. Oh my God.

The war on terrorism is not the only manifestation of heightened levels of our national fear. This week Presidents George W. Bush and Vladimir Putin will sign an arms-reduction agreement—the Moscow Treaty—that includes an American-sponsored provision allowing for the indefinite mothballing of thousands of disarmed nuclear weapons. Notice this. The United States, breaking with the primordial assumption of nuclear arms control, is now saying that the overkill supply of warheads must be preserved against future threats—as yet entirely unimagined. This marks the end of the hope, long shared by conservatives and liberals alike, that human beings might eventually wean themselves of these terrible weapons altogether. After such a reduction to the absurd of "reduction," we should call this and subsequent treaties not "START" but "STASH."

Bush has, in one stroke, reversed the single most positive foreign policy track of our lifetimes—and he has done it out of fear.

Here is the irony: the surest way to make the world an even more dangerous place is to posit danger as the most important thing about it. This week's treaty is the clearest case in point. America's determination to preserve thousands of excess nuclear warheads means that now Russia, despite its firm preference for elimination, will certainly preserve them as well. And what will happen over time to those warheads? When the urgency of keeping such material out of the hands of rogue elements is clear, the American move away from full elimination of nukes, especially as duplicated in Russia, makes no sense. But that very irrationality is the revelation.

We are like a nation that has had a psychological break, descending into rank paranoia. The destruction of the Twin Towers shows that there are things to be afraid of, but our government's mad responses are making us more vulnerable to such things, not less. The war on terrorism has strengthened the hand of those who hate America. The U.S. example of "overwhelming force" has pushed the Middle East into the abyss and has dragged India-Pakistan to its very edge. The only real protections against cross-border terrorism are international structures of criminal justice, like the recently established International Criminal Court, yet an "unsigning" United States slaps the court down with contempt. Since September, we have squandered our wealth and focus on a huge war, while entirely neglecting police work and intelligence at home and abroad. Hence the vagueness of the current warning. And how dare our government set off alarms about Cuba's putative bioterrorism project, while it has done nothing to apprehend the anthrax killer? Oh and—forgive me, just asking—where is Osama?

The Bush administration's warning about Castro's interest in bioterrorism could seem blatantly timed to deflect political pressures arising from Jimmy Carter's trip to Havana. Vice President Richard Cheney's agitated Sunday alarm about imminent terrorist attacks could seem timed to defuse last week's long overdue political offensive by Democrats. The president's rejection, in principle, of arms "reduction" could seem to serve his larger political and economic purpose of restoring the American war industry to its place of preeminence. The president and his closest advisers, in other words, could be cynically exaggerating threats to our national security for their narrow purposes.

But it may be worse than that. The shape of their dread is useful to them in these ways, but, also, like the mentally disturbed, they seem convinced that any danger they imagine is real. Our nation is being led by men and women who are at the mercy of their fears. That they work hard to keep the American people afraid might seem to suggest that they want merely to deflect any second-guessing about the course they have set, but in fact our fear reinforces theirs. Fear has become Washington's absolute and is shaping its every response to the future. America is being led by cowards.

American Mortality

July 2, 2002

We celebrate beginnings, whether of persons or nations, as a way of honoring our place in time. The joyful rituals of the Fourth of July, observed nowhere more happily than in Boston, remind us of the day when our country came into being. This week we feast on summer food, listen to patriotic music, send up flares, and, perhaps, choke up for a moment on the high emotion of love for this country.

But to acknowledge that the United States of America has a beginning, and is thus bound by the rules of time, is implicitly to recall that this nation will, equally, have an end. What the Fourth of July celebrates, at bottom, is American mortality. Like every birthday celebration, it defies the human temptation to imagine oneself as living forever. There was a time past when we did not exist, and there is a

time future when, again, we will not exist. To remember the one is
to anticipate the other. And everything that America accomplishes
and signifies must be measured, finally, against this radical transience
within which it all occurs.

What could be more obvious than that? you ask. And yet, the
truth of our national mortality constantly eludes us. The ultimate
demise of the United States of America is deeply unsettling, even if
only in prospect. This is more true of our nation, perhaps, than of
others, precisely because we define ourselves in terms more of the
future than of the past. The greatness of Britain, say, or Greece, is
tied to what it was, which is why immigrants to those countries, not
sharing the past, take on national identity with difficulty. American
greatness is always tied to what the nation is becoming, which is why
immigrants here feel readily commissioned to create that greatness.
The American future belongs equally to everyone.

But what if the future is finite? Which is another way of asking
about death. At Gettysburg, Abraham Lincoln suggested that our
hallowed dead will not have died "in vain" only if, in the future, "the
great task remaining before us" is accomplished. Lincoln thus gave
voice to a basic American assumption: that present experience is
justified only by future outcomes. But if ever the Union "perishes
from the earth," will all those who died for it in the past have died
"in vain"? In a world that remains bound by the rules of time and
mortality, no matter how cloaked by patriotic fervor, is the charac-
teristically American idea of boundlessness inevitably self-
defeating? If the United States has defined the future as its only
absolute, what happens when the future, too, is revealed as relative?
This forward-looking ideology has been an engine of both industry
and social justice, but is it nevertheless built on a contradiction? And
why shouldn't Americans have looked for ways to avoid the bite of
such questions?

Enter God. Here is the context in which to understand the use to
which we have put our civic religion. When we claim to be a nation
"under God"—and it was Lincoln who first used that phrase, at Gettysburg—or when we blithely pray "God bless America," assuming

that God's blessing for this country is unique, we are appropriating for ourselves divine attributes of infinity and immortality that, in fact, have no place on earth. And notice, we do this when our future seems most at risk (1863, 1954, 2001), the American variation on faith in foxholes. It should be no surprise that in the current period of acute national anxiety, we have resumed our emphatic dependency on God-talk, and no surprise that a court that presumed to question it should have been so efficiently slapped down last week. We Americans feel vulnerable enough without surrendering the sense of transcendent protection that derives from public expression of our felt connection to God.

Thus, much more is at stake in our public appeals to "God" than constitutional questions about church and state. Every nation has a way of invoking the divinity, and every army goes into battle under the patronage of some god or other. Nothing new in that. But the American appeal is different because of the function "God" serves as a solution to the American problem. We prefer to think of ourselves as "the indispensable nation," hoping to postpone the inevitable reckoning with an opposite truth for as long as we can. "God" is our postponement.

On this earth, within the limits of time, no nation is indispensable. No nation is forever. When it comes to the human condition, no nation is exceptional. And if one nation is "under God," it is only because every nation is. Therefore, the joy with which we celebrate our nation's beginning must inform, equally, a sense that our nation's eventual end marks us as part of the human family, which remains our true glory.

The Coming War in Iraq

July 23, 2002

We Americans find ourselves in the extraordinary position of witnessing our government's slow but certain movement toward a major war with Iraq. Such open maneuvering, with clear statements of intention from the Bush administration, the leaking of war plans from the Pentagon, and the acquiescence of Congress, could not have happened when U.S. power was balanced, and therefore checked, by the Soviet Union, nor when that power was mitigated by Washington's regard for world opinion. Now the only conceivable check on the sole superpower is the will of its own people, manifest through politics, which is why we must urgently take up the subject ourselves.

It can be agreed that Saddam Hussein is a danger to his neighbors, an enemy to his own people, and a threat to world peace. But on this page last Saturday the former chief U.N. weapons inspector in Iraq, Scott Ritter, expressed grave skepticism about the Bush contention that Hussein so threatens the United States with weapons of mass destruction that war is justified. Ritter proposed congressional hearings to "ask the Bush administration tough questions" about its purposes. Here are some questions that occur to me:

- Having lived with Hussein as a mortal enemy for more than a decade, is the urgency of replacing him now a result less of real evidence of increased threat than of the "us-versus-them" mindset that drives the war on terrorism? Is the cause of war something Hussein is doing, or is it something we are imagining?
- Does the bellicosity of the Bush administration eliminate the alternatives to war? For example, "containment and deterrence," which worked against the Soviet Union and have so far worked against Hussein, depend on the multilateral coopera-

tion of other nations. But Bush's chest-thumping war talk, even short of actual invasion, is destroying that cooperation.

- When America's goal shifts from one of moderating Hussein's behavior to the openly expressed purpose of regime change, what does Hussein have to lose? And when Hussein knows an invading American force is surely coming, does he not have to "use or lose" whatever weapons he has? Isn't Washington forcing him to respond with his worst?

- What effect will a major American war against Iraq have on the broader conflict between Islam and the West? If al Qaeda grew out of the humiliations attached to the Gulf War, what will grow out of the new humiliation of a massive American imposition on Iraq, including the necessity of a long-term American occupation?

- What is the relationship between the urgent American project in Iraq and the staggering lack of American interest in the worsening Israeli-Palestinian crisis? Is Bush using the former problem as an excuse to avoid grappling with the latter one? How is it in Israel's interest to invite Hussein to unleash his scud missiles again? And what is the hope for improved U.S.-Arab relations so long as Palestinians are left in misery?

- What does it say about the United States that we are about to become a "first-strike" nation? Abandoning multilateralism, have we abandoned diplomacy as well? Is war no longer a last resort, taken in self-defense, but a routine method of getting our way, since no one can stop us? Has the time come for us to reverse the National Security Act of 1947, and go back to calling the Defense Department the War Department?

- Does a war against Iraq, with its risk of inflaming the "clash of civilizations" and its likely weakening of ties between the United States and our allies, make our nation all the more vulnerable to terrorist attacks? If the only real way to track down al Qaeda and prevent future attacks is through the very multilateralism that the Bush war will weaken, isn't Bush still enacting the script written by Osama bin Laden?

- What does a longer view of war making tell us? Recall that Hussein began as an American client (as bin Laden did) when we were fighting other wars; isn't he an argument for finally breaking with the myth that war solves more problems than it creates? If we came to that conclusion, wouldn't other forceful ways of resisting Hussein's tyranny emerge? And in the long run, who is to say they would not be far more effective?

The obvious difference between Iraq and America is that this nation is a democracy. That means that we U.S citizens are responsible for the behavior of George W. Bush in ways that the people of Iraq are not responsible for Saddam Hussein. There is good reason to believe that Bush, in his highly personal, irrational, and thoroughly Manichaean campaign against Hussein, has set the very world on a course toward disaster. No one can change that course but us.

Lies, Damned Lies

July 30, 2002

"My dear fellow citizens," Václav Havel said in his inaugural address as Czech president, "for forty years on this day you heard from my predecessors the same thing in a number of variations: how our country is flourishing, how many millions of tons of steel we produce, how happy we all are, how we trust our government, and what prospects lie ahead of us. I assume you did not propose me for this office so that I, too, should lie to you."

That was 1990. It seems a quaint time, back when public lying was defined as one of the key differences between the Soviet empire and America. Public lying is now revealed as endemic to what capitalism has become in the United States, with Havel's summary of the Stalinist deceptions reading like a standard CEO report to share-holders. This discovery of a basic dishonesty in the heart of "free en-terprise" can shock us into moral maturity.

The worst effect of the cold war on the American mind was the bipolar thinking it encouraged. We allowed ourselves to believe that the world could be divided between the essentially virtuous and the radically evil. We operated for a generation on the assumption that human beings behind the Iron Curtain were in the grip of Satan, while those of us in the West were entrusted "here on earth," as John Kennedy put it in his inaugural, with God's own work. Thus, we de-fined Kremlin intentions as imperialist expansionism, while our own global reach aimed only at free markets. That we spent the bulk of our treasure and the best of our intellectual effort preparing to blow up the world seemed, in the moral alchemy of deterrence, an act of high virtue. Not trusting Soviet signatures on treaties, nor imagining the mundane goodwill of Russian people, we were certain that the totalitarian enemy could be brought down only by eventual world violence. Simplistic moral thinking is always apocalyptic.

We knew, meanwhile, that we and our leaders were capable of ly-ing, but in the American narrative, public deceptions like Watergate have been counted as exceptions which proved the rule of American innocence. Jimmy Carter, in running for office on the slogan "I will never lie to you," made explicit what we expect from presidents—and from everyone in authority. And was the self-anointed nation ever more itself than in feeling so morally superior to the disgraced Bill Clinton?

But the main moral failure of CEOs—and U.S. presidents—does not consist in the conscious venality of thinking one thing while say-ing another. The disorder is deeper than that, for it is far more likely that such leaders are convinced of the false justifications they offer. That the justifications are profoundly self-serving, of course, is part of why the leaders are convinced. When George W. Bush recently broke America's promise on the ABM Treaty, that did not make us a nation of liars, he told us, but of realists. And, incidentally, his sole-power agenda was advanced.

The pattern is wide. Executives who want only to put the numbers "in a better light" end by cooking the books. Politicians who harmlessly aim to tell voters what they want to hear wind up having no core grasp of what is true. Religious leaders who maintain the *appearance* of virtue as an absolute value lose the capacity to recognize their own fallibility. But in all of this, such figures are behaving only like members of the human species, for the tendency toward grievous self-deception is universal.

Thus, husbands and wives can go years without realizing they have no intimacy. The overweight can fool themselves about their health problem. Drinkers can deny what their lives have become. Compulsive workers can enslave themselves to a false dream of success. Life-wrecking depression can pass itself off as selfless worry. Greed can seem like ambition. The pursuit of happiness is killing us. The most damaging lies are the ones we tell ourselves.

Today's nationwide rude awakening understandably prompts broad outrage at deceptive leaders, but that must not be our only response. During the cold war we exempted ourselves from the kind of moral scrutiny that could have prevented the spreading of this poison cloud. The lies of business (Madison Avenue), of government (the Missile Gap), of culture (Forever Young), and of religion (God Bless America) were built into our system, but we could not see them as lies because of the split in our thinking. In this time of ethical reckoning, will we again smugly divide the world between the good and the evil?

Yes, we can insist on a purging of public lies—a true reform. But we repeat a major blunder if we conclude that the problem of self-serving deception belongs to someone else. "When I talk about the contaminated moral atmosphere," Havel presumed to tell his fellow citizens, "I mean all of us."

A Mistake, and a Crime

August 6, 2002

"I made one great mistake in my life," Albert Einstein admitted, "when I signed the letter to President Roosevelt recommending that atom bombs be made." The letter was brought to the president in the fall of 1939, within weeks of the beginning of the war in Europe. Einstein and other scientists were worried that Hitler had embarked on an atomic bomb project, which is why Einstein's comment continued, "But there was some justification—the danger that the Germans would make them." (My source for this quote, and inspiration for this column, is Martin J. Sherwin's milestone book, *A World Destroyed*.)

Motivated by an urgent impulse to achieve the atomic weapon before Hitler, a collection of the world's most brilliant physicists went to work. The first self-sustaining chain reaction was created at the University of Chicago in December of 1942, but then, unknown to the scientists, a strange thing happened. Winning the race against the Nazis stopped being the paramount concern. As the policy chiefs of the Manhattan Project began to see exclusive possession of the bomb as a source of tremendous diplomatic power, they recognized its potential as an unprecedented political check on the Soviet Union after the war. The bomb had a new, if as yet unadmitted, purpose.

In November 1944, the United States discovered that Germany's atomic program was embryonic: there was no real threat of a Nazi bomb. Sherwin suggests that this crucial intelligence may have been kept from the scientists working on the bomb "in order not to dampen their enthusiasm." By this point in the war, there was no longer any real danger of an Allied defeat, yet the Manhattan Project proceeded with more urgency than ever. The policy chiefs had an eye as much on a postwar rivalry with the Soviet Union as on the endgame with Germany and Japan, which gave them a whole new motive for using the bomb as soon as possible.

Today marks the anniversary of the American atomic bomb falling on Hiroshima. The unfinished debate about whether that attack, and the subsequent bombing of Nagasaki, were justified has always focused narrowly on the question of the war with Japan. Didn't the atomic bomb, in effect, spare the lives of all the leathernecks and GIs who would otherwise have landed on the beaches of the die-hard island nation? What else could Truman have done? These questions have stymied the American conscience, making it impossible to seriously reckon with that crossing of the nuclear threshold, which in turn inhibits our moral reckoning with our present nuclear arsenal.

But what if the invasion of an all-but-defanged Japan was, and remains, a red herring? What if, just as the Nazi threat fell by the wayside, the Japanese threat was not the real issue by then either? What if, by the summer of 1945, the overriding purpose of the atomic bomb was not to end a conflict against Japan but to control the shape of an anticipated conflict with the Soviet Union? What if it was not Emperor Hirohito we were mainly trying to terrorize but Premier Joseph Stalin? Not a last shot against the Axis powers but a first shot against the Kremlin?

In war and politics, there are never one-factor answers to complex questions. In truth, the atomic bomb was both a last shot and a first shot. The point of my asking is simply to suggest that, as a people insisting on a narrative in which Hiroshima marked the end of a conflict instead of the beginning of one, we have given ourselves a pass on a far more troubling question. If we used the nuclear weapon as much to send a signal to the Soviet Union as to end World War II, all the wickedness unfolding from that use—not only the arms race but the demonic new idea that national power can properly depend on the threat of mass destruction—belongs to us. If Saddam Hussein wants weapons of mass destruction for the sake of the strategic diplomatic power they will give him, he is playing by rules written in Washington. There are two ways to use the nuke: as a source of world destruction and as a source of world power. We did the former at the end of World War II, which was the exact beginning of the cold war. We have been doing the latter every day since. And why should Hussein not want to imitate us?

The bombing of Hiroshima was a great crime. That the United States of America has yet to confront it as such not only leaves the past with unfinished business but undercuts the possibility of present moral clarity about the exercise of American power and leaves the earth's future tied to a fuse that we set burning fifty-seven years ago today.

Catholic Collapse and U.S. Foreign Policy

August 13, 2002

Priests abusing children. Bishops protecting the abusers instead of the victims. The corruption exposed. What effect will the collapse of American Catholic moral authority have on U.S. foreign policy? Some might dismiss that as the question of an obsessive Catholic who sees everything through the narrow lens of a parochial church problem. Indeed, the media's preoccupation with the Catholic scandal can seem a distraction from the more grievous problem of George W. Bush's warmongering. But, in fact, the issues are related. American Catholicism's confrontation with its own flawed character can mitigate a broader American self-righteousness, to the benefit of the world.

Roman Catholic moral absolutism has been a pillar of U.S. foreign policy since the beginning of the cold war. Indeed, Catholicism joined the American consensus only as that consensus jelled around an anticommunism that smacked, as the statesman Bernard Baruch warned in 1947, of "religious war." Nothing wrong with that, President Truman might have said. His foreign policy aimed to embody nothing less, he said, than the Sermon on the Mount. The religious character of America's new crusade prompted Truman to issue his most belligerent anti-Soviet call to arms at Cardinal Francis Spellman's annual St. Patrick's Day dinner in 1948.

Spellman became the champion of American anticommunism. Every Catholic seemed enlisted. Hence Fulton J. Sheen as a media celebrity; hence Senator Joseph McCarthy as a tribune of ideological purity. This quasi-religious politics gave a sacred edge to U.S. strategy and made Spellman the most influential Catholic bishop in American history. He then helped shape perceptions of the postcolonial crisis in Vietnam as centrally about Catholic anticommunism and helped his protégé Ngo Dinh Diem become premier in 1954. Overwhelmingly Buddhist, South Vietnam was seen in America as a mainly Catholic country, with Catholics seen fighting for all that was good, and protesting Buddhists seen linked with evil Communists from the North. In fact, Diem was waging a Catholic religious war against his own people, but the moralist worldview prevented that tragic reality from coming through. The American misadventure in Vietnam began with this mistake. (When Diem was assassinated in 1963, he wore the disguise of a priest.)

The absolutism of Catholic anticommunism was tempered by Pope John XXIII, who questioned America's reliance on nuclear deterrence and fostered U.S.-Soviet détente. A Catholic peace movement helped end the Vietnam War, and a broad Catholic constituency for dissent emerged, with even the bishops joining in nuclear skepticism by 1983. But unnuanced Catholic moralism made a public comeback when Pope John Paul II's apocalyptic view of Communism meshed with Ronald Reagan's. CIA funds went to the right-wing Contras in Nicaragua through Catholic Church channels, for example, even as the Vatican undercut Catholics allied with Latin American liberation. U.S. priests and nuns were ordered out of (left-wing) politics, and Catholic bishops resumed their function as mascots of the American consensus. So firmly were American Catholics again rooted in the sense of their nation's purity that not even bishops seemed to notice as John Paul II began to object to Washington's wars. The Indispensable Nation was immune to criticism from outside, incapable of self-criticism.

With the Catholic Church's blessing, the word *evil*, as applied to enemies, became a staple of American rhetoric fifty years ago. That tradition has been reinvigorated by George W. Bush, along a new axis. Bush's ideological soul mate in all of this was Boston's Cardinal Bernard Law, whose particular imprimatur Bush sought during the 2000 election campaign. The cardinal's worldview of good and evil in absolute ontological conflict mirrored Bush's, with each man certain of his own alliance with good.

No more. Cardinal Law's disgrace as a protector of abusers is complete. And see how Bush keeps his distance from the men in red robes now. The priestly child abuse-and-cover-up scandal has fully discredited the church's claim to be a moral exemplar. Its function as a pillar of American exceptionalism is ended. As legitimizing patrons of the cause of righteousness, the American Catholic bishops are about as useful as Enron executives. Yet the church scandal continues. Catholic prelates, who still speak in legalese, threaten dissenting clergy, reject alternative financial donations, and forbid concerned laity to gather in church halls, only show how total is their moral failure. The collapse of this self-obsessed clerical establishment is a literal Catholic purgatory, but the purging is right and just for the church.

It can be a good thing for the nation, too. The ongoing revelations of the hierarchy's self-deceit, cruelty, and grievous crimes should remind every person that every institution is morally deficient— America included. Evil is not an axis but an orbit encircling the planet, a universal problem.

The Sermon on the Mount as American foreign policy? President Truman, in claiming for himself and his successors the role of the preacher of that sermon—the role, that is, of Jesus Christ—may not have noticed how, in Matthew, that sermon includes the question "Why do you see the speck that is in your brother's eye, but do not see the log that is in your own?"

So Who Do I Think I Am?

August 20, 2002

On a Tuesday ten years ago, I began to appear on this page as a regular columnist, not imagining what a controversial role it would be. Among the columns that drew unexpected criticism was one I wrote about our family dog, Sophie. My description of jogging with her on the pathways along the Charles River included the sentence "I glance down at Sophie, off the leash, yet reliably two feet away." As numerous readers pointed out, that was an admission of my being in technical violation of the leash laws, although Sophie was steadily at my heel. Respondents assumed, wrongly, that I am one of those self-centered dog owners who, ignoring the law, also neglects to clean up after my dog. Columnists routinely presume to judge and condemn such bad citizens. Wasn't I one of them? Who, they asked in effect, do you think you are?

Sophie is still our cherished family member, but she is, as the vet just told us, a geriatric patient now. Her jogging days are over. As part of her elder-canine checkup, we had to supply an early morning urine sample, which is how I came to be following her the other day, stooped over with a plastic pie lid in hand. Passersby were mystified to watch me trailing Sophie, trying to catch drops of her urine before they hit the pavement. Talk about anal compulsive. And it was then that I thought of my dog-column critics and wished they could see me now.

As I browse through my files, looking at the subjects I have addressed over the years, I recognize a common thread, from the first regular column I wrote in 1992—"War No More"—to the column I wrote last week—"Catholic Collapse and U.S. Foreign Policy." I have been preoccupied with the dangers of good-versus-evil moralism, yet immediately I recognize, also, the danger of such a preoccupation. *Who do you think you are?* What's to keep the critic of sanctimonious moralizing from being a sanctimonious moralizer? "Why do you see the speck that is in your brother's eye," I presumed to ask last week, quoting Matthew, "but do not see the log that is in your own?" Asking that question of myself, I think of Bob Dylan's refrain: "In a soldier's stance I aimed my hand / at the mongrel dogs who teach. / Fearing not, I become my enemy / in the instant that I preach."

And what disclaimers do I owe my reader? In assuming the "soldier's stance" of an objective truth-teller, should I more blatantly emphasize the odd, continuing relevance of my own history? Writing skeptically about the shocking bellicosity of our government, should I acknowledge more forthrightly my unfinished psychological tensions with my late father, an air force general, our split over Vietnam? When I criticize the Catholic hierarchy, should I more consistently admit the collapse of the fervent idealism that took me into the priesthood as a young man? In truth, whether the subject is war or politics or religion—it is all intensely personal with me. Is that my problem? Or is it my solution?

Who do you think you are? That question is always asked as a way of silencing. It implies that only certain voices have the right to be heard, the voices that affirm things as they are, keeping the powerful in power. The voices that belong, on matters of war, only to warriors; of religion, only to the clerical elite. That question wickedly exploits the truth of the human condition—that no one is free from hypocrisy. Yet it falsely implies the opposite, that certain perfect creatures stand above the would-be critic and only they have the right to criticize. Of course, they are the ones who ask the silencing question in the first place. Except when, perversely, we ask it of ourselves.

After ten years of writing this column, I understand better than before that we human beings are alike in our limitations, and we owe it to each other not to, in Dylan's word, *preach*. A column, certainly, is not a pulpit. But I also understand that we human beings are alike in being responsible for this world. No one is exempt from the obligations to judge and to speak. Every voice has a right to be heard. A column is a privileged microphone, that's all. Thank you for letting me have it.

Who do you think you are? When it comes to war, I am an American citizen saying no. When it comes to religion, I am a Catholic believer aware that all God's creatures are imperfect. When it comes to life in the city, I am a dog's friend, the one with the plastic pie lid.

7

DRUMBEAT

On June 1, 2002, the president began to articulate a new Bush Doctrine at West Point. "For much of the last century, America's defense relied on Cold War doctrines of deterrence and containment. . . . But new threats also require new thinking." Deterrence and containment were no longer enough. In response to "shadowy terrorist networks" and "unbalanced dictators," America had to be more aggressive, especially given the transcendent nature of the unfolding global crisis. "We are in a conflict between good and evil, and America will call evil by its name." The drumbeat had begun.

The National Security Strategy of the United States, a full theology of the Bush Doctrine, was published the following October. It was an official proclamation of America's programmatic willingness to launch "preventive" wars. The doctrine did not say whether such a right could be claimed by other nations. The Bush Doctrine implicitly asserted that military initiatives would replace diplomacy; that the United States was entirely and appropriately prepared to act alone; that the virtue of American purposes was self-evident; and that America's unchallenged power was justification enough for taking any preemptive action desired. These assertions of "new thinking," representing a profound break with twentieth-century foreign policy, were made by fiat, without consulting allies, and without debate in Congress.

The abstractions of the Bush Doctrine found their concrete focus in the figure of Saddam Hussein. Calling evil by its name meant calling it by his. No longer would deterrence and containment form the strategic response to his—or any other "evildoer's"—machinations. Preventive war meant preventing Hussein. No one explained how he had replaced Osama bin Laden in the crosshairs of America's gun. Osama bin Laden, in fact, was no longer discussed.

Inarticulate and Proud of It

August 27, 2002

"I'm a patient man," President Bush said the other day. He was dressed in cowboy clothes. "And when I say I'm a patient man," he added, somewhat impatiently, "I mean I'm a patient man." The president was responding to reporters' attempts to make sense of the administration's scorching but confusing rhetoric about Iraq. His declaration of patience amended his declarations of war, seeking to douse expectations of imminent attack, while promising that hostile action will come eventually.

The nation is beholding something that can only be called weird. Ever since Bush announced his new doctrine of preventive war last spring, his administration has been engaged in an unprecedented war of words aimed at Saddam Hussein. In the beginning, the justification for regime change in Baghdad was entirely a matter of the threat Hussein represents, but no more. Now the justification includes protecting the integrity of *America's* threat. We have to go to war now because we said we would. Language is no longer an expression of purpose but the shaper of purpose.

The United States, in fact, is in a crisis of language. This is what it means to have a president who, proudly inarticulate, has no real understanding of the relationship between words and acts, between rhetoric and intention. Consider his heated boast about his own patience. I saw his declaration on the evening news, and it was clear that, as he began that second sentence, seeking to emphasize the first, he meant to find another way of displaying his determination. But he was, as usual, at a literal loss for words. And so he fell back on empty repetition. "When I say I'm a patient man, I mean I'm a patient man."

George W. Bush mistakes tautology for explanation, a habit of mind marking his entire administration. Bush governs by assertion instead of persuasion. Whether the United States seeks to exercise power over the Taliban, or over Ariel Sharon and Yasir Arafat, or over Russia, or over its European allies, or even over its own citizens, the method is the same. Washington doesn't waste a moment trying to convince the Taliban to side with us against bin Laden. Washington rejects Arafat as a dialogue partner and forgoes any effort to influence Sharon. Washington presents Moscow with ultimatums on arms-control treaties. Washington rejects the International Criminal Court, instead of trying to help shape its development. On the home front, Washington claims emergency martial law exemptions from traditional court procedures. In every case, Washington is avoiding the need to explain its position with the clarity and logic necessary to change minds and win support. Instead of convincing, Washington coerces. And why? Obviously, because Washington apes the style of a president who has no capacity for the use of language as a mode of leadership.

The problem comes when, having sought to lead through the imperative voice, instead of the exhortatory or the explanatory, nothing changes. The world is beginning to act like America's sullen teenager, refusing to obey orders. Bin Laden at large. The Middle East in escalation. A nuclear arms race on the cusp of resumption. A global summit in Johannesburg enraged at U.S. arrogance. Even Europe openly contemptuous. And at home, the anthrax killer unidentified. Citizens at risk. The economy shaken. In the face of such failure, there is nothing for the imperative voice to do but grow louder. "The level of threats has increased dramatically," a Human Rights Watch official observed, concerning recent U.S. attacks on the ICC. "And threat inflation is a sign of a policy gone amok."

The post-9-11 mantra is "United we stand." But not so. The United States is a splintered, lost country where words have been emptied of meaning. That is a symptom of posttraumatic stress syndrome, our national malady. We have been unable to give expression to terrible experiences. Our worst fears remain subliminal, but we recognize them in each other's eyes. In mirroring this unarticulated desperation, our tautological president has been the perfect emblem of the American condition. He is the maestro of disconnect between words and experience. Having emptied the word *evil* of meaning (Iran is evil but also our ally), Bush is now—incredibly—emptying the word *war* of meaning, too.

His vacuous reflection of our mute anguish can be consoling because familiar—hence the high poll numbers—but it is the farthest thing from what the country needs. Mawkish bluster in cowboy clothes does nothing to nurture a community of purpose. It does the opposite.

As a candidate, George W. Bush openly displayed his willful illiteracy. At a loss for words and proud of it. Many voters were charmed. Others were appalled. Few understood, however, that this abdication of leadership by the intelligent use of language would be dangerous to democracy at home, a grievous threat to peace abroad.

The War Anniversary

September 10, 2002

September 11. The heart-wrenching anniversary deserves, amid so much else, an urgent meditation on the subject of war. A nation at war, on the cusp of wider war, we are in danger of defining ourselves by war entire—all within the mystical aura of this shattering date. Are we being true to what was actually laid bare a year ago tomorrow? Do we worthily memorialize those who died so violently by making them patrons of unending violence?

War is not machines. War is not threats. War is not strategy, tactics, martial music, or the proper source of a political party's advantage. War is not a way of proving manhood. To say that war is hell, implying a realm apart, is also wrong. Wars are fought no more in hell than in heaven. Wars are fought, alas, on the very earth. Those who carry its weight are the last to know of war's transcendent meanings. They are deaf to its music. Just war, unjust war—all the same to them because they are dead.

"As I look back over the five years of my service as secretary of war [1940–45]," Henry L. Stimson wrote after World War II, "I see too many stern and heart-rending decisions to be willing to pretend that war is anything else than what it is. The face of war is the face of death; death is an inevitable part of every order that a wartime leader gives." Do our wartime leaders know this today? The cavalier belligerence with which President Bush and Cheney-Rumsfeld-Rice speak of America's impending war against Iraq raises the key question: do they know that death is about to define our nation's purpose? Deaths of soldiers. Deaths of old men, women, and children. Deaths of Arabs, Americans, perhaps Israelis. Deaths of the many who will die in consequential violence of legitimized "preventive war."

Tomorrow the rebuilt Pentagon will be rededicated. The marvel of its repair in one year recalls the greater marvel of its original construction in sixteen months, a feat supervised by Henry Stimson. But the building was the least of his achievements, all of which were reduced in the end to a vivid sense of the actuality of war. He had overseen the entire U.S. campaign with unflinching resolve—even to the ordering of its nuclear conclusion. Yet war reversed itself in him. The atomic bombs, he wrote, "made it wholly clear that we must never have another war. This is the lesson men and leaders everywhere must learn."

A year ago tomorrow, the face of death stared back at America. For a few moments, endlessly replayed, the horror of war was anything but abstract. For months afterward, the individual faces of September's lost men and women stared out from the newspaper pages that gave us their names and stories. We felt a fitting rage aimed at their murderers, but knew also that rage can dishonor the dead by making them faceless victims again. Named and mourned, the September dead were our epiphany of war's actuality. The force of such death, real death, must lead—Stimson's lesson—to the reversal of what causes it.

Did the world change a year ago? Claiming it did, Bush pursues war more energetically than ever. Yet is that the sign of true change? Secretary Stimson was certain that the world had changed in August 1945. For sure he had changed. In his last act as secretary of war, he made a shocking proposal to President Truman. Thinking of the bomb he had himself built and used, Stimson urged Truman to make an immediate diplomatic approach to the Soviet Union, to avoid "a secret armament race of a rather desperate character." The secretary wanted a U.S.-Soviet covenant that would stop work on atomic weapons at once, impound existing bombs, renounce future use, and openly share atomic research for peaceful purposes. All of this with the notoriously unreliable Stalin? Stimson anticipated the objection. Before his service in World War II, he had been secretary of war (1911–13) as guns were primed for World War I, and secretary of state (1929–33) as Hitler came to power. "The chief lesson I have learned in a long life," he told Truman, "is that the only way you can make a man trustworthy is to trust him."

Stimson's radical proposal was rejected, he retired a week later, and the desperate arms race ensued. But the Stimson proposal stands as a marker both of the road not taken at that crucial juncture and of the road that yet remains open ahead of humanity. War is unnecessary death, period. Once a leader has seen its true face, the resolution of conflict by other means will be that leader's undying purpose. Henry L. Stimson haunts our choices. He made his proposal on September 11, 1945.

Good Doubt, Bad Faith

September 17, 2002

A famous prayer includes the line "Where there is doubt, let me sow faith." Doubt is usually regarded as something to repent. Nothing deadens the human spirit like skepticism. Doubt can undermine resolve, and it can make heroic action impossible. Even more undercutting, doubt can poison the self, leaving one suspicious of one's own motives. In that circumstance, doubt can paralyze. But not even that is the worst of it. When one's broader community is taken over by a swelling certitude, doubt can be taken as a sign of bad faith, rendering the doubter ineffectual and alone.

On the question of the threatened war with Iraq, the tide of certitude is swelling in America and perhaps around the world. Doubt begins to seem disloyal at home, foolish abroad. That is why, since President Bush's speech at the United Nations last week, open expressions of doubt about America's new definition of itself as a first-strike warrior nation have been dropping away. Formerly contrary world leaders express support for the characterization of Saddam Hussein as an immediate global threat requiring urgent action. Once skeptical columnists and editorial writers suddenly take the necessity of an unfolding American military offensive for granted. Democrats in Congress are trading criticism for endorsement. A political consensus in favor of war against Iraq seems to be jelling—despite the fact that the Bush administration has in no way made a case. A primitive rhetoric of absolute assertion has been enough.

Standing before the United Nations General Assembly last week, President Bush said that Hussein represents a mortal global threat, which can be dealt with only by martial force. In fact, neither case was argued, much less proven. Hussein may or may not possess usable weapons of mass destruction; even what meager evidence has been cited is in dispute. If Hussein does possess such weapons, he may or may not intend to use them; he was successfully deterred from using them in the past. Apparently, questions like this do not matter.

A more general question has to do with how to influence Hussein. His behavior may or may not be able to be influenced for the better by diplomacy or other nonviolent pressures, but war, or even the imminent threat of war, would seem to guarantee behavior for the worse. That promises disaster, especially for Israel, if Bush's gravest charges about Hussein's arsenal and his readiness to empty it are true. But apparently this doesn't matter either. Bush has yet to explain how the world is served by giving the dictator nothing to lose. Why has behavior change been trumped by regime change? These questions have remained unanswered through all of the recent talk, but what is striking now is how many fewer voices are asking them.

The real subject of President Bush's U.N. speech was not Iraq's malfeasance but America's indomitable will. Why is Iraq a mortal threat requiring violent overthrow? Because America says so. Why are nations stifling their doubts to join this campaign? Because America has told them to. Nations—whether France or Saudi Arabia—cannot afford to be on the losing side of an American war. Bush changed the subject at the U.N. from the war's justification to its inevitability, and its justification ceased to matter. The positive response to Bush's speech was a measure not of his personal resolve, nor of his leadership, but of the meaning of the new American hegemony. This is what the raw power of the world's only superpower looks like.

Similarly within the United States. Political power is diffuse and unfocused on every subject except war. Once war defines the national purpose, war itself is no longer considered a proper subject for debate—not in the media, not in Congress. By showing up at the U.N. last week, and giving a nod to multilateralism, Bush shrewdly blunted the one point of criticism most domestic opponents of war had been prepared to make. If France won't forthrightly oppose an unprovoked campaign to overthrow Hussein, how can the Democrats? An unnecessary multilateral war is still unnecessary, but again Bush could preempt war opposition with war's inevitability. Get on the train.

What, then, are skeptics to do? First, be clear on what has happened. Objections to the war have not been addressed; they have been bowled over by rhetorical assertion. The assertion has been empty, but oddly that has made it more powerful. How do you rationally consider the pros and cons of a course of action with someone for whom the cons simply do not exist? The responsibility of the skeptic is clear: to remain engaged in the debate, even if by insisting that the debate is not over. The American war against Iraq must be opposed. It must be stopped. Where there is faith in its justice or in its inevitability, sow doubt.

The President's Nuclear Threat

October 1, 2002

The National Security Strategy of the United States, the document published by the Bush administration last week, explains the rush to war, lays bare how much more dangerous the world is under Bush, and shows that neither he nor his advisers understand the history they have lived through. In a statement full of disturbing assertions, perhaps the most troubling is the sweeping dismissal of nuclear non-proliferation agreements among nations in favor of "proactive coun-terproliferation efforts" that will now originate in Washington.

A myopic fixation on unproven fears about the capabilities and in-tentions of Iraq, Iran, and North Korea has blinded the Bush admin-istration to one of the great contemporary triumphs of American-led diplomacy. Far from being a failure, the nonproliferation regime, orig-inating with the Nuclear Nonproliferation Treaty of 1970, has been a success, the partiality of which underscores its significance. As I first learned in conversation with nonproliferation expert James Walsh of Harvard's Kennedy School, the true wonder of nuclear weapons is how few nations have come to possess them, how many nations have renounced nukes altogether.

In 1970, five nations openly possessed nuclear weapons, but many others stood on the nuclear threshold. Since then Israel, India, and Pakistan have joined the club, but consider what else happened. Argentina and Brazil, mutually suspicious, both embarked upon nu-clear weapons development, but then renounced it. South Africa did likewise, and so did Taiwan. After the breakup of the Soviet Union, Ukraine, Kazakhstan, and Belarus could have clung to remnant nu-clear capacity and expanded on it, but all three did the opposite. In 1994, even demonized North Korea, responding to diplomatic pres-sure from the United States, halted plutonium production, and South Korea stayed on the nuclear sideline. When India exploded three nukes in May of 1998, the American intelligence establish-ment was, as usual, completely surprised, but the real surprise should have been that India, having tested its first nuke in 1974, had waited so long.

Nonproliferation defined the international order. The exceptions only prove the point. We could very easily be living in a world with nuclear weapons as common, say, as high-tech fighter aircraft—with countries like Egypt, Indonesia, Australia, and numerous others

armed with nukes. Pakistan's nuclear capacity, despite grave impoverishment, is a signal of how widely dispersed the weapon could be.
The nations that renounced nuclear ambition, and the 167 nations
that renewed the NPT in 1995, have done this not out of a preference for powerlessness but out of commitment to two foundational
principles. The first is the ideal of ultimate nuclear disarmament.
The cornerstone of the NPT is article 6, in which the five possessor
states (the United States, Russia, China, France, Britain) agree "to
pursue negotiations in good faith on effective measures relating to
cessation of the nuclear arms race at an early date, and to nuclear
disarmament."

That process has proceeded in fits and starts, but until now it has
remained at the center of international hope. In last week's statement, Bush renounced the ideal of eventual nuclear disarmament,
by renouncing any "intention of allowing any foreign power to catch
up with the huge lead the United States has opened since the fall of
the Soviet Union more than a decade ago." American military supremacy, based on nukes, is forever. And so, therefore, is the inherently destabilizing gulf between nuclear haves and have-nots.

The second principle that allowed nonproliferation to take hold is
the idea of democracy. The Bush strategy claims to be at the service
of democracy, but what Bush fails to grasp is that you can't have
democracy *within* nations while repudiating democratic values *among*
nations. The NPT worked because it embodied the idea that nations,
even if unequal in power or treasure, are mutually accountable, devoted to common standards, and bound by shared commitments. The
main structure of democracy among nations consists precisely in that
web of treaties (including the ABM, Kyoto, Comprehensive Test Ban,
ICC, and Nuclear Nonproliferation treaties) that is brushed away by
Bush's "distinctly American internationalism."

"We will not hesitate to act alone," Bush declares, promising to
extend American sway by "convincing or compelling states to accept
their sovereign responsibilities." The United States has become a ludicrous self-contradiction: a dictator state dictating democracy. And
how does Bush imagine other nations will respond? It is certainly

true that no power will compete with us for world dominance, but in the nuclear age total throw weight is irrelevant. Other nations will inevitably respond to this unprecedented American swagger exactly by pursuing nuclear capability—if only to force Washington to treat them with respect. Proliferation squared. With nuclear know-how dispersed, and especially with Russian nuclear materials and capabilities headed to market, the only possible protection from eventual nuclear disaster is precisely the tissue of international agreement that the United States has just crushed and trashed, like used Kleenex.

Antiwar Then, Antiwar Now

October 8, 2002

In 1971, Washington was shocked when a throng of battle-scarred veterans showed up to protest the war in Vietnam. They camped on the Mall, and the Nixon administration quickly obtained a ruling from Chief Justice Warren Burger ordering the veterans to clear out. They refused. Would they be arrested? It was then that Senator Edward M. Kennedy boldly went to the Mall where the antiwar veterans had pitched their tents and sleeping bags. "You have served your country well abroad," he told them, "and will serve it even better here in Washington." Kennedy's public support of the illegal demonstrators was key in turning the tide of opinion—and then law—in the veterans' favor, and a crucial blow against the war was struck. (See *Home to War* by Gerald Nicosia.)

Ted Kennedy is doing it again. "I started my career at a time when there was a war that was important to end," he said to me as we sat together last Saturday. "And now—not that I am finishing my career—there is a war that requires us to relearn those lessons of history." A few minutes later, in Harvard's Sanders Theater, Kennedy delivered a stirring address at the induction ceremony of the American Academy of Arts and Sciences, perhaps the strongest criticism of the move toward war in Iraq yet made by a leading politician, although you would not know that from the way the speech was ignored in the drumbeating media.

Instead of focusing on the details of the pro-war resolution that Congress will likely approve this week, Kennedy honed in on "a more fundamental debate that is only just beginning—an all-important debate about how, when and where in the years ahead our country will use its unsurpassed military might." Iraq is simply the first case in point.

Responding to the Bush administration's recently published *National Security Strategy of the United States*, Kennedy carefully dissected the radical assumptions that are driving the nation toward war. First, he showed that by equating the two quite distinct purposes of "prevention" and "preemption," Bush is leading America to embrace a course of action it has long condemned in others. "Traditionally," Kennedy said, " 'preemptive' action refers to times when states react to an imminent threat of attack." He offered Israel's response to the border-moves of Egypt and Syria in 1967 as an example of justified preemption. By contrast, the Japanese attack on Pearl Harbor, intending to undercut a potential "capability that could someday become threatening," was a "preventive" action. "The coldly premeditated nature of preventive attacks and preventive wars makes them anathema to well-established principles against aggression."

To Kennedy, preventive war is still anathema, and his denunciation of the Bush embrace of preventive war against Iraq draws its edge from the fact that President John Kennedy, in 1961 and 1962, rejected the argument for preventive war against the Soviet Union, protecting a moral boundary. "For 175 years," Edward Kennedy quotes Robert Kennedy as saying, "we have not been that kind of country."

Are we now? The Bush administration's new doctrine, Kennedy

said, "asserts that global realities now legitimize preventive war and make it a strategic necessity. The document openly contemplates preventive attacks against groups or states, even absent the threat of imminent attack. . . . I strongly oppose any such extreme doctrine."

The second feature of Bush's radical new approach that Kennedy lambasted was its assumption that the United States is somehow exempt from the rules it "expect[s] others to obey." Kennedy reiterated an old cliché of public morality—"Might does not make right!"—but in the present context, his reference rang with prophetic relevance. The hubris of overwhelming power is corrupting the nation. "America cannot write its own rules for the modern world. To attempt to do so would be unilateralism run amok." Bush is undercutting the war on terrorism, destroying alliances, setting dangerous precedents, and eviscerating America's moral legitimacy.

Again daring to go where few of his colleagues venture, Kennedy defined all of this by its proper name: "The administration's doctrine is a call for twenty-first-century American imperialism that no other nation can or should accept." The debate in Congress this week is centered on Saddam Hussein and Iraq, but what is really at stake are basic structures of the American idea. The name Kennedy is properly attached to this nation's noblest impulse, and it is fitting that the last of the brothers is raising his voice in its defense.

The afternoon of his speech, the senator and I were sitting in a Somerville café. A customer approached our rear-corner table to say, "Senator, I want to thank you for all you're doing to stand up for us against this rush to war."

I asked her name, and if I could quote her. "Lucy Borodkin," she said firmly. "And you certainly can."

8

HOSTAGE

In the autumn of 2002, terrorists became hostage takers. Unknown snipers took the entire Washington metropolitan area hostage, and then Chechen guerrilla fighters took Moscow hostage by seizing a theater full of people. But George W. Bush, in dismantling the structures of international order that had been put in place over fifty years, proved to be a hostage taker, too.

Through that fall, President Bush prepared for a moment that many thought would never really come, and then on December 17, he did it. He ordered the first actual deployment of an antimissile system—the long-deferred Reagan dream of Star Wars. In Alaska, California, and on Aegis destroyers in the open ocean would be based a first generation of antiballistic missile interceptors, costing almost $18 billion over two years—and paving the way for more of the same. Six days before Bush's announcement the interceptor had been tested, and for the third time it had failed. The fact that scientists were nearly unanimous in saying that such a system could never be made reliable did nothing to deter Bush. He justified his action, as he had more or less every other action of the preceding year, by pointing to September 11.

This deployment marked the crossing of yet another threshold. He was officially abandoning the cold war's breakthrough recognition: in the nuclear age, "defensive" measures, like the missile shield, inevitably spark offensive measures, undermining national security instead of adding to it. This idea may seem counterintuitive, and it certainly opens into a worldview based on paradox instead of conflict. Only the renunciation of defense, institutionalized in the Anti-Ballistic Missile Treaty and now rejected by Bush, led to détente, arms reduction, the halt of nuclear proliferation, and, ultimately, toward a post-cold-war dream of peace. Now, that insight, and the diplomatic accomplishments to which it led, were repudiated. A threshold, therefore, in reverse. With one initiative after another, President Bush dragged the human race back into the minefield from which, at the millennium, it had just seemed to escape.

Threshold Period

October 17, 2002

That an official of the Federal Republic of Germany was sacked last month for comparing George W. Bush to Adolf Hitler was proper, but not because of the insult to Bush. The uniqueness of Hitler's malevolence must always be insisted upon. Whatever one's problems with Bush, it banalizes evil to equate him with the author of the Final Solution. Germans must be particularly careful not to do this.

Historical analogies can often mislead, as the numerous dead ends beyond the signpost of "appeasement" show. How many people have needlessly died in the name of avoiding another Munich? But humans are nevertheless condemned to understand the present in the light of the past, especially when events are radically unprecedented. It seems clear that, with the American president intent upon a new program of moralistic imperialism, beginning with a war in Iraq, we are in what might be called a threshold period, leading from one conception of society to another as yet undefined one. The ominous situation requires us to ask: when have we stood in such a threshold before?

For Americans of my generation, the years between 1963 and 1965 leap to mind. It was then that decisions taken in Washington established a momentum of violence that ran unchecked for a decade. By the time U.S. citizens realized what was being done in their names, it was too late to stop the momentum until it ran down on its own timetable. America before the war in Vietnam was a very different place from America after. To say nothing of the transformation of Vietnam. A historic threshold had been crossed, but what everyone saw by 1975, very few had seen in the pivotal period of 1963–65.

What characterized that threshold? Four things:

- Low-grade social panic. American citizens had just suffered through two traumas: the near apocalypse of nuclear war over Cuba and then the shattering of national self-confidence with the assassination of President Kennedy.
- The mainstreaming of previously "extremist" ideas. Lyndon Johnson was elected in 1964 as the "peace candidate," but he immediately embraced the rampant belligerence of Barry Goldwater, his vanquished rival. Savage violence was promoted with hyperrationality as the "moderate" course.
- The surrender by legislators of their constitutional authority. Congress ceded emergency powers to the executive branch with the Gulf of Tonkin resolution, and political opposition to the war—from Eugene McCarthy to George McGovern—would be permanently marginalized.
- The recasting of patriotism to mean conformity. National self-criticism was defined as disloyalty. America—love it or leave it.

To list such defining notes of a threshold period in the past is to recognize them in the present. Our social panic today is tied to terrorism.

Formerly extreme ideas (contempt for the U.N., unilateralism, carelessness about civil liberties) animate Washington now. The U.S. Congress has just given Bush nearly unrestricted license to use force. Citizens are detached, dissenters are marginalized, and a momentum toward permanent war is set loose.

But to enumerate such characteristics of the time is to recall another threshold period, one to which we must return again and again—even though this act of memory can seem offensive for a reason already noted. Between 1933 and 1935, the world changed, although how it changed was not clear until the horrible decade that followed had run its course. The notes of that threshold period are familiar. The 1933 social panic in Germany was tied to economic distress and to active dread of terrorism—Communist terrorism. (Hitler was elected on March 5, 1933, two days after the Reichstag was burned, a national horror blamed on Communists.) The once widely denounced ideas of Nazism, especially the political exploitation of antisemitism, quickly found a place in mainstream attitudes. (Few objected to the Nazis' April 1, 1933, offensive against Jews.) German legislators entirely ceded their responsibility to Hitler by passing the "Enabling Act" in April. The last opposition party—the Center Party—dismantled itself. The broad population of Germany quickly accommodated the new hysterical nationalism, despite excesses few would have affirmed earlier. A threshold was crossed.

The point of this analogy is not to compare Hitler and Bush, any more than the 1963–65 analogy is to compare Johnson and Bush. The question is not about leadership but about societies that allow themselves to be radically transformed without substantial debate. The question is about what is lost when traditional restraints are abandoned, and about what follows when the momentum toward open-ended war is set loose. The question is about what the cost for prideful world primacy entails, and who pays it. The question is about what happens when national consensus is hijacked by fringe politics, and when the very people empowered to object say nothing. The question, in other words, is not about Bush but about us.

Taken Hostage

October 29, 2002

You keep thinking of the people in that Moscow theater, how their jeopardy seemed so familiar to you. Once, an ordeal like that— masked captors, the bombs, the ticking clock—would have been unimaginable outside of novels, but no more. Indeed, as you watched the drama unfold, you thought of theaters in your own country and realized that now they, too, will be installing metal detectors. When will you be taken hostage, forced to wait in terror, sharing an orchestra pit for a latrine, fathoming the motives of your masked enemies, secretly using your cell phone, weeping with anxiety, whispering to your fellow prisoners, until you are all overcome by gas, perhaps to be rescued into the nightmare of having survived?

The cruelty of strangers, however motivated, takes your breath away—but that, too, seems like something close at hand. Just moments before Chechen guerrillas seized the Moscow theater, weren't you obsessively imagining yourself in Washington, D.C., with the snipers at large? The seized theater, in that case, was the very city. For weeks you have not pumped gas without looking around at the lost innocence of the world. How long is it since you felt safe?

What was it like in Moscow? You take the story of Pierre Bezukhov as an instance, how he was stunned to find himself captured by fanatical invaders. When they announced their intention to begin shooting their prisoners, Bezukhov was put in the line, number six. He felt, you read, "as if part of his soul had been torn away. He lost the power of thinking or understanding. He could only hear and see. And he had only one wish—that the frightful thing that had to happen should happen quickly." Bezukhov was forced to watch as his fellow captives were shot dead, one after the other, a horror beyond anything he had ever experienced. He never expected to be spared, but he was—and then came the real surprise. Instead of feeling sweet relief at having escaped murder, he was even more devastated. "It was as if the mainspring of his life, on which everything depended and which made everything appear alive, had suddenly been wrenched out and everything had collapsed into a heap of meaningless rubbish. . . . His faith in the right ordering of the universe, in humanity, in his own soul, and in God, had been destroyed."

Pierre Bezukhov, of course, is the central figure of Leo Tolstoy's *War and Peace*, and the marauding hostage takers are French invaders, not Chechens. That Tolstoy's war of 1812 can have such pointed resonance reminds you what the great novel is for. Its revelations apply forever. You needn't be directly a casualty of terror to have part of your soul ripped out. You needn't even read the novel. You, too, through the mere newspaper and television, have felt the mainspring of order tampered with by recent horrors.

Pierre Bezukhov came to his trauma from a life of privilege, not unlike yours, and it chastens you to realize that wanton cruelty and random violence define the limits of life for most human beings. Nevertheless, the cumulative effect of this year's traumas, and the even greater ones that threaten from the shadows, have left you shaken to the core. Not only that. Your faith in the "right ordering of the universe" has been tied to a hope that your own nation's purposes, however ambiguous, are still more aligned to that ordering than not. Yet now you worry that some mainspring has been wrenched, also, out of America's moral intuition, threatening to reduce the nation's traditional regard for others—defined variously by prudent statecraft, a preference of diplomacy over war, an innate generosity, the dream of democracy—to a heap of meaningless rubbish called American Empire.

What does it do to you—not only to witness at close hand (as close as the TV on the kitchen counter) the manifestation of breathtaking cruelty, but to feel yourself next in line as its victim? Does it harden you to such cruelty? Prepare you to become cruel yourself? The sniper in Washington, the hostage takers in Moscow, the suicide-bombers, the berserk commandos, and the high-tech wizards of laser bombs above Iraq are all on the same continuum. Defense becomes offense, the protection of your children becomes the murder of another's, his threat becomes your preemption. You kill to stop the killing. Why should you not feel like a stranger in a strange land, abandoned by God?

"What does all this mean?" Tolstoy asks in his epilogue. "Why did it happen? What made those people burn houses and slay their fellow men? What were the causes of these events? What force made men act so? These are the instinctive, plain, and most legitimate questions humanity asks itself." So why should you not ask them? And why should your soul not be troubled—to find itself taken hostage again by war?

The Purpose of the War

November 5, 2002

Confusion still reigns over America's war aim, and this week's home-stretch debate at the U.N. Security Council shows it. Does the Bush administration want "regime change" or disarmament? Despite the president's callow equation last month—"Disarmament *is* regime change"—not only are the two purposes different, but they can work against each other. Such confusion is typical of the careless Bush mind, but in this circumstance it is dangerous. Perhaps there is something to learn from another time when public and private perceptions of America's war aim became confused at the crucial moment—with tragic results.

Beginning with an agreement made at Casablanca in 1943, the purpose of the Allied war was "unconditional surrender" of the Axis

enemies. After the utter destruction of Germany, Japan began to put
out "peace feelers" in the spring and early summer of 1945, seeking
clarification of Allied objectives. Of particular concern to the Japanese was the fate of the emperor, a concern no doubt exacerbated by
the grotesque deaths of Hitler and Mussolini. To his people, Hirohito was no mere Führer or duce, but a divine personage, the object
of worship. Would he be tried as a war criminal? Would he be executed? Forced from his throne? What unthinkable dishonor awaited
him? Could these questions be negotiated? The answer from the Allies was no: Truman repeated "unconditional surrender" in early
June.

But senior U.S. officials debated in secret what "unconditional
surrender" actually meant, knowing that the all-but-defeated Japanese fighting force would die to its last man rather than betray the
emperor. Indeed, the emperor's word would be necessary to get
them to lay down their arms. But there was no public mitigation of
terms. At the end of July, with "totality and severity," in Secretary of
State James F. Byrnes's phrase, the demand for "unconditional surrender" was reiterated from Potsdam. The Japanese die-hard fatalism
that would follow was factored into the massive cost of an anticipated Allied invasion of the island homeland, which in turn was
used to justify the dropping of the two A-bombs. Because the Japanese wanted to protect their emperor, and because America refused
to negotiate the point—no retreat from "unconditional surrender"—
the nuclear age began.

And then what happened? On August 10, the day after Nagasaki
was bombed, a message came from Tokyo accepting the terms of the
Potsdam Declaration, but "with the understanding that the said Declaration does not comprise any demand which prejudices the pre-
rogatives of His Majesty as a sovereign ruler." All Japanese resistance
would cease, but only assuming the emperor would be spared—as
emperor. Byrnes, for one, wanted to refuse the offer because it was
not unconditional, and "we might be exposed to the criticism that
we had receded from the totality and severity of the Potsdam Decla-

ration." He was overruled and the war ended, yet the question of that "receding" would stand. Having just obliterated Hiroshima and Nagasaki for the sake of an absolute victory, didn't the attached Japanese condition relativize it? If we would agree to the emperor's survival as emperor after the bombs, why would we not do so before? We maintained the mental and spiritual absolutism required to incinerate two entire cities—but only long enough to accomplish the incineration. Was the shock of what we had done the source of our sudden—and humane—flexibility? Was even Washington aware that Hiroshima and Nagasaki had tipped a moral scale? In the horror of what we had done, the emperor's fate, like the Japanese surrender with a condition attached, could seem a mere detail. For two and a half years "unconditional surrender" had defined our stated war aim, but in the end we accepted something less. (Hirohito did not renounce his divine status until 1946. He reigned until his death in 1989.) How might World War II have ended if America had sooner found and indicated a readiness to yield this point of transcendent honor? How many bodies are buried in this question?

"Regime change" is another way of saying "unconditional surrender." To Saddam Hussein's ear, the phrases must be synonymous. It may be progress that the quite different, less absolute, war aim of disarmament is also announced, but, except in Bush's mind, the American position may not reflect confusion. Perhaps the contrasting notes being struck by Washington—Donald Rumsfeld "total and severe," Colin Powell relatively flexible—represent a deliberate blurring of national purpose at the service of obtaining the U.N. Security Council endorsement this week. Once a resolution passes—any resolution will do—"regime change" will surely resume its place of primacy. As before, Washington will hold to its stated purpose until the momentum of war trumps everything else, until even the White House, the Pentagon, and our shamefully pliant Congress are at last appalled by what such rampant absolutism actually costs in human life.

Toeing the Fault Line of Fear

November 18, 2002

"Are you safer today than a year ago?" a *New York Times* headline asked the other day, and a TV news reporter was asking persons in the street, "How safe do you think we really are?" In recent days, perhaps because the purported voice of Osama bin Laden announced his resurrection, government warnings have heightened national anxiety again. When casual talk touches on public questions, the pleasures of conversation give way to worry. That we are a people poised to go to war against an unpredictable adversary in an inflamed region adds to our unease. Meanwhile, al Qaeda has taken on the dimensions of a mythic enemy. Our ignorance of its actual makeup makes it seem omnipotent.

What is *safety* anyway? More than the absence of immediate physical threat, the word refers to a feeling. Indeed, one might say the word refers to a delusion, for in truth it is the business of life on the earth to be dangerous. What humans ultimately long to be safe from is the threat of death—and yet every human is dying. We clothe ourselves in denial of mortality, paying as little heed to the iron law of time as we can. Life requires these mental tricks: that we embark upon each day as if it will go on forever; that we take up our mundane tasks as if they have ultimate significance; that we act as though our necessarily imperfect love for one another will eliminate loneliness; that we ignore the radical contingency of existence in favor of a feeling of being "safe." There is nothing wrong in all of this. The waking dream of a snug immortality is a necessary, even ingenious, adaptation to an earthbound finitude, unrelenting consciousness of which would be immobilizing. The feeling of being safe, in other words, may have nothing to do with our actual condition in a tragic universe, but it is essential to the human act of turning tragedy into hope.

But a longing for safety can be carried too far, and such a wish can be unworthily exploited by government. In the name of American safety, the once unthinkable is being done: in Yemen two weeks ago the CIA unapologetically killed six labeled terrorists, a legitimizing of extrajudicial execution. Assassination abroad is being openly proposed, and totalitarian controls at home are being installed. Under cover of escalating citizen anxiety, the Bush administration is masterfully reshaping both foreign and domestic policy—according to preset ideological dispositions. The policies promise "safety," but Bush's recast America feels less safe than ever.

Why are we so afraid? That question drives the disturbing and important new Michael Moore movie *Bowling for Columbine*. An absurd dynamic of fear peculiar to America—fear prompting reactions that make fear worse—is captured in the movie's display of how gun violence generates gun purchasing which generates more gun violence. That irrational cycle defines the U.S. gun obsession—and the U.S. war economy. What lies beneath such fear? Moore suggests that the unreckoned crime of slavery and the resulting unhealed wound of racial antagonism underwrite the readiness of fearful American whites to bring loaded weapons within range of their children.

The obsessive quest for "national security" has been a version of the same impulse on a larger scale. During the cold war, the demonized Communists turned our own nuclear weapons against us. As with the aftermath of slavery, the threat involved an unreckoned moral catastrophe of our own making. The nightmare scenario of incinerated cities so devastated us, even if subliminally, because we had already incinerated cities ourselves. In each terrifying case— slavery and nuclear war—merciless enemies are feared as striking back for crimes that deserve no mercy.

Could something similar be at work in our fear of terrorism today? One needn't recognize Osama bin Laden as a tribune of the dispossessed to acknowledge the vast gulf between privilege and desperation as the very precondition of terrorism. Here is the true meaning of the phrase "Gulf War": safety-obsessed Americans on one side of the gulf, most of the imperiled human race on the other. This disastrous inequality is not of our making, exactly, but our prosperity derives in part from the worsening of the lives of those who do not share it. (Our greenhouse gases lead to their floods; our war economy supplies their rogue armies with highly destructive weapons; our oil-thirst empowers their tyrants. And so on.)

Why don't we feel safe? For the reason American whites don't feel safe after slavery; the reason nuclear weapons traumatize us above all. We are conditioned to be terrorized by terrorism because it moves along a fault line for which we ourselves share responsibility. The fault line widens. And we do nothing to close it. The favored niche of fear is an uneasy conscience, and from its sure knowledge there is no escape.

A Missile Cover-up at MIT?

December 2, 2002

Last month the air force general in charge of developing the missile defense system declared that the elusive technology had finally proven itself. "We no longer need to experiment, to demonstrate or prevaricate," Lieutenant General Ronald Kadish said. "We need to get on with this."

But the record of Pentagon assertions in favor of missile defense has been unreliable, to say the least. A project that is bringing many tens of billions of dollars into military-industrial coffers carries an irresistible bias in its own behalf, and history shows that neither the Defense Department nor its contractors are reliable evaluators of the science and technology on which President Bush's vaunted "shield" must stand. Leave aside for the moment the disturbing question of whether U.S. initiatives toward missile defense will ignite a mortal new arms race with China and others. The remaining question of feasibility is grave enough. Can the nation afford $100 billion for a system that won't work? Can the government put the lives of citizens at risk behind a shield that will not protect?

Such questions are too important to leave to the obviously biased evaluators of the Pentagon and the defense industry. That is why the scientific claims of the Missile Defense Agency and its contractors must be examined by disinterested experts in the scientific community. On such independence rests the health of the U.S. economy, the safety of the nation, and the integrity of science itself when so much else has been corrupted. These are the stakes of a dispute that has been brewing at the Massachusetts Institute of Technology for more than a year.

Theodore A. Postol is a professor of science, technology, and national security policy at MIT. He earned a reputation as a debunker of the Patriot missile's Gulf War performance and then as a skeptic of missile defense. He challenged whether the system under design could ever reliably distinguish between incoming warheads and decoys. At particular issue was a 1997 test conducted and deemed successful by the defense contractor TRW. After that "success" was questioned by federal investigators, MIT's Lincoln Laboratory was hired to evaluate it. In 1999 Lincoln Lab affirmed TRW's results. Soon thereafter Postol objected, challenging not only the Pentagon and its contractor—but his own university. The Government Accounting Office investigated and concluded that Postol was right in pointing out flaws in the TRW test, but Postol's charge had gone beyond flaws to fraud. "Lincoln Lab," he said to me over coffee recently, "covered up a program-stopping flaw in the missile defense system. A great university involved in a cover-up?"

In April of 2001, Postol went to MIT authorities about the matter, and then early this year he went public, raising the grave question whether Lincoln Lab was collusive in TRW's deception. Postol argued that the "success" of the experiment depended on a match between observed phenomena and predicted phenomena. Had TRW fraudulently substituted one for the other? Had Lincoln Lab knowingly covered up that substitution? Had Lincoln Lab misled federal investigators? Had top MIT officials ignored and distorted these charges? Postol demanded an investigation. Last February, MIT launched an in-house inquiry into Postol's charges. (The *Boston Globe* called for an independent investigation at that time, asking MIT "to reconsider this self-protecting institutional reflex.")

The internal MIT inquiry into its own conduct was concluded last month, and it called for the outside investigation Postol had been demanding all along. That recommendation has now gone to MIT's top officials, and what it will lead to remains to be seen. Postol, for his part, has already reached a conclusion and is hoping for a congressional intervention. In letters he sent in late October to Congressman Howard Berman (D-California) and Senator Charles Grassley (R-Iowa), coauthors of the False Claims Act, Postol wrote, "In effect, Lincoln verified and certified as accurate bookkeeping arithmetic when Lincoln knew that the bookkeeping practices were fraudulent."

This might sound like a reprise of the Enron scandal, when both a company and its watchdog accountants were caught lying—a corruption not only of a basic system but also of the system's oversight mechanism. But Enron, finally, involved only money. The corruption that Postol alleges goes to the quick of scientific integrity, to the dead center of the academy's relationship to government, and, even more crucial, to the method by which future American defense strategies will be devised.

The independent investigation demanded by the courageous Professor Postol is long overdue. His demands might seem like disloyalty to a besieged university protective of its reputation. They might seem like mere "prevarication" to a Pentagon wanting "to get on" with missile defense. But to America there can be nothing esoteric about the truth, especially when falsehood, igniting an arms race, can pave the road to war.

What the Seven Died For

February 4, 2003

The brave astronauts who lost their lives last Saturday were pressing the literal limit of what separates the earth from all else that is. In dying, they remind us of the primordial truth that human beings exist to press such limits, even knowing that the results are often tragic. Space flight has been tamed no more than the human project has itself been purged of risk. When women and men consciously defy that risk for the sake of the universal impulse to know and to find, and when they then die doing so—we, the rest of their kind, rightly respond as one family, honoring them as exemplars of human nobility.

The vast blue in which the *Columbia* crew died has always drawn the human gaze in the quest for something more. Surely that is why, from the beginning, humans have populated the sky with angels, gods, and heroes. In our own time the sky has gone from being the place out of which fire falls—the realm of bombs and missiles—to being the place in which the earthly borders over which wars are fought become invisible and therefore meaningless. That, after all, was the "earthrise" epiphany, the picture taken by the moonwalkers a generation ago of the blue-green ball hanging in the void, our fragile planet as an oasis of life and hope in an otherwise indifferent cosmos. And then, marvel of marvels, that borderless dream of one earth became institutionalized in the joint Russian-American space station, which the *Columbia* and other shuttles regarded as an outermost home.

Space exploration defined the cold war at its most dangerous— from *Sputnik* in 1957, announcing the Soviet capacity to rain H-bombs on the United States, to John Kennedy's retaliatory race to

the moon, which sparked a final American military dominance. Ultimately, a counterimpulse, rooted in common humility before the
vast unknown, led Washington and Moscow to cross an even bolder
space frontier—into a realm of cooperation. Transforming "throw
weight" and "force projection," the enemies became partners in the
very enterprise that had most endangered the earth.

That partnership is enshrined in the space station where even
now a Russian and two Americans face perilous uncertainty after
the *Columbia* disaster. Their common plight reminds us that in
nothing was the reversal of the cold war more absolute than the
transformation of space from nationalistically demarcated battlefield
to transnational field of human investigation. That good tradition
was being honored last week by the presence of Israel's lone astro-
naut aboard the *Columbia*, a successor to participants from other
nations.

One of the things that makes the sky newly dangerous is the
resurgent temptation to elevate armed borders into the air and beyond, a reiteration of the ancient trumping of the human with the
tribal. That impulse is reflected in the initiatives, sponsored by Secretary of Defense Donald Rumsfeld, toward a weaponization of
space, under the so-called U.S. Space Command. Defying a nearly
unanimous U.N. consensus, the Pentagon is staking claims on the
"high frontier," a corollary of current U.S. strategies toward global
military dominance. The Bush administration's missile defense program is the first stage of this expansion. Space-based laser weapons,
"sentry satellites," orbiting "kill vehicles," plutonium-powered space
probes—all are an appalling, if little-noted, coming of age of Star
Wars. Nothing would more thoroughly betray the humane spirit of
the *Columbia* astronauts than a retreat from international space
partnership-for-peace in the name of one nation's space-based hegemony. That it would be America's only makes the very thought of
such betrayal more grotesque.

Today, in the formal memorial service for the lost *Columbia* astronauts in Houston, and in the coming days of mourning and reflection, our nation's heart will be full. Again and again, we will see,

in the broadcast image, the blue sky cut by the white arc of sudden devastation. We will see the faces of the dead men and women, of their bereaved families. We will see faces of newly stunned Israelis. And what will all of this prompt in the American heart? Will we come out of this grief more alive to the fragility of all human life and therefore to its preciousness? Will we recognize in the world outpouring of empathy a signal that international commonality must now transcend every narrow notion of "national security"?

When our eyes drift skyward today, what will we see? What about the refusal of the very air, not to mention outer space, to define itself by anything but the color blue? The dense, deep, endless blue in which, as our noble astronauts keep telling us, the exquisite planet earth hangs—hangs there without even a thread to hold it up. All that this lovely sphere in the otherwise indifferent void hangs by is human courage. May those who have just taught us this again rest in peace.

9

MORAL MEMORY

By the end of 2002, it was clear that recollections of 9-11 had been shaped into a "national memory," a defining note for a new political framework; that state-sanctioned commemoration had trumped all personal experience of grief and loss. This public paradigm featured evil foreign enemies and noble Americans (firefighters, policemen, airline passengers). Characters who did not fit into this narrative framework, like the anthrax killer who turned out not to be foreign, and, eventually, a foreign villain who proved too wily to capture, were simply deleted from the collective narrative. Saddam Hussein replaced Osama bin Laden. A story was being told about the terrorist attacks that justified a particular course set by the nation's leaders. Complexities were filtered out and countermemories forgotten. This had happened before. In Europe, after World War II, heroic memories of resistance blocked out memories of collaboration and cowardice. After the Vietnam War, in the United States, memories of that war—and its great memorial in Washington—emphasized American suffering, with no acknowledgment of the far more catastrophic Vietnamese experience.

The Bush-sponsored version of the past aimed toward action in the present, and on October 10, 2002, that action was affirmed by the passage of House Joint Resolution 144: "To authorize the use of United States Armed Forces against Iraq." But that same day, a counternote was struck when an opponent of the resolution, former president Jimmy Carter, was named winner of the Nobel Peace Prize. In his acceptance remarks, Carter expressly repudiated the Bush project: "For powerful countries to adopt a principle of preventive war," Carter said, "may well set an example that can have catastrophic consequences." The debate was not only about American purposes in the present and future but about uses of the past as justification for those purposes.

———

Philip Berrigan

December 10, 2002

Philip Berrigan is dead. His family and friends buried him yesterday in Baltimore. Most people who remember Philip Berrigan associate him with the long-ago draft-board raids that made him famous in the 1960s. Fewer people know that he committed eight major acts of civil disobedience between 1980 and 1999—literal acts of disarmament, which cost him years in prison. But the image of the smiling, white-haired man in handcuffs can be misleading. Far from being a marginal figure whose time is long past, Philip Berrigan, even in death, has extraordinary relevance for two of today's most urgent questions.

The first has to do with the Catholic priesthood. Once, the pressures facing the Catholic Church would have seemed a parochial matter, but the moral conflagration that is melting the inner girders of this institution has begun to threaten the very structure of authority in society. Catholics continue to be staggered by the abuse-cover-up scandal, with each further revelation of the hierarchy's obtuseness—and the priesthood's hollowness. Early on, others watched the church's immorality play with detached fascination, but lately even non-Catholics have sensed a dangerous, societywide shuddering. If the Catholic Church can fall, what can't? In fact, the social order is all one tower—and it, too, can come down.

Philip Berrigan lived a life that offers an image of redemption to the Catholic priesthood. In particular, he showed what the vow of obedience really means. With his Jesuit brother Daniel, he found himself in conflict with a hierarchy that was, in effect, a cosponsor of an immoral war. (Cardinal Francis Spellman: "Nothing less than victory will do!") Berrigan's challenge was as much to the church as to the nation. The church, too, is subject to biblical judgment; the church, too, is fallen. And by refusing to heed those who equated his prophetic critique with disloyalty, affirming his Catholic faith to the end, and ignoring those who would excommunicate him, Berrigan showed the way for Catholics today. In defying corrupt authority, he rescued the principle of authority. To stand against a morally bankrupt Catholic power structure is the highest manifestation of Catholic love. Philip Berrigan, married and the father of two magnificent daughters and a magnificent son, never stopped being an exemplary priest.

But his significance is far broader than that. While most Americans were in willful denial about their nation's hubristic devotion to "overwhelming force" based on nuclear weapons, Berrigan was endlessly sounding alarms. When the cold war ended, and with it the threat that had pushed the world to the brink of an abyss, America alone declined to step back. The "indispensable nation" would be armed to the teeth. Berrigan protested, directly assaulting missiles, destroyers, warplanes, and uranium warheads. The war culture/economy, he warned, will spark a momentum toward mass violence that will be its own justification, and it will be unstoppable.

And lo, behold where we have come. The imminent invasion of Iraq is an exact instance of what Berrigan predicted: America going to war not because it needs to but because it can. And Berrigan would insist that this crisis originates not with the eccentric machismo of George W. Bush (Berrigan challenged Carter, Reagan, Bush Sr., and Clinton) but with the universal American fantasy that "national security" can depend on weapons of mass destruction. On this point, Saddam Hussein is our mirror image, which must be why we hate him so. Berrigan was often dismissed as a pacifist idealist, but the current crisis reveals him to have been a shrewd realist. The weapons we accumulate, instead of protecting us, are themselves the source of our mortal danger.

Americans should not condescend to the troubled Catholic Church. The nation and the religion are enshrouded in the same moral fog. For years, Catholics—both bishops and laity equally at the mercy of a corrupt clericalism—looked the other way while pathological priests abused children. Now some would like to blame the cowardly leaders, fire them, and get back to normal. But what if "normal" is the problem? What if the entire system of church triumphalism (sex-hating, woman-hating, power-mad) must be dismantled?

Equally grave questions address the American war culture. The attack on Iraq must be opposed, but must not everything that has brought our nation to this threshold of violent imperialism be reexamined? Why, over the last dozen years, have we done so little to step back from the nuclear abyss? Why is the ideal of international law so weightless in Washington? How can we expect other nations not to imitate our unchecked reliance on weapons of mass destruction? When did this vast American militarism become "normal"?

These are questions on which Philip Berrigan had the nerve to stake his life, as a Catholic and an American. As a priest and a prophet. *Phil is dead.* We loved him. *Phil is dead.* His voice is still there to be heard. *Phil is dead.* May he rest, yes, in peace.

The Christmas Bombing

December 24, 2002

Christmas Eve seems made for memory. I remember being wedged among my brothers, all of us between our parents, in the crowded balcony of St. Mary's Church for Midnight Mass. The aroma of incense, the hissing of a nearby radiator, the unpadded kneeler hard against my knees, my mother's rosary beads swaying below her tan gloves. The best part of Christmas Eve was the cold, clean air into which we walked coming out of church, the ride home in the car, the exotic feeling of being out so late. The worst part: how impossible it was to keep my eyes from fluttering shut even as my brothers debated whether Santa Claus would come to a house whose occupants were all away at Mass.

But as the music of bells and carols yield to the drums of a mounting military cadence, America about to go to war, another Christmas memory intrudes. This year marks the thirtieth anniversary of the Christmas bombing of North Vietnam. For people of a certain age, the thought of that unprecedented air assault, lasting from December 18 to 30, intermittently disturbs the tranquillity of the otherwise holy season. How staggered we were at reports of the bombs falling day and night on cities across North Vietnam. Hanoi and Haiphong were especially hard hit. American pilots flew nearly four thousand sorties, including more than seven hundred by high-flying B-52s. Those "area bombers," incapable of precision, had never been used against cities before. That they were used now was a sure sign that this was terror bombing pure and simple. Washington said its penultimate air campaign was necessary because Hanoi had balked at the peace talks, but most of the balking was obviously coming from Washington's Saigon ally. Everyone could see that the bombing was a final venting of frustration and rage by a superpower faced with ignominious defeat.

The reason to remember the Christmas bombing of 1972 is not to feel morally superior to those responsible for it. Rather, it is to understand something basic to the experience of war. Here is the most important truth of this memory: those who ordered and carried out the brutal attacks against population centers at the end of the Vietnam War would never have done so at the beginning. What Nixon commanded in 1972 he would have condemned in 1969. The war transformed America's moral sensibility; the war deadened it. It had happened before. In 1939, the American president pleaded with the nations that had gone to war in Europe: "Under no circumstance," FDR said, "undertake the bombardment from the air of civilian populations or of unfortified cities." By the end of that war, the U.S. Army Air Force had defined itself as an instrument of urban destruction, replacing cities with piles of rubble (81 of Japan's largest 120 cities were obliterated from the air, even before Hiroshima). What Washington abhorred at the beginning was taken for granted by the end.

The dynamic of war transcends the ability of warriors to resist it. In war, choices routinely lead to unanticipated consequences, which present wholly unimagined new choices, which involve further consequences, leading finally to choices to which warriors would never have given assent at the start. Because of this human inability to foresee or control descent into savagery once killing begins, the only way to keep war "humane" is not to embark on it in the first place.

But sometimes the coming moral horror presents itself in prospect with clarity and force. When President Bush announces, as he did two weeks ago, an American readiness to use nuclear weapons in retaliation against any use by Saddam Hussein of chemical or biological weapons against U.S. forces, he is, in effect, ceding to Hussein the primacy of moral judgment. He is saying that, under certain foreseeable circumstances, which may or may not be likely, the United States will join Iraq in crossing the threshold into the ethical abyss of mass destruction. By raising the specter of nuclear use, President Bush is already defining the war he is about to initiate as a war without moral limit. Having imagined choices and consequences to that extent, alas, he does not seem to have considered what will follow from an American return to the exercise of power by nuclear terror: a savage century. To his credit, though, the president has given the world and his nation a fair description of what he imagines he might do. A fair warning, and not only to Hussein.

Have we heard it? On this Christmas Eve, which is nearly the eve of an aggressive American war, the nation goes down on its knees to pray for peace. We worship memories of our own virtue. What lies we tell ourselves! Santa Claus is coming tonight. We are the forces of good arrayed against evil. Yes, and Nixon's Christmas bombing brought us peace with honor.

The Last Year

December 31, 2002

What if we could know for certain that the coming year would be the world's last year? Abstracting from the way in which the climax of history would occur, and leaving aside all visions of apocalypse, how would it change our approach to life and time if we knew that one year from today everything would end? To ask such a question is an outlandish exercise, yet its drama is implicit in the cycle of the calendar. The last day of the year is fraught because, if we bother to notice, it offers just such a foretaste of the last day of all. Why else, at New Year's, do we try to remember what we care about most? Why else do we resolve to reorganize our lives accordingly? Why else, for that matter, do we get smashed?

What would the known limit of time mean to us as Americans? How would we give expression to our national purpose if we could see the common end coming? Only one more year to let the world know what the American dream really amounts to. The first question, of course, is about war and peace. Would it make sense to go forward with plans to launch attacks against Iraq, especially since the stated purpose of the war is to prevent Iraq from behaving badly in the distant future? If there is no distant future, what then? And what about America's role in the conflict between Israel and the Palestinians? Would we be content to continue sitting on the sidelines with these antagonists locked in their death struggle? Or would we feel a new urgency to help them break it?

It is the unpredictability of the open-ended future that makes America feel insecure. Our obsession with "national security" would dissolve in the light of a limited future, and we would see very clearly that what defines our relationship to the rest of the world is our excessive wealth. Instead of protecting it, in the new circumstance, wouldn't we see our affluence as the great source of a new agenda? Our perceptions would shift. The threatening "other" would emerge as fellow human beings in need. North Koreans, for example, would stop being the faceless Communist horde they have been for fifty years, and would become instead a collection of mothers, fathers, and children who cannot heat their homes. Nuclear energy, nuclear bombs—the dispute would give way to the main fact of North Korean life today, which is that everybody there is cold. With only one year to go, wouldn't we want to help them into the great luxury of warmth in winter? Send the people oil because without it they freeze?

Seeing the world through a lens defined by human need instead of by mortal threat, and having no use over the long haul for our cache of riches, nor therefore for the weapons that protect it, wouldn't America spend its treasure so that the hungry would know for once the simple satisfaction of a full stomach? Wouldn't we open up our storerooms and give away the surplus medicine, blankets, clothing, utensils, books, bread? And wouldn't we discover to our shame how much of that hoarded bread had gone stale because we had more than we ourselves could eat?

As individuals, what would we do with our last year? Certain things are obvious. Wouldn't we shore up our relationships, making sure everyone we love knows it? Those whom we have wounded—wouldn't we make it up to them? Instead of living to work, wouldn't we work to live? Wouldn't we abandon our habit of postponement, allowing into our lives at last the beauty, quiet, pleasure, good company, and chosen solitude that have been eluding us? Without worries tied to a long-term future, wouldn't the present moment reclaim its value? And wouldn't we live every such moment attuned to its transience, newly aware that what makes human experience tragic is the very thing that makes it beautiful?

We are fragmented people, hopelessly at the mercy of multiple, often conflicting purposes. A mundane dualism defines our existence (body versus soul, public versus private, ideal versus real), leaving us neither here nor there. With our last year as a source of ferocious concentration, wouldn't we reclaim a unity of purpose? Organizing our time around one single reason for being? Which would be what? Wealth? Fame? Pleasure? Control? Happiness? Justice? Or might it be love?

It is only a New Year's exercise, to imagine that a year from today the sun goes down for the last time. According to tradition, that would make a year from tomorrow Judgment Day, but what the exercise shows is that the judgments that matter happen now. The new year will, in all likelihood, not be the world's last, but wouldn't the world be a better place if we, its beloved humans, lived as though it were?

The Twenty-ninth Day

January 14, 2003

Consider the lilies, Jesus said—but he was thinking of the field. The lesson for the political season just under way comes from the lilies of the pond, water lilies. It is an old French riddle. "At first there is only one lily pad in the pond, but the next day it doubles, and thereafter each of its descendants doubles. The pond completely fills up with lily pads in thirty days. When is the pond exactly half full? Answer: on the twenty-ninth day."

The entomologist Edward O. Wilson uses this riddle to illustrate the urgency of our ecological crisis. "Because Earth is finite in many resources that determine the quality of life—including arable soil, nutrients, fresh water, and space for natural ecosystems—doubling of consumption at constant intervals can bring disaster with shocking suddenness. Even when a nonrenewable resource has been only half used, it is still only one interval away from the end." The twenty-ninth day can feel like a normal day—look how much room is left in the pond—but it can actually be the eve of catastrophe. Only those who are paying close attention may see the dire significance of the day, but by then their biggest problem is the complacency of those who do not know what time it is.

On the twenty-ninth day, the pond is half choked to death, but it seems okay. Surely we have another twenty-nine days to fix the problem. But do we? How this lesson applies to the earth's dwindling resources is obvious, but it has meaning in other areas as well. Apply the image of the exponentially reproducing lily pads to the phenomenon of human aggressiveness. Am I imagining it, or has there been a doubling and redoubling of world belligerence since September 11, 2001? Last January, the United States issued the

Nuclear Posture Review, which effectively abandoned the long-standing (and treaty-mandated) commitment to move toward ultimate elimination of nuclear weapons. That emphatic American legitimizing of its own weapons of mass destruction surely led to a doubling and redoubling of an attitude of reliance on weapons of mass destruction around the pond, especially once their significance for the exercise of power was made explicit by the publication of *The National Security Strategy of the United States* in October 2002.

Last week, in a demonstration of lily pad–like reproduction, India issued its own nuclear posture statement, and the rumbles from Pakistan immediately doubled. The two nations stake a mutually threatening claim to power that is the very child of the claim staked in Washington. (Indeed, Pakistan's terrifying refusal to join India in renouncing the first use of nuclear weapons is itself patterned on—and legitimized by—the permanent U.S. refusal to renounce first use.) In this environment of exponentially expanding belligerence, who does not shudder to hear the North Koreans evoke the specter of World War III? With such shocking new levels of war preparation roiling Asia, imagine what decisions are quietly being made in Beijing and Tokyo. Meanwhile, Israelis and Palestinians take for granted a level of weaponized contempt that would have been unthinkable not long ago, and, yes, there too the family vine of dead-or-alive militarism is rooted in Washington. That these world developments approach climax exactly when the United States finally orders the deployment of its war-fighting army to the Middle East—coincidence? America may or may not be the indispensable nation, but when it comes to war, it is certainly the generating lily pad. And this week the pond is more than half full.

Not only war. There is an exponentially growing coarseness of life in the United States. That homeless people are sleeping in doorways again is a sure sign that the American sense of civic kinship is being choked. That protections of law are shrinking is another. We are constantly invited to care about ourselves and our kind, with no concern for those in other circumstances. The great symbol of this is the shrinking role of government as the guarantor, and if necessary provider, of essential human needs. Tax cuts may or may not be economic stimulators, but they are certainly deathblows to clinics, schools, libraries, laboratories, food banks—and the impulse of the young to make careers in public service. Imagine our nation as an overgrown pond in which a few lily pads have ample sunlight and room to flourish, while all the others are drowning in the fetid dark. For a while yet, the privileged lilies can maintain the illusion that they are not tied to all the rest, equally doomed.

War abroad. Coarseness at home. Ecological disaster, too. On the twenty-ninth day, things may not seem so bad; but are we more than "one interval away from the end"? This urgent question must define the political season that begins now—the overdue challenge to George W. Bush, whose policies are choking the nation and the world.

PART THREE

AS TO WAR

10

IRAQ

On March 17, 2003, George W. Bush addressed the nation: "My fellow citizens, events in Iraq have now reached the final days of decision. . . . We are now acting because the risks of inaction would be far greater." Referring to weapons of mass destruction, Bush said, "With these capabilities Saddam Hussein and his terrorist allies could choose the moment of deadly conflict when they are strongest." And with a clear reference to 9-11, he added, "We choose to meet that threat now, where it arises, before it can appear suddenly in our skies and cities."

Widespread American support for the war was mostly based on that 9-11 link, and on dread of those Iraqi "capabilities." Neither existed, as most people in the world, and an active minority in the United States, assumed. The legality of the war was called into question, in particular, by Germany and France. Even in countries whose leaders were supportive of Bush, like Spain, Italy, and nations of the "new Europe," popular majorities were solidly antiwar. Before the attack on Iraq had actually commenced, the streets of the globe's major cities were full of protesters—an unprecedented outpouring of protest.

Two days after the president's speech, Operation Iraqi Freedom was launched. According to monitoring physicians' groups, the war resulted in up to 55,000 deaths, including about 10,000 civilians. By early 2004, over 525 Americans had been killed, with about 2,700 wounded, many of them permanently impaired. (American casualty figures in Vietnam did not reach this level until 1965, after two years of involvement.) The war led to further degradations of Iraq's environment, social infrastructure, civil order, medical care system, and nutritional well-being. Most Iraqis reportedly approved of the removal of Saddam Hussein, but the Bush administration's justification for the war was tied not to human rights or democracy, but to the illusory threat posed by weapons of mass destruction. Saddam Hussein, for eight months, eluded capture.

Outside Iraq, passions among Arab and Muslim extremists were inflamed. In Sunni regions of Iraq, support for the missing Saddam began to be openly expressed. Resistance to the American occupation slowly spread from the Sunni-controlled center of Iraq toward areas of Shi'ite dominance. Instead of "final days," the war was the beginning of a new chaos.

At the United Nations

February 11, 2003

Don't be fooled by Colin Powell. With testimony before the U.N. Security Council last week, the secretary of state brought many formerly ambivalent politicians and pundits into the war party. But that is a measure of how callow the entire American debate over war against Iraq has been. The question is not whether Saddam Hussein is up to no good. Powell's indictment confirmed the Iraqi's malfeasance, although with no surprises and no demonstration of immediate threat. The question, rather, is what to do about Hussein's malevolence.

Don't be fooled by Donald Rumsfeld, either. The secretary of defense said in Munich on Saturday, "The risks of war need to be balanced against the risks of doing nothing while Iraq pursues weapons of mass destruction." Just as Powell fudged on what the question is, Rumsfeld fudged on there being no alternative to war. Ongoing and ever more robust inspections, like those proposed by France and Germany, are an alternative to war. Containment is an alternative to war. And an aggressive application of the principles of international law is an alternative to war.

Colin Powell's prosecutorial summary of the case against Hussein should have been prelude not to further warmongering but to a legal indictment of the Iraqi leader for crimes against humanity. In what court, you ask, and under what jurisdiction? America's imminent war takes on an absurd—and also tragic—character in the light of what else is happening right now. Last week the International Criminal Court was initiated with the formal election of judges. Next month the court will be official. Its purpose is to deal exactly with offenses like those of which Hussein stands accused. A forceful indictment in such a forum, followed by a trial, verdict, and world-enforced sentence, has an unprecedented potential for a laserlike release of transforming moral energy. The court intends on the world scene what has already happened within nations—the replacement of violent force with the force of law. A true alternative to war.

But the 139 nations that signed the ICC agreement no longer include the United States, since George W. Bush "unsigned" that treaty early in his term. The U.S. refusal to participate in the new world court makes it irrelevant to the present crisis, but that refusal also lays bare the world's gravest problem: America's contempt for the creation of alternatives to war.

The most important reason to be skeptical of the Bush administration's claim of necessity has nothing to do with Hussein. It has to do with Bush's own palpable predisposition in favor of war, and

when the casus belli is in dispute, predisposition counts for everything. Powell's performance at the U.N. was compared to American
ambassador Adlai Stevenson's in 1962, but war was averted in the
Cuban crisis, as it had been in the Berlin crisis the year before, precisely because John F. Kennedy's predisposition inclined him away
from war, not toward it. Kennedy's inaugural address, which is often
misremembered as a cold-war call to arms, was a straightforward
challenge to create new structures of peace. He proposed a litany of
political change: an extension of the "writ" of the United Nations; an
ending of the arms race; a replacing of the "balance of power [with]
a new world of law"; a new trust in negotiation ("never fear to negotiate"); an affirmation that "civility is not a sign of weakness." On
each of those points—the U.N., the arms race, international law, negotiations, even civility—the Bush administration has reversed the
momentum that began with Kennedy.

And as for war, in the most misremembered passage of all,
Kennedy made his repudiation explicit: "Now the trumpet summons
us again—not as a call to bear arms, though arms we need, not as a
call to battle, though embattled we are, but the call to bear the burden of a long twilight struggle, year in and year out . . . a struggle
against the common enemies of man: tyranny, poverty, disease, and
war itself."

War itself the enemy. Not the sentiment of "idealists" but the
supremely pragmatic conclusion of men and women who saw the
horrors of war played out in the twentieth century. In rejecting
Bush's war, France and Germany honor that memory today, as do the
creators of the International Criminal Court. "War never again!"
Pope Paul VI declared—also at the United Nations—in 1965. When
he cried, "No more war!" a generation of world leaders cheered
him—all but one. Then, too, in that autumn of Rolling Thunder, an
American president defied the universal longing for another way.
But the pope, in his U.N. speech, did not hesitate to cite "a great man
now departed, John Kennedy," against the warmonger in Washington, and neither do I. "Mankind must put an end to war," the pope
recalled Kennedy saying, "or war will put an end to mankind."

The Age of Innocence

February 18, 2003

"This is the patent age of new inventions / For killing bodies and for saving souls," Lord Byron wrote. "All propagated with the best intentions." The lines serve as an epigraph for Graham Greene's *The Quiet American*. That novel first appeared in 1955, but a filmed version arrived in theaters last week, a timely renewal of its prophetic relevance. Michael Caine's performance as Thomas Fowler, the opium-ridden British journalist who jousts with—and befriends—an American intelligence operative, just received an Oscar nomination. Americans may go to this movie for the superlative acting, but in the "patent age" of a coming war, they may find something more.

Graham Greene was a connoisseur not of good and evil but of innocence and corruption. The dangers of the latter are well known—here is Greene's great theme—but the former is especially to be feared. In his novels, Greene was obsessed with that moral paradox. In *The Power and the Glory* the well-meaning police lieutenant is a source of death and chaos, while the deeply flawed fugitive priest brings those he encounters more fully alive. Scobie, the hero of the *The Heart of the Matter,* suffers "corruption by pity" and embodies the tragedy of Europe's intrusions into Africa. *The Honorary Consul,* in which an American is kidnapped by revolutionaries in Argentina, features a main character for whom "caring is the only dangerous thing." And always, innocence, which Greene defines in *The Quiet American* as "a dumb leper who has lost his bell, wandering the world, meaning no harm." A leper is the title character in *The Burnt-Out Case,* set in the Congo, where the question—the hero's name is Querry—is between dumb innocence and nihilism.

One can tell the brutal story of European colonialism as a saga of the dangers of good intentions. (The Belgians, after all, embarked on their genocide in the Congo in the name of the eradication of slavery.) Good intentions always cloak a more ambiguous agenda, and as an Englishman who came of age while the noble savageries of the trenches played out during World War I (the "war to end war"), Greene knew that very well.

Yet it was when he applied this critique to the nascent American impulse in Vietnam that Greene achieved his literary masterpiece and his sharpest political critique. Alden Pyle, the "quiet American" of the title, is a man whose bookshelf includes idealistic political titles like *The Challenge to Democracy*, but "tucked away" on the same shelf is *The Physiology of Marriage*, indicating his pathetic innocence when it comes to sexuality. Pyle is drawn to Fowler's mistress, a beautiful "Annamite" woman named Phuong. Pyle wants to rescue her from Fowler, who embodies the corruptions of "the old Europe," to use a phrase current in Washington. Pyle wants to rescue Phuong's nation too, aiming to create a virtuous "third force" that is neither communism nor colonialism. "We are the old colonial peoples, Pyle," Fowler admits, "but we've learned a bit of reality, we've learned not to play with matches. This Third Force—it comes out of a book."

Yet to bring it about, Pyle supplies not only matches but explosives. After a horrendous blood-spattered bombing, Fowler tells Pyle, "You've got the Third Force and national democracy all over your right shoe." Fowler sees what will come in the wake of the American intervention, but Pyle does not. "He was impregnably armoured by his good intentions and his ignorance." Fowler, with no particular sense of virtue, finally takes action against Pyle and becomes implicated in his murder. With the American dead, Fowler's mistress has no choice but to return to him. The last line of the novel reads, "Everything had gone right with me since he had died, but how I wished there existed someone to whom I could say that I was sorry."

Greene's is a bleak vision, as if the only choice is between ignorant, damaging innocence and complicitous but self-aware corruption. *The Quiet American* is nowhere more prophetic than in that simple name Greene gave to the woman who motivates both men.

The name Phuong, Fowler says, "means Phoenix, but nothing nowadays is fabulous, and nothing rises from its ashes." What Greene could not have known in 1952–55 when he wrote the novel is that the ultimate circle of hell into which Pyle's CIA successors would descend, still from idealism, would be the late-1960s assassination-murder program called Operation Phoenix. Operation Phuong.

Vietnam haunts our national spirit because America's violence was so well motivated—destroying villages, yes, but only to save them. Vietnam teaches that good intentions are not enough. In the patent age of new inventions, there must equally be the knowledge—we have it from Greene but also from the American generation that fulfilled his prophecy—that saving souls by killing bodies is impossible. Beware a nation announcing its innocence en route to war.

Watch the War with Both Eyes

February 25, 2003

Because the circle of chaos was closing in on the realm, the hero went to the troll and, forcibly subduing him, demanded to know the secret of drawing order out of chaos. The troll replied, "Give me your left eye and I'll tell you." Because the hero loved his threatened people so much, he did not hesitate. He gouged out his own left eye and gave it to the troll, who then said, "The secret of order over chaos is: Watch with both eyes."

This story, from the late novelist John Gardner, perfectly illustrates the American problem. We are embarking on war with only one eye watching. That eye sees Iraq, Hussein, the threat of terrorism, a break with "old Europe," the frightening foreground of the post-9-11 world. But what we are not seeing is the larger background where far more deadly dangers lurk. We have no eye on the very real possibility that this swaggering war, coupled with the entire "us-or-them" spirit of American foreign policy, will decisively force Russia and China back into the armed hostility of a bygone era. A restoration of that enmity will return both powers, independently or together, to the bunker of rampant nuclear threat—the only way to check Washington's unipolar and unilateral exercise of power. Ironically, that the world survived the nuclear terror of the cold war seems to have made the American people assume that no such threat can ever reappear, which is the only reason the far lesser dangers of Hussein and al Qaeda can have so traumatized us.

But superpower nuclear danger is making a comeback. It is well known that the United States, Russia, and, to a lesser degree, China maintain globe-destroying nuclear arsenals. But what has not been sufficiently noted is that the nuclear powers have stopped working toward the elimination of nukes and are again depending on them as guarantors of national sway. That was clear a year ago in Washington with the Pentagon's Nuclear Posture Review, but not only there. While Leonid Brezhnev (responding to the worldwide nuclear-freeze movement) declared in 1982 that Moscow would never be the first to use nuclear weapons, Vladimir Putin (responding to NATO's 1999 air war against Serbia) renounced that promise in 2000. Mikhail Gorbachev proposed in 1986 the elimination of all nuclear weapons; Putin's "new concept of security," like Bush's new "strategic doctrine," assumes their permanence.

And so with China. When Washington renounced the ABM Treaty last year, Beijing could reasonably assume that new U.S. missile defense would undercut the deterrent value of China's comparatively small nuclear arsenal, forcing an escalation of offensive capacity. The militarization of China's nascent space program becomes inevitable in response to the Pentagon's resuscitated Star Wars. The arms race in orbit.

What we have here—Russia bristling at American moves into central Asia; China ever wary of American-armed Taiwan—are the preconditions for a renewed cold war—and worse. This is the background to which our missing eye makes us blind. The war in Iraq will open into all these horrors, which can rapidly spread. Russia's quickened belligerence will unsettle eastern Europe and Germany, which, distrusting America, may finally pursue nukes of its own. China's escalations will spark India's, increasing pressure on Japan, at last, to embrace nuclear weapons. Already smoldering fires in North Korea and Pakistan can easily ignite. A domino theory—the falling of nuclear abstinence before mass proliferation—will be proven true after all. The new chain reaction.

Watching with two eyes, we would see that in dealing with Saddam Hussein, no nation's convictions matter more than those of Russia and China. Why? Simply because Russia and China can, with us, set in motion forces to destroy the world. It is more crucial than ever, building on the near-miraculous peaceful outcome of the cold war, to erect structures of trust and mutuality with these two former enemies. Yet the opposite is happening. If Washington were deliberately to set out to alienate Moscow and Beijing, its policy would look exactly like the Bush administration's.

Americans seem hardly to have noticed that both Russia and China oppose the U.S. plan to invade Iraq—opposition that should weigh far more than that, even, of France or Germany. Faced with this display of what can only appear as American imperial assault, Russia and China have good reason to feel directly threatened. They can be expected to hasten the construction of a counterforce aimed at limiting Washington, renewing a level of catastrophic threat that will make today's war on terrorism—and even tomorrow's war on Iraq—look like the good old days. To watch the looming U.S. aggression with both eyes is to oppose it.

A War Policy in Collapse

March 4, 2003

What a difference a month makes. On February 5, Secretary of State Colin Powell made the Bush administration's case against Iraq with a show of authority that moved many officials and pundits out of ambivalence and into acceptance. The war came to seem inevitable, which then prompted millions of people to express their opposition in streets around the globe. Over subsequent weeks, the debate between hawks and doves took on the strident character of ideologues beating each other with fixed positions. The sputtering rage of war opponents and the grandiose abstractions of war advocates both seemed disconnected from the relentless marshaling of troops. War was coming. Further argument was fruitless. The time seemed to have arrived, finally, for a columnist to change the subject.

And then the events of last week. Within a period of a few days, the war policy of the Bush administration suddenly showed signs of incipient collapse. No one of these developments, by itself, marks the ultimate reversal of fortune for Bush, but taken together they indicate that the law of "unintended consequences," which famously unravels the best laid plans of warriors, may apply this time before the war formally begins. Unraveling is under way. Consider what happened as February rolled into March:

- Tony Blair forcefully criticized George W. Bush for his obstinacy on environmental issues, a truly odd piece of timing for such criticism from a staunch ally, yet a clear effort to get some distance from Washington. Why now?
- The president's father chose to give a speech affirming the importance both of multinational cooperation and of realism in dealing with the likes of Saddam Hussein. To say, as the elder

Bush did, that getting rid of Hussein in 1991 was not the most important thing is to raise the question why it has become the absolute now.

- For the first time since the crisis started, Iraq actually began to disarm, destroying Al Samoud 2 missiles, and apparently preparing to bring weapons inspectors into the secret of anthrax and nerve agents. The Bush administration could have claimed this as a victory on which to mount further pressure toward disarmament.

- Instead, the confirmed destruction of Iraqi arms prompted Washington to couple its call for disarmament with the old, diplomatically discredited demand for regime change. Even an Iraq purged of weapons of mass destruction would not be enough to avoid war. Predictably, Iraq then asked, in effect, why Hussein should take steps to disarm if his government is doomed in any case. Bush's inconsistency on this point—disarmament or regime change?—undermined the early case for war. That it reappears now, obliterating Powell's argument of a month ago, is fatal to the moral integrity of the pro-war position.

- The Russian foreign minister declared his nation's readiness to use its veto in the Security Council to thwart American hopes for a United Nations sanction for the war.

- Despite the offer of many billions in aid, the Turkish parliament refused to approve American requests to mount offensive operations from bases in Turkey—the single largest blow against U.S. war plans yet. This failure of Bush diplomacy, eliminating a second front, will be paid for in American lives.

- The capture in Pakistan of Khalid Shaikh Mohammed, a senior al Qaeda operative, should have been only good news to the Bush administration, but it highlighted the difference between the pursuit of 9-11 culprits and the unrelated war against Iraq. Osama bin Laden, yes. Saddam Hussein, no.

- Administration officials, contradicting military projections and then refusing in testimony before Congress to estimate costs of war and postwar efforts, put on display either the administration's inadequate preparation or its determination, through secrecy, to thwart democratic procedures—choose one.

• In other developments, all highlighting Washington's panicky ineptness, the Philippines rejected the help of arriving U.S. combat forces, North Korea apparently prepared to start up plutonium production, and Secretary of Defense Donald Rumsfeld ordered the actual deployment of missile defense units in California and Alaska, making the absurd (and as of now illegal) claim that further tests are unnecessary.

All of this points to an administration whose policies are confused and whose implementations are incompetent. The efficiency with which the U.S. military is moving into position for attack is impressive; thousands of uniformed Americans are preparing to carry out the orders of their civilian superiors with diligence and courage. But the hollowness of that civilian leadership, laid bare in the disarray of last week's news, is breathtaking. That the United States of America should be on the brink of such an ill-conceived, unnecessary war is itself a crime. The hope now is that—even before the war has officially begun—its true character is already manifesting itself, which could be enough, at last, to stop it.

A Meditation on War

March 11, 2003

Until the war begins, one must insist that it is not inevitable. The conventional wisdom is that the United States, having already deployed its massive fighting force, cannot back down from the assault against Iraq without humiliation—and a grievous loss of "credibility."

But that "wisdom" fails to take into account the most basic fact of military strategy. "Violence is most purposive and most successful," as the theorist Thomas C. Schelling wrote, "when it is threatened and not used. Successful threats are those that do not have to be carried out." The Bush administration seems confused about this, as if the movement from threat to action is inexorable. Why else would Washington manifest such consistent indifference to the obvious success its threats have been having with Saddam Hussein? The tyrant has steadily bent to Washington's will and shows every sign, despite his bluster, of continuing to do so.

To put the question another way: why has Washington not declared victory, explaining that this slow yielding by Iraq to a range of pressures—the inspector Hans Blix on one side, General Tommy Franks on the other—is what victory looks like now? Instead of a loss of credibility, this solution short of open warfare could be said to represent the triumph of lethal threat combined with political process, a supreme example of military force used with real power. Essential to that power is restraint. But instead of laying claim to this accomplishment and building on it, Washington seems intent on squandering its achievement and going to war—despite the steady accumulation of good reasons not to. Why?

The horrors of war have moved to the forefront of the common mind as D-day draws nearer. But those who would stop the war are up against more than Washington's belligerent obsession with Saddam. Below all of the Bush administration's stated reasons for the necessary movement from threat to violence, the clear inadequacy of those reasons suggests that something else must be at work. What could it be? That question requires hard thinking about the other side of war—not its horrors but its attractions. Could it be that an unconscious wish to be at war—any war—has been driving George W. Bush and his circle all along?

Pierre Teilhard de Chardin, the great priest-scientist, served as a medic in the trenches of World War I. He saw war's horror up close. But he saw the other thing, too. "The front cannot but attract us," he wrote, "because it is, in one way, the extreme boundary between what you are already aware of, and what is still in the process of formation. Not only do you see there things that you experience nowhere else, but you also see emerge from within yourself an underlying stream of clarity, energy, and freedom that is to be found hardly anywhere else in ordinary life."

It seems clear that Bush's sense of himself as a war president, a man of "the front," is the source of "clarity, energy, and freedom" that would otherwise never be his. Leaders and whole nations have gone to war exactly as a way out of the ambiguities and alienations of "ordinary life." They have defined their purposes in the high rhetoric of honor and glory, while satisfying the basest of needs, which is to escape from mediocrity. President Bush would not be the first leader to take his people into war for such a reason, nor would America be the first country to welcome it for such a reason. Indeed, for a time the entire nation might draw a kind of vivid sustenance from being at the "extreme boundary" where human performance is acute, choices heroic, "the fog of peace" replaced by a crystal vision of life's preciousness made possible, ironically, by its being wasted. As those old enough to remember Vietnam know—those honest enough to admit it—this extreme boundary would become the realm as much of those who hate violence as of those who indulge it. A life built around high-intensity opposition to war can also be a life rescued from the mediocrity of mundane experience.

There is a painful truth here that all must acknowledge. If this nation does indeed move, against all reason, from threat to violence, "clarity, energy, and freedom" will belong as much to those whose purpose is to stop the war as to those who fight it. "This exaltation is accompanied by a certain pain," Teilhard observed. "Nevertheless it is indeed an exaltation. And that's why one likes the front in spite of everything, and misses it." What Teilhard confesses liking here, and missing, was the place where 10 million men died, and another 20 million were wounded and maimed. Yet of all the horrors of war, isn't this the most grotesque—that human beings, even exemplary ones like Teilhard, can like it?

At War in Iraq

March 25, 2003

Look at what America has become. We are moving on steel treads across a harsh landscape as a creature of destruction, kicking up clouds of unreality through which we see illusions of our efficiency and virtue. The extravagance of our nation's claims for itself is staggering. We can decide alone when the use of overwhelming violence is justified. Before the onslaught of our weapons, enemy resistance will be nil. The display of "shock and awe," an unprecedented bombardment aimed less at human beings and buildings than at the human imagination, will bend the world to our will. Unlike all previous powers in history, we can wage war humanely. Our success will be so complete that no other nation will challenge us—or imitate us. The time for complexity is past: you are for us or against us. Either way, your world will be a far safer place when we are finished. Those who opposed this war will sheepishly return to the fold, the flock of our dominance. We are so good.

Young Americans in uniform are now dying for this cloud of illusion—dying of it—and so are Iraqis of all ages and stations. When the dying begins, the arguments leading up to the war cease to have resonance. Who is debating anymore the hazards of intervention, the relationship of ends and means, the question of whether Sadddam Hussein is Osama bin Laden's partner or nemesis? Those who opposed the war on the grounds that its good effects would be outweighed by unintended disasters—chemical attacks, oil wells aflame, riots in the street across the globe—are now in the position, only, of praying to have been wrong. Those who opposed it more broadly, as a reckless act of hubris whether successful or not, are still saying no without waiting for outcomes. Yet all are braced today for the Battle of Baghdad, hardly breathing.

Americans overwhelmingly support this war, apparently—but do we understand it? The bombardment that has already been carried out, for example: more bombs dropped already than in the forty days of Desert Storm. Let's assume for a moment that civilian casualties have indeed been kept to a minimum by the "coalition's" precision weapons. Still, what are we seeing through the lenses of news cameras mounted on hotel rooftops on the "safe" side of the river? What do those raging fires, all that smoke, signify? If Washington were the target of a "shock and awe" campaign, the U.S. Capitol would now be rubble, as would all of the federal triangle, that nest of becolumned buildings along seven blocks of Pennsylvania Avenue. The White House would be a smoldering ruin (as would Camp David—and the Bush ranch house in Crawford, Texas). The Pentagon, of course, would be a fetid sinkhole, in-rushing waters of the adjacent Potomac River having snuffed the burning abyss. The vice president's residence at the head of Embassy Row near the National Cathedral would be in ruins. Bolling Air Force Base and Andrews Air Force Base on the Maryland side of the Potomac would be aflame. Fort Myers and the navy annex on the ridge of Arlington; Fort McNair and the marine barracks in southeast Washington; the naval hospital in Bethesda, and Walter Reed Hospital in northwest Washington—all on fire. CIA headquarters in McLean, Virginia, would be a smoking scar on the landscape. This is the description of a "limited" campaign, targets chosen "humanely" according to a strategy of "decapitation." We can leave until later the question of who and how many are dead and wounded.

And what, exactly, would justify such destruction? Make it an act of virtue? And is it possible to imagine that such violence could be wreaked in a spirit of cold detachment, by controllers sitting at panels and screens dozens, hundreds, even thousands of miles distant? And in what way would such "decapitation" spark in the American people anything but a horror to make memories of 9-11 seem a pleasant dream? If our nation, in other words, were on the receiving end of "shock and awe," we would have no trouble seeing through the cloud of illusion and recognizing it for exactly what it is: terrorism, pure and simple.

The broadcast airways above America are full, already, of the language of glory and eventual triumph. But it all depends on the story we tell ourselves. Are we the new masters of morality and power, imposing our order on a world that will someday be grateful to us? Are we the victors, at last, over self-deceit and pride, crushing opposition only because it forces us to? Have we overcome the inefficiencies and inbuilt momentums of violence so that at last it can be used humanely? If so, the glory and triumph are right and just. If not, all that we represent today are vainglory and triumphalism.

11

QUESTIONS

The chaos of the Middle East threatened to become global and even more lethal in the first half of 2003. America's initiatives abroad began to backfire, and questions tied to the Bush administration's foreign policy follies had a way of curling back onto the nation. One of the most egregious examples involved North Korea, which President Bush had labeled part of the Axis of Evil in his 2002 State of the Union address. Later that year, an unexpected note of anti-American dissent was struck by South Korean voters when they elected as president Roh Moo Hyun, a human rights activist and critic of Washington. President Bush spoke openly of "toppling" North Korean president Kim Jong Il. Then, simultaneously with the March 19, 2003, launch of Operation Iraqi Freedom, the United States and South Korea engaged in a long-scheduled joint military exercise called Foal Eagle, which could only have been intended to exacerbate tensions on the Korean peninsula.

Within days of that, North Korea, bankrupt, its people on the edge of starvation, ordered increases in its already sky-high military expenditures. In the same period, Secretary of Defense Donald Rumsfeld circulated a secret—soon to be leaked—Pentagon memo that advocated regime change in Pyongyang. Here it was: the "preventive war" against Iraq seemed then but a prelude to just such an initiative against North Korea. But actions cause reactions: in April, North Korea announced that it had begun reprocessing spent fuel rods into plutonium. This penultimate move to a nuclear weapon was clearly North Korea's response to Bush and his war in Iraq. It was symbolic of the administration's grave failure to understand the inevitably proliferating effect of its entire "national security strategy," which ranged from regime change to threatening bluster to an ongoing attachment to America's own nuclear arsenal.

South Korea, the supposed beneficiary of the longtime American commitment, and of thirty-seven thousand U.S. combat soldiers deployed on its territory, raised resounding questions about Washington's entire approach. Seoul's new "sunshine" policy was focused on seeking closer ties with Pyongyang, not confrontation—and not desolation throughout the Korean peninsula. Nowhere was the rejection of the Bush Doctrine more poignant. Thousands of South Koreans took to the streets in defiance of the United States, their great protector. This palpable repudiation of the American approach by the people most supposed to benefit from it had the effect of stopping it cold. There would be no regime change in Pyongyang. Questions can be powerful.

An April Fools' Day Surprise

April 1, 2003

On April Fools' Day thirty-five years ago, morning newspapers trumpeted the exceedingly unlikely story that Lyndon B. Johnson had announced his intention not to seek reelection as president of the

United States. It was not a joke. On television the night before, the beleaguered president had insisted on his determination to bring the war in Vietnam to an end. He said he was ordering a halt to the bombing of North Vietnam above the twentieth parallel, and that he was ready for negotiations. Johnson emphasized his wish for peace by renouncing his own political ambition. It seemed that an end to the war was at last possible.

"For four days in April," the reporter Charles Kaiser wrote, "joy took the place of anger in America, as hope replaced despair." News from the war across the previous months had indeed been staggering: the brutal siege at Khe Sanh; the Tet Offensive; General William Westmoreland's plea for more troops beyond the 550,000 he already had ("I desperately need reinforcements"); a bitter throng of war opponents storming the Pentagon; the betrayal felt by war supporters embodied in the resignation of Secretary of Defense Robert McNamara. The nation was terribly divided. The war had come to signify all that was wrong. That is why every American heart could lift at that morning's front-page news.

Whatever his intentions at the start, the president's war policy had shown itself to be a mix of incompetence, deceit, hyperviolence, arrogance toward critics abroad, contempt for dissent at home. But that war policy was also a corrupt and flimsy illusion that had now been discredited. Finally, the United States would not destroy Vietnam to save it. Johnson's withdrawal meant that American decency could triumph after all. I myself was moved to write a letter to President Johnson, whom I had reviled. I thanked him for his magnanimity.

Four days later, with the murder of Martin Luther King Jr., the sky fell on America. In that one event, in ways we could not grasp at the time, our nascent hope was dashed, and with it our sense of possible recovery. The assassination went far beyond the death of one man, and its implications transcended the particular struggle with which he was identified. As the riots that broke out after King's murder demonstrated, the racial division in America was even deeper than believed. Only days before, the Kerner Commission had released its bleak finding that the nation had become two nations, divided by race—and King's death proved it. The Great Society was a false dream, and events of subsequent weeks (the Poor People's Campaign, student riots, Robert Kennedy's murder, chaos at the Democratic convention in Chicago, Richard Nixon elected president on a lie about "secret peace") laid bare all the ways that America was at war with itself. And, of course, Vietnam resumed its place as the heartbeat of tragedy. Negotiations opened in Paris but would go nowhere for years. The war was not half over. Peace on April 1—we should have known better.

Those sad events are commonplace memories, essential to what sinks our hearts at the mention of "the sixties." Indeed, they represent a collapse of democratic hope from which, in truth, the United States of America has not recovered. The war against Iraq thus floats on undercurrents of depression that are long familiar, but is a countercurrent of hope still flowing as well? Thirty-five years ago today, Americans woke up to a moral recognition that was as powerful as it would be transitory. It demands to be noted. The president had effectively admitted what the entire nation, across the left-right argument, already intuited: that the intervention in Vietnam was a mistake, whether defined in moral or tactical terms. There would be no "winning." Further escalation, therefore, would be wrong. That subsequent leaders failed to fulfill the promise of this recognition (Nixon, Kissinger, and the chimera of "peace with honor") should not take away from what it signified.

When LBJ said, "Accordingly, I shall not seek . . . ," he was responding to nothing less than the will of the people as already manifest in polling places, in street demonstrations, on news broadcasts, and in a million living-room arguments. Johnson's decision, that is, was a triumph of democracy. The war had to end. The people knew it. And now the president did, too. Politics as moral reckoning. No wonder, for a few days that April, the nation was exhilarated.

It is April again. The war machine is loose, apparently unstoppable. An escalating air war, a rush of reinforcements, an enemy that surprises, demonstrators in the streets, a nation divided. But as before, Washington's war policy is made in fantasyland—and is even now being exposed as such. This anniversary suggests that an on-track war machine can be derailed. A prideful president can be brought down. An April Fools' Day when peace became a joke can be redeemed. Stop the war!

The Answer Is No

April 8, 2003

Are you unmoved by the loss of the young Americans who have died in Iraq? Or indifferent to the devastation now felt by their families? Or less than worried sick by what awaits the stalwart individuals poised to enter Baghdad?

Are you surprised that many of Saddam Hussein's defenders have fought ruthlessly and lawlessly? Do the discoveries of mutilated corpses in Basra establish something new? Are you confident that chemical or biological weapons won't yet be unleashed? Or sure that those weapons have not already been dispersed among others who hate America?

Do the deaths of noncombatant Iraqis mean less to you than the fate of your own forces? Are Iraqi children less precious than other children? Are the conscripted young men who make up the bulk of the Iraqi army deserving of being smashed and killed? Are their families less grief-struck than American families? Do Baath Party leaders care for the huddled people behind whom they hide? Did war planners not know that the mass of people would face death, maiming, homelessness well before the leading clique is cornered? Does it help a bereaved Iraqi family to be told its anguish is "collateral"?

Would the war unfold this way if the age groups traded places—with the middle-aged decision makers on both sides leading the charge, while wide-eyed twenty-year-olds remained safely behind the lines? Would the war be popular if it involved any real danger of homeland America's suffering war's direct consequences: demolished neighborhoods, orphaned babies, thousands homeless, disease from bad water, hospitals overwhelmed? Would the war have even begun if such consequences remotely threatened Boston, say, or New York? Can a people who have never been subjected to invasion, occupation, or all-out terror bombing begin to imagine what such things actually do to bodies and souls?

Does Washington stand ready to universalize its policies of preventive war and unilateral violation of sovereignty as new principles of international order available to all nations? Would Washington welcome such behavior from Moscow, say, or Beijing? Will the short-term definition of victory in Iraq survive its long-term global consequences, when "humanitarian" aggression becomes common behavior among nations? As for consequences local to Iraq, will America fare any better as an occupying force than Israel does in the West Bank and in Gaza? Is victory really the opposite of defeat?

In the age of world-destroying weapons, does violence lead to international balance and domestic security? Have the ancient laws of vengeance and vendetta been suspended? Will war at last put an end to war? Does the exercise of overwhelming force by a strong nation against a weak one slow proliferation of nuclear weapons if it gives other weak nations an urgent new reason to obtain such weapons? Does the larger context implied by the preceding question seem even to be in the minds of U.S. war planners?

If American purposes are innocent, aiming only at the obliteration of disorder, does that make the new disorder that follows every such act of obliteration any less cruel? If, on the other hand, American purposes are selfish, aiming at economic hegemony and world power, does a war thus waged protect what makes America America? Do American motives, whether good or ill, matter in the slightest to those who are dead?

Can aggressive war be waged by those who grasp the bottomless tragedy of the human condition, how every story—whether one person's or a nation's—ends in death? How every untimely death wounds the absolute, and how unnecessary death is itself the mortal enemy? Knowing that, could America so willingly enter into the alliance with death that is war? Could America kill those children? Could America send its own young women and men to die? Could America, for that matter, so ruthlessly maul an army mainly of draftees who have no choice? Could America, more broadly, license future wars like this one, sowing seeds of untimely death into winds that now blow across Iran, Turkey, Israel, Palestine, Saudi Arabia, Egypt—around the very globe to Korea, Pakistan, India? Does a hair-trigger obsession with an Axis of Evil, in other words, align America with the Axis of Human Good?

Does your nation any longer know that it, too, is part of the human family? That that family is now warning of a fatal loss of trust in the ideal for which the American flag has so long stood? Are that flag and all who have carried it honored by what is being done under its sign today?

These many questions boil down to three: Was this war necessary at the start? Is it a just war now? If the one heartbreaking answer was somehow to lead America to change course, away from war toward law and life again, would the dead have died in vain?

A Nation Lost

April 22, 2003

Even before conclusions can be drawn about the war in Iraq (Saddam Hussein? Weapons of mass destruction? Iraqi stability? Cost to civilians? Syria?), a home-front consensus is jelling around a radical revision of America's meaning in the world. Centered on coercive unilateralism, the new doctrine assumes that the United States not only stands apart from other countries but stands above them. The primitive tribalism of boys at football games—"We're number one!"—has been transformed into an axiom of U.S. strategic theory. Military force has replaced democratic idealism as the main source of national influence. Formerly conceived of as essentially defensive, American armed services are now unapologetically on the offense. Aggression is prevention. Diplomacy is reduced to making the case for impending war and then putting the best face on war's denouement. The aim of all this is not world dominance but world order. That world order in the new age in fact requires American dominance is an unintended consequence of America's power-altruism. That "we're number one" makes the world safe for everybody—if only they accept it.

This new vision is clear, its advocates are powerful, and with Iraq its main blocks are in place, with obvious implications for countries as geographically dispersed as Iran and North Korea. What are the elements of an alternative vision? In a world traumatized by terrorist threat, weapons proliferation, and the dread-sensationalism of Fox and CNN, disruption is infinitely magnified. When such horror strikes, whether from Twin Towers collapsing or twin snipers shooting strangers, can human beings put faith in something other than overwhelming force? What strategies should critics of the new American doctrine of coercive unilateralism employ in opposing it? Learning from the past, I think of several:

- Don't cede the language of morality to the right wing. Manichaean bipolarity oversimplifies good and evil, but some things should still be done because they are right, or opposed because they are wrong. Critics of the intended new Pax Americana should not hesitate to say that long-agreed ethical principles are being violated. It is wrong to break treaties, as America is doing in its treatment of POWs in Cuba. It is wrong to wage aggressive war, as America now openly does. To make decisions for or against such policies on purely pragmatic grounds is to break the crucial link between means and ends, as if an outcome (regime change) can justify whatever was done to accomplish it. In the long run, the only truly pragmatic act is the moral act.

- Be openly skeptical of "homeland security." The American tradition prefers the risks associated with liberty to the risks associated with bureaucratic state control. The new Homeland Security State threatens the kind of excess that came with the National Security State after World War II. It was the National Security Act of 1947, after all, that laid the groundwork for the univocal bureaucratizing of government, based in the Pentagon, that marginalized internal debate and eliminated the natural checks of multiple power centers. "National security," defined by anti-Communist paranoia at home and abroad, was false security. "Homeland security" promises to be a paranoid reprise.

- Be suspicious of foreign policy based on "worst-case" thinking. During the cold war, the United States made fearful assessments of Soviet capabilities and intentions that turned out to be entirely false—assessments that shaped policy. Low-level intelligence estimates regularly reported mere possibilities of hostile threat, which, reported up the chain of command, were invariably transformed into certain facts. Thus, Soviet troop strength was wildly overestimated in the beginning of the era; Soviet missile strength was overestimated in the middle; Soviet political strength was overestimated at the end. The result was an American-driven nuclear arms race, the effects of which still threaten the world. The Soviet worst-case existed only in Washington's fantasy. And now it seems that the Saddam worst-case resides in the same place. A nation that is so driven by fear will always find things to be afraid of. That nation's gravest threat arises, of course, from what it then does to defend itself.

• Beware of war as an organizing principle of society. It should be a source of alarm, not pride, that the United States is drawing such cohesive sustenance from the Iraqi war. Photographic celebrations of our young warriors, glorifications of released American prisoners, heroic rituals of the war dead all take on the character of crass exploitation of the men and women in uniform. First they were forced into a dubious circumstance, and now they are themselves being mythologized as its main ex post facto justification—as if America went to Iraq not to seize Saddam (disappeared), or to dispose of weapons of mass destruction (missing), or to save the Iraqi people (chaos) but "to support the troops." War thus becomes its own justification. Such confusion on this grave point, as on the others, signifies a nation lost.

Moral Awareness in Korea

April 29, 2003

"Forgetfulness is the way to exile," the legend reads at Yad Vashem. "Remembrance is the way to redemption." Yad Vashem is the Holocaust memorial in Jerusalem, and today is Holocaust Remembrance Day. Jews everywhere pause to think of the 6 million Jews slaughtered by the Nazis, and in Israel itself everything stops for a long moment of silence. If Jews have a reason to remember what happened in the heart of Europe between 1933 and 1945, how much more so do non-Jews.

Remembrance can advance narrow agendas—revenge, exceptionalism, victimhood, guilt—but remembrance can also lead to understanding and change. Memory is a main source of moral awareness, a way of finally coming to terms with what we do without meaning to; a way of facing the truth that even apparently virtuous action can be grounded in prejudice or selfishness. More than that, memory as moral reflection can offer, in the political philosopher Hannah Arendt's phrase, "the possible redemption from the predicament of irreversibility." In relation to the Holocaust, this means that non-Jews remember that greatest of moral failures in order to grasp the full meaning of the antisemitism that led to it. The point of doing that, of course, is to repent of such prejudice and to root out its sources. Remembrance is thus an offer of freedom from the tyranny not only of the past but of the present: things need not be what they are. Moral memory creates a better future.

The permanent relevance of this way of thinking becomes clear when we apply it to the looming conflict between the United States and North Korea. This is not to make comparisons with the Holocaust, but rather to learn from the mode of moral awareness that the Holocaust makes possible. As the confrontation between Washington and Pyongyang escalates, achieving "redemption from the predicament of irreversibility" takes on a global urgency. Americans owe it to the near and far future to remember that this conflict originated as a cold-war proxy fight between the United States and the Soviet Union—a brutal explosion of misunderstanding and miscalculation for which both sides bore responsibility. Unfolding between 1950 and 1953, the Korean War reinforced the worst impulses of America's belligerent insecurity. It drove the development of the H-bomb and made decision makers deaf to the pleas of scientists like J. Robert Oppenheimer who wanted to stop it. That Oppenheimer was then himself a Red-scare scapegoat defines the extent of the tragedy, for the Korean War was waged at home, too. It piqued the fever of the anti-Communist paranoia that blinded American policy makers for a generation, leading not only to Vietnam but to a decades-long misperception of Soviet intentions and capabilities.

When Dwight D. Eisenhower became president in January 1953, he escalated the rhetoric of threat in a way that fixed the cold war as a permanent feature of international relations. When Joseph Stalin died that March, Eisenhower refused the opening offered by the new Soviet leader, Georgy Malenkov. Instead, Ike conveyed his readiness to resolve the Korean conflict by using nuclear weapons— "without inhibition in our use of weapons" is the phrase he used in his memoirs—so that when the Chinese and Soviets finally did agree to a truce that July, Washington could miss the signal that a post-Stalin communism would be different. Assuming that Moscow and Beijing had bowed before the threat of nuclear war, Washington took their yielding as confirmation of its deadly choice to build American influence around the Bomb. That justified a shocking growth in U.S. dependence on nuclear weapons, the significance of which has been made clear to me by writers like John Steinbrunner, James T. Patterson, and Janne E. Nolan. In 1950, the United States possessed about 250 nukes; a decade later that figure had mush-roomed to something like 10,000. Moral memory requires us to rec-ognize that growth itself as the central failure of America's response to the cold war.

Now the Bomb is the point of conflict between the United States and North Korea. If Americans had done a better job of reckoning with the moral legacy of our own nuclear dependency, we would see more clearly how Pyongyang's unacceptable nuclear agenda origi-nates in Washington. U.S. officials would be less moralistic, and all Americans would grasp the tragedy of our post-cold-war renewal of dependence on the nuclear arsenal.

None of this is to exempt from judgment the corrupt tyranny that presides over North Korea, nor is it to downplay the threat rep-resented by North Korean nuclear blackmail. But the conflict be-tween Washington and Pyongyang is by no means a simple matter of good versus evil. The present danger springs from America's actions as much as from North Korea's, and only a full reckoning with the blind foolishness of that past, however well intentioned it was, can prepare for a different, wiser future.

The Absolute Weapon

May 13, 2003

Last week the Senate Armed Services Committee voted to allow the development of low-yield nuclear weapons—a reversal of a ban that had been in effect since 1993. According to press reports, the committee also approved funding to study bunker-busting nuclear weapons, as well as funding to speed up preparations for underground nuclear testing. These decisions, taken in response to Bush administration requests, come as no surprise in the light of the Nuclear Posture Review that was released in January 2002, but they amount to first steps in the implementation of the administration's radical new nuclear policy.

As the *New York Times* reported, the Senate committee proposals are slated to be considered by the House Armed Services Committee today, and then by the full Senate next week. In each of these forums, Democrats should vigorously oppose the Bush administration's dangerous attempts to reshape America's relationship to nuclear weapons. Here is why:

- The proposals relativize "the absolute weapon." In 1946, only a few months after Hiroshima was bombed, the political theorist Bernard Brodie published a book with that phrase as its title— a first statement of the fact that nuclear weapons are unique, have changed warfare forever, and must always be considered apart. That became the consensus of international statecraft, a key to the fact that nuclear weapons were never used during the cold war. Any blurring of the distinction between nuclear weapons and conventional weapons was understood to move the world across the nuclear threshold again—to disaster. It is that consensus that the Bush administration is overturning by lumping conventional and nuclear weapons together as "offensive strike weapons," and by proposing to develop "usable" low-yield nukes as part of the standard arsenal.

- These proposals, if enacted, will exacerbate "the security dilemma," a phrase referring to the built-in paradox that was laid bare by the cold war. "An increase in one state's security," as the political scientist Robert Jervis put it, "will automatically and inadvertently decrease that of others." The dynamic is inevitable: when one state enhances its military capacity, other states take steps to match it. Compared to the hugely expensive and unchallenged conventional force that America now possesses, nuclear capacity (like chemical and biological capacity) is cheap and relatively easily achieved. The security dilemma squared.

- These proposals, if enacted, would violate clause 6 of the Nuclear Nonproliferation Treaty, which commits the United States (like other nuclear powers) to work toward the elimination of nuclear weapons, not toward their normalization. The Bush administration's effective abandonment of the nonproliferation regime may be its single gravest folly—and in violating the NPT, the administration would be violating the law of the United States. In Bush's defense, one Republican senator said last week, "Experience has shown that nonproliferation treaties really don't have any effect on countries like North Korea, India, and Pakistan." But what about countries like Brazil, South Africa, or Sweden? Do we really want a world in which every nation is given urgent new cause to nuclearize its arsenal? The United States meets the challenge of so-called nuclear rogues by behaving like one.

- All of this makes the United States less secure, not more. Indeed, the very idea of *national security* has become mythical. The only meaning *national security* can have now assumes an international mutuality, a system of acknowledged—and treaty-enforced—interdependence among states that will check the armed nihilism of nonstate actors, which is the real threat in the world today. The Bush administration's nuclear policy moves in exactly the opposite direction, keeping in place an outmoded system of nationalist rivalry that has nearly destroyed the globe twice. Those who think of America's new dominance as "empire" are stuck in the nineteenth century; our vast power will not protect us in a world where, because of new technologies and information systems, methods of mass disruption and violence are cheap and unstoppable.

• These proposals represent a complete failure to imagine what such moves look like to other nations, both our friends and adversaries. As the war in Iraq shows, the United States is the one country in the world for which further nuclear capacity is entirely superfluous. Others must then ask: why is the United States preparing to take such steps? Washington's motive may be the moral good of an orderly world, but its self-anointed militarism can only look to others, friends included, like arrogant swagger. Is this really what the United States has become?

As the presidential election season gets under way, the differences between Democrats and Republicans are muted, as if Democrats are reluctant to draw attention to their inbred opposition to Bush's various revolutions. But his radical overthrow of nuclear caution is by far the gravest issue facing this nation. We know what Republicans will do about it. Beginning today, the urgent question is: what about the Democrats?

12

RECOGNITIONS

On May 1, 2003, President Bush landed on the deck of the aircraft carrier USS *Abraham Lincoln* and addressed the troops in front of a large banner that declared "Mission Accomplished." He said, "My fellow Americans, major combat operations in Iraq have ended. In the battle of Iraq, the United States and our allies have prevailed."

Even to its fiercest proponents, it was soon evident, however, that the American war in Iraq had not been successful. As postwar violence and chaos mounted, the costs of what was now being called "reconstruction" showed every sign of being greater than any possible benefit. In October, Bush himself repudiated the "Mission Accomplished" sign, claiming it had been put up by members of the aircraft carrier crew. Later, the White House had to acknowledge that the sign was made at its order.

In front of that sign, on the carrier deck, Bush had boasted, "From distant bases or ships at sea, we sent planes and missiles that could destroy an enemy division or strike a single bunker." But such weapons could do nothing to or for the grief-struck hearts and skeptical minds of those for whom the war, purportedly, had been fought. Before long, that reality sank in. The easy talk of "empire" that marked Bush Doctrine rhetoric throughout 2002 had all but disappeared by mid-2003. In the long run, the most important result of Operation Iraqi Freedom may lie in what it did *not* lead to. The idea that overwhelming military preeminence meant a self-anointed United States could impose its idea of order on the world was efficiently exposed in Iraq as blatant illusion.

Other things had become clear as well. The government of Ariel Sharon, having followed Washington's lead into the realm of "dead or alive," had made Israel more vulnerable than ever, as even tough-minded veterans of its security forces began to point out. Inflamed Islamic militancy, joined to a shocking resurgence of antisemitism, put all Jews in a new place of risk. In America, political differences were radicalized. Dishonesty was exposed as a mark of the Bush administration's war policy, even as Bush prevarications on education, the environment, health care, taxes, and budget deficits were also laid bare. But these terrible outcomes of Bush Doctrine misadventures pale beside what could have resulted at home and abroad if the Bush project in Iraq had been the "cakewalk" for which its proponents had already prepared the victory music.

Bad Weather over America

May 27, 2003

When will the bad weather end? Why the distance between what is and what ought to be? Where are Saddam Hussein's weapons of mass destruction? If he was such a threat, why did his army perform so poorly? Does it matter where he is? If the war in Iraq was not about oil, why does the United States insist on its indefinite control? If the war was, instead, about democracy, why are the Iraqi people, including

Saddam's proven enemies, excluded from authority? Is Iraq to be like Afghanistan, where warlords rule and heroin thrives? Are there more suicide-bombers now than ever? Has the American war on terrorism advanced safety? How did relations between the United States and its European allies become so fragile? Will history recognize the twenty-first-century Anglo-American combine as a mere continuation of the nineteenth-century British empire? What do good intentions count for if they cut a wake of wreckage? And is the bad weather the result of an atmospheric low that will not lift without the answers?

Why are taxes being cut when teachers and librarians are being laid off? What happened to campaign finance reform? Why is the United States more divided by race than ever? When did its citizens ever decide to forgo privacy? How can low-income wage earners support their families? How much longer will the middle class be able to afford health insurance? Why are Americans eating so much bad food? Does prime-time television hold a mirror up to the nation? Who teaches children to bring guns to school? What happens to teenagers who fulfill every graduation requirement except the test they can't pass? How many more will fail that test because their teachers were laid off?

Such impossible questions go a long way toward explaining the American mood. We cannot answer them, so we do not ask them, and the emotional weather is lousy. Thus, the patently false ebullience of George W. Bush—the doubtless man—is the perfect emblem of a nation so adrift that it dares not look twice at its real condition. Whatever the technical reasons for it, the economy that refuses to recover matches perfectly a broad psychological stagnation that precludes self-knowledge. Why are Americans incapable of looking directly at what we are doing and what we are becoming? Abroad, the United States wages war on such vaporous pretexts that when they dissipate in the first breeze of mourners wailing, Americans take no notice. A strong tradition of multilateral internationalism is overthrown without political controversy or even debate. An old liberal dream of world federalism, nations united as democratic partners in global governance, is replaced by a program of American unipolarity, world government administered by fiat from Washington. And who in Washington questions this?

At home, an anxious sadness underlies the civic life. Careers feel terribly uncertain. Leisure is a forgotten luxury, which is not all bad because blank spaces in the datebook spark insecurities most of all. Intimate relationships are burdened by what is not discussed, and the confessional to which many people might once have carried such secrets is now dangerous. The Catholic crisis, cutting an entire community loose from moorings of authority and meaning, directly affects only a part of the national population, yet it, too, seems very American. The sadness is as religious as it is political.

In America each boon seems now to carry a curse. Is our freedom secured? Yes, by a government that can eavesdrop on every conversation. Are we well fed? Yes, to the point of obesity. Is our medical care superb? To the point of bankruptcy. Are we the most heavily armed people in history? Frighteningly so. Does the unprecedented success of the national project over the last generation bode well for the next generation? Obviously not. Can we dare to ask why?

An answer is apparent this very day in Iraq. The distance between what is and what ought to be is so vast there that only an act of communal self-blinding can keep Americans ignorant of it. The dark national mood has many causes, but one cries out to be reckoned with immediately. The Iraqi war was a pack of lies, and Washington's war on terrorism is a cynical manipulation of fears for the sake of power. So far, the citizens of the United States have willfully participated in this Bush-led charade. We have done so out of the very insecurity they tell us not to feel, as if the charade, however much it wrecks the world, will protect us. But our underlying sadness indicates what we need to know. America was not meant to be like this. We are no longer ourselves. The bad weather will not end until we face this cold truth and change it.

Antisemitism and Israel

May 20, 2003

With breathtaking cynicism, Hamas blew a hole this weekend in the road to peace between Israelis and Palestinians—four suicide-murder attacks in twelve hours, including a particularly savage one in Jerusalem. The Bush-Sharon meeting scheduled for today in Washington was called off, Israel clamped a total closure on the West Bank, and the challenge facing Palestinian peacemakers became far more daunting. Everyone who loves Israel, while also affirming Palestinian hopes, is disheartened.

It is possible to condemn the broad Palestinian surrender to the nihilist fringe that sponsors such brutality without falling into an endemic anti-Palestinian bigotry. That the proper Palestinian demand for justice is so soaked in blood severely undercuts its claim on the world's conscience, and it is no manifestation of racial hatred to say so. But criticism of Israel is more complex. The "overwhelming force" occupation by Israel of the West Bank and Gaza, with attendant strategies of collective punishment, extrajudicial assassination, and the ongoing policy of salting disputed territory with the "facts" of Jewish settlements, deserves to be denounced and often is—by many Israelis and American Jews, as well as by others who make clear that their opposition is to Israel's policy, not to its Jewishness.

But it is likewise true that criticism of Israel is increasingly animated by the ancient bigotry of antisemitism. This shows up most obviously in some Arab countries, but also in Europe and America where political criticism of the Sharon government morphs into transcendent scorn. Urgent conferences have convened on the subject of resurgent antisemitism here and abroad. Understanding this ugly phenomenon is important for three reasons: to oppose antisemitism, to affirm a normalcy for Israel, like other states, that takes criticism of the exercise of power for granted, and to defuse one of the explosive elements that keeps the Israeli-Palestinian dispute so volatile.

Two features of anti-Semitic thinking come into play here. The first might be called the celebration of "the ideal Jew," which accomplishes a denigration by means of an exaltation. Jews as they exist are measured against Jews as they should exist, and are always found wanting. This can involve a New Testament assumption that God's chosen people should certainly have recognized Jesus as Messiah; a medieval Christian rage against the Talmud as denial of the sufficiency for Jews of the Old Testament; an Enlightenment-era resentment against Jewish "clannishness" that complicates Jewish citizenship; or the contemporary contrast between the socialist idealism of the kibbutzim and the compromised realpolitik of the post-1948 state of Israel. In every case, the imagined Jew is used to justify contempt for the real Jew. Israelis are thus commonly measured against standards of justice that Palestinians would not match, and neither, for that matter, would the administration of George W. Bush. After all, Bush's "overwhelming force" is the license for Sharon's.

A second, related signal of anti-Semitic thinking is the tendency to define "the Jews" univocally, as if this group is only one thing. Thus, criticisms of Israel are routinely mounted from outside Israel with little attention to the expressly Jewish voices *within* Israel that steadfastly raise issues of Palestinian suffering. It is true, as polls show, that in the present climate of terror, the Sharon government draws wide support from the Israeli electorate; it is equally true that majorities of Israelis still favor compromise for peace, dismantling of settlements, and a viable Palestinian state. When Israel is harshly judged, one might ask: Which Israel? The Israel of the *Jerusalem Post* or the Israel of *Ha'aretz*? Of Likud or Labor? Which Jews? Ariel Sharon or columnist Thomas Friedman? Senator Joseph Lieberman or publisher Michael Lerner?

The inability of many of Israel's critics to refrain from sweeping condemnation of "the Jews" repeats the originating Christian mistake—perceiving "the Jews" in such univocally negative ways that Jesus was no longer recognized as belonging to this people. And it is important to acknowledge that a particularly Christian prejudice sometimes powers this sweep, as is clear every time an Israel Defense Force siege of Palestinian militant positions in Bethlehem is characterized as "the Jews" against Jesus once again.

Antisemitism is back, and perhaps not surprisingly. Despite the American government's disclaimers, the war on terrorism, with its attendant war against Iraq, has been cast, alas, as a momentous conflict between "the West and the rest." It feels, indeed, like a new Crusade. The first Crusade (1096) initiated a war not only against Islam in the flashpoint city (then as now) of Jerusalem but against Jews in the heart of Europe. The first pogroms occurred along the Rhine that year. As I have emphasized before, the flip side of a massive assault against an enemy outside is paranoid fear of an enemy inside. Today, in Europe and America, that fear identifies Muslims and immigrants from Arab nations as suspect, but in Western civilization the enemy inside par excellence has been the Jew. To be aware of this twin dynamic is to be alert to its grave danger, which is the first step in finally defeating it.

Palestinian Pain and Hope

June 3, 2003

The refusal of the Bush administration to involve itself in resolving the conflict between Israelis and Palestinians has been one of the worst consequences of the 9-11 terror attacks. Here's hoping that President Bush's meeting tomorrow with Israeli leader Ariel Sharon and Palestinian leader Mahmoud Abbas in Jordan marks a change in the attitudes not only of the two antagonists but of Washington as well.

When Americans felt vulnerable to the devastation wrought by suicidal terrorists, they found a new way of identifying with citizens of Israel, where suicide-bombers wreak such regular havoc. Washington's hyperbelligerent reaction to terrorists reinforced the Sharon government's response. A traditional alliance between the United States and the Jewish state was intensified. After September 11, an Israeli friend told me, "Now you know what it feels like," and it was true.

But another question arises: having empathized with Israeli feelings of vulnerability, do Americans have any real idea of what Palestinians have been experiencing? Leave aside the complexities of the political dispute to focus on its less well known human consequences. The character of Palestinians has been perceived stereotypically, as if every citizen of East Jerusalem or Ramallah is ready to murder innocents—or dispatch their children to do so. The terrorists have clouded Palestinian claims, but they and their supporters represent a mere fraction of the Palestinian population in Israel, the West Bank, and Gaza. Suicide-murder represents a horror to those millions, too. It is to them Americans must now turn in empathy. Their experience must be acknowledged. If Americans grasped the full dimensions of Palestinian suffering, they would insist that the U.S. government make an effort to end it by renewing the work of peace.

The still point around which a compassionate American imagination might most productively turn is the plight of Palestinian children. Americans read news reports of the widespread malnutrition that has come to plague a significant proportion of the babies and youngsters of the West Bank and Gaza, but do they really take in what that word *malnutrition* defines? The severely underweight child. The tortured mother. The doctor at a loss to help. The teacher aware of the impossibility of the child's learning. The father driven to depths of shame and despair. Relief workers unable to deliver what is needed. All of this multiplied by thousands. More than a million people in the West Bank and Gaza, including hundreds of thousands in refugee camps, depend on agencies for food, but need outpaces aid. Levels of destitution among some Palestinians have begun to approach those of the world's poorest nations.

All of this follows the border closings and restrictions on movement that have cut off Palestinians from their work, leading to a collapse of the economy. Unemployed young men abound, a recruiting pool for Hamas. But clampdowns have other effects, too. Curfews imposed by the occupying Israelis routinely subject great numbers of Palestinians to an effective house arrest, leading to a culture of claustrophobia. Gaza, in particular, can seem the site of a vast incarceration. Children bear the brunt of this also, as families and communities fracture under such inhumane stresses. Meanwhile, violence flares around even the most innocent, with all too many children having been collateral casualties of the conflict. They have seen their fathers, brothers, uncles, and sometimes mothers killed—often up close, for the battle zones of this war are neighborhoods. Its weapons, in addition to guns, aircraft, and tanks, are bulldozers, which have demolished hundreds of Palestinian homes. How many of those demolitions included the precious corners in which children had, until then, felt safe?

War is a realm in which brutality becomes mundane, but a simple destruction of trees can be almost as shocking as assaults on human life. When ancient olive groves are bulldozed, with the loss of noble stands of trees that have borne fruit for generations and should have continued to do so for generations to come, the Palestinian heart can be pierced to the pulse. And when equally ancient claims of proud families to land and homes are dismissed with the wave of an eviction notice, the blow goes far deeper than the words *real estate* imply. What is at stake for men and women whose histories are denied and whose place in the world is taken away is nothing less than the order of existence itself. In addition to all else, this harried people lives on an enforced edge of meaninglessness.

Most Palestinians refuse to define themselves by enmity. They reject the temptation to shape nationhood only from revenge. That is what it means that their leaders take places at a table of peace tomorrow. Will they be understood? Will their experience be acknowledged? Much must happen, in other words, before Palestinians turn to the overdue delegation from Washington and say, "Now you know what it feels like."

Millennial War

June 17, 2003

Now that Americans have begun facing the fact that, in the absence of Iraqi weapons of mass destruction, the stated purpose of the war was false, a new question presents itself: why, actually, did the United States go to war? And why, even now, do citizens of the United States apparently feel so little compunction about having waged war without justification? A prominent U.S. senator and candidate for president can ask tough questions about the Bush administration's falsification of WMD intelligence data, even while still affirming his own vote in favor of the war that data supposedly made necessary. What is going on here?

Many forms of human behavior can involve stated purposes and hidden purposes. When the former are debunked, attention necessarily shifts to the latter. Hidden motivations for war making are well known and much discussed—from Homer to Freud. (See authors like Ernest Becker and Lawrence LeShan.) War gives otherwise alienated human beings a sense of cohesion. War, by dividing reality into realms of good and evil, purges unconscious guilt and reinforces feelings of virtue. War offers redemption from the burdens of mundane existence. War justifies the creation of victims whose negation provides the thrill of victory, which is itself experienced as an opening to transcendence. And so on.

We post-Freudian Americans normally consider ourselves beyond such primitive impulses, which is why the United States prides itself on going to war only for good and solid reasons. But that is what makes the debate over the missing weapons of mass destruction salient. If the war can no longer be justified as an authentic act of "prevention," why do Americans still feel fine about it? It does not take a psychoanalyst to see that something powerful is moving below the surface of the American psyche. Two things suggest themselves. We are lost in time. And we are lost in space. War helps to locate us in both.

Recall the overwhelming anxiety with which we watched the clock tick down to the mythic moment of January 1, 2000. We anticipated unknown disasters, even if we attached them to the "rational" problem of Y2K, a computer glitch that threatened everything from power grids to air traffic control. In hindsight, we can recognize that, despite our sophistication, we were gripped by a millennial panic worthy of our ancestors of a thousand years ago. Apocalyptic fear consists in the expectation that the end of time has drawn near, and every creature conscious of the passage of time is vulnerable to it. (I am particularly instructed on apocalyptic time by Richard Fenn in the current issue of *Daedalus*.) It is human, that is, to be mightily afraid of the end of time, and that mythic prospect worked on the American unconscious with Y2K. The millennial catastrophe was a threat we thought we had survived—until 9-11. And as was true in Christendom at the previous millennium, our instant, if unconscious, response was to launch crusades. Millennial crusades aim to eliminate disorders which, in other times, human beings find ways to live with.

And so also space. It is well known that American free-market capitalism and information technologies are at the center of a new globalization, but these innovations have obliterated traditional definitions of place. Today, with instantaneous access to experience everywhere available not only through computers but through cell phones, the boundary between here and there is no longer clear. This development is momentous because that boundary has served as the first marker in human consciousness, the primal source of identity and meaning. Persons become who they are—members of family, tribe, people, nation—by pacing out territory and discovering who shares it. But what is territory in the age of television? Migration, mass media, McWorld, the mall—the very structures of contemporary life are sources of dislocation. Human beings across the world are left wondering: where am I? But Americans, assuming a natural right to dominance, find an answer by staking a claim to the globe itself. The aim of our wars launched in uncertain time is to redefine uncertain space. America is the world. Everyplace is our place.

It does not matter, therefore, if Saddam Hussein's weapons of mass destruction turn up. It does not matter if the Bush administration's prewar justifications were the result of intelligence ineptitude or outright lies. It does not matter whether the post-9-11 wars against Afghanistan and Iraq were related to the purposes offered. It does not matter, apparently, even if there are more dubiously justified American wars to come.

But it matters that we are thus a people in the grip of millennial, apocalyptic impulses, which we are determined to deny. That we are so primitive makes us human. That we are so blind makes us dangerous.

To Love America

July 1, 2003

It was the point of fireworks when you were young. In those days, each backyard had its own celebration of the Fourth of July, and your dad, like all the others, presided over the lighting of the Roman candles, the volcano cones, and firecrackers. He saw to the distribution of sparklers with which you and your brothers wrote your names on the air. All that fire felt dangerous, but it did not frighten you because your father was in charge.

Fireworks were exclusive to the Fourth of July, which is how you knew what they meant: America is a great nation. Color in the sky was a joyous celebration of that greatness. You grew up with a fervent love of your country, which you never felt more fully than on its birthday. In those years, America's greatness had just been demonstrated by the victory over fascism, and even as a child you grasped the mortal stakes of the conflict with Joseph Stalin, and were not wrong. But the threshold into adulthood was set by disturbing recognitions. Having grown up playing "Cowboys and Indians," one day you wondered: Where are all those Indians now? And why are all the colored kids in that other school? And then, while crouched under your desk for the "duck and cover" drill, it hit you that Stalin's atomic bomb and America's were the same thing.

Your first real fight with your father was over Martin Luther King Jr. You started to insist, "Doctor King says that if America is ever to be a great nation—" But your father cut you off: "America already is a great nation." The furious conviction with which he said this made you think that you and he no longer believed the same thing, but now you understand that you were both right.

You celebrate the greatness of America this week, with gratitude and pride. But also with a mature understanding that greatness does not preclude grievous failure, nor does it consist in static perfection that is above criticism. Since those midsummer nights of Roman candles and sparklers in the backyard, your country has redefined itself again and again. "Colored people" are not mere colored people anymore, and just as assumptions of racial dominance—dominance by white Europeans—were central to the founding of America, the overturning of those assumptions has accomplished nothing less than America's reinvention. That is why you were right to see Martin Luther King Jr. as the tribune of changes that go far beyond a narrowly conceived civil rights agenda. Expansive attitudes toward gender and ethnicity; a readiness to face dark secrets of the nation's past and repent of them; an authentic tolerance for various ways of being different; a recognition that violence is a particular American plague, even if Americans still widely disagree about its implications at home and abroad—all of this marks the national mind in ways that were unthinkable not so long ago.

What made it true to say, as your father did, that America was already a great nation is that America has long contained within itself—"We hold these truths . . ."—principles of its own self-criticism. Martin Luther King Jr. could demand radical change from within the American context, not against it. By appealing to America's own noblest idea of itself as a way of demanding a new greatness, King was building on the greatness that was already there. The founding Americans are thus honored not for having established the just society but for erecting structures of mind and union within which the just society can continuously be pursued. You have seen this happen in the span of your own life, and so had your father in his.

It is not news that America stands sorely in need of criticism today. Yielding to the old temptation of a new triumphalism; putting its trust in violent power; glorifying possession to the point where the dispossessed are left behind; cloaking national insecurity with thin patriotism; treating criticism as disloyalty. But there's the point. The peculiarly American demonstration of love of country consists in the readiness to hold the nation to its own higher standard. America, by definition, continually falls short of itself.

These Fourth of July abstractions have an urgent implication for today. The misbegotten Iraqi conflict has now entered its guerrilla phase and is steadily killing young people, including Americans. Voices of protest from around the world will grow louder as this hemorrhaging worsens, but the criticism that can actually rescue Americans and Iraqis from this disaster must come from within. The capacity of your nation to face such failure and, in the name of its own best self, to end it is why your father taught you to love America. That capacity for self-criticism and change is what you celebrate this week.

13

LOST

Just as George W. Bush declared victory in Iraq, the full extent of the American loss was beginning to show itself. The entire post-9-11 enterprise was coming apart. Afghanistan, with the exception of a narrowly drawn enclave centered in the capital city, Kabul, had declined into a nation of warlordism, tribal conflict, and unchecked criminality. A revived Taliban movement, a revived heroin trade, and a broad humanitarian crisis among Afghans had become main notes of the new situation. If al Qaeda was dispersed from its bases there, it was in no way vanquished. The American defeat embodied in Osama bin Laden's still being at large was far more than symbolic. In the Arab world—indeed, throughout the whole House of Islam—bin Laden's stature was in the process of being transformed from a marginal miscreant to a modern-day Saladin, the hero who vanquished crusaders. Bush's war on terrorism, by defining bin Laden as a martial adversary instead of as a sadistic criminal, had elevated him to mythic status. The "war" on terrorism, in that sense, was lost the day Bush declared it.

And remarkably enough, Bush managed to do something similar with Saddam Hussein, before his capture. For eight crucial months in the war of the imagination—the true battlefield—Saddam's survival gave the lie to every claim of American victory. The ragtag guerrilla war his supporters began waging almost immediately after our war "ended" depended, for example, on well-placed and secured stocks of munitions whose very existence showed far shrewder preparation than anything the Pentagon did with postwar Iraq in mind. Indeed, one great scandal of the American occupation has been how poorly equipped, trained, and protected were America's young soldiers for the landscape of battle, political as well as military, that they faced.

Every war is, first, an intelligence war, and on every front of that conflict, America has lost. The 9-11 attacks themselves displayed the incompetence of America's foreign and domestic intelligence services. Then followed the rank failures to understand Taliban capabilities, anticipate al Qaeda resources in Pakistan, assess Hussein's actual intentions and resources, and, especially, provide meaningful analysis of his *lack* of weapons of mass destruction. Bush is fighting his war on every front blind! No wonder it is lost.

Ridding the World of Evil

July 8, 2003

In the Gothic splendor of the National Cathedral, that liturgy of trauma in September of 2001, George W. Bush made the most stirring—and ominous—declaration of his presidency. "Just three days removed from these events," he said, "Americans do not yet have the distance of history. But our responsibility to history is already clear: to answer these attacks and rid the world of evil."

The statement fell on the ears of most Americans, perhaps, as mere rhetoric of the high pulpit, but as the "distance of history" lengthens, events show that in those few words the president redefined his raison d'être and that of the nation—nothing less than to "rid the world of evil." The unprecedented initiatives taken from Washington in the last two years are incomprehensible except in the context of this purpose. President Bush, one sees now, meant exactly what he said. Something entirely new, for America at least, is animating its government. The greatest power the earth has ever seen is now expressly mobilized against the world's most ancient mystery. What human beings have proven incapable of doing ever before, George W. Bush has taken on as his personal mission, aiming to accomplish it in one election cycle, two at most.

What the president may not know is that the worst manifestations of evil have been the blowback, precisely, of efforts to be rid of it. If one can refer to the personification of evil, Satan's great trick consists in turning the fierce energy of such purification back upon itself. Across the distance of history, the most noble ambition has invariably led to the most ignoble deeds. This is because the certitude of nobility overrides the moral qualm that adheres to less transcendent enterprises. The record of this deadly paradox is written in the full range of literature, by authors from Sophocles to Fyodor Dostoyevsky to Ursula Le Guin, each of whom raises the perennial question: what is permitted to be done in the name of "ridding the world of evil"?

Is lying allowed? Torture? The killing of children? Or, less drastically, the militarization of civic society? The launching of dubious wars? But wars are never dubious at their launchings. The recognition of complexity—moral as well as martial—comes only with "the distance of history," and it is that perspective that has begun to press itself upon the American conscience now. Having forthrightly set out to rid the world of evil, first in Afghanistan, then in Iraq, has the United States, willy-nilly, become an instrument of evil? Lying (weapons of mass deception). Torture (if only by U.S. surrogates). The killing of children ("collaterally," but inevitably). The vulgarization of patriotism (last week's orgy of bunting). The imposition of chaos (and calling it freedom). The destruction of alliances ("First

Iraq, then France"). The invitation to other nations to behave in like fashion (good-bye, Chechnya). The inexorable escalation ("Bring 'em on!"). The made-in-Washington pantheon of mythologized enemies (first Osama, now Saddam). The transmutation of ordinary young Americans (into dead heroes). How does all of this, or any of it, "rid the world of evil"?

Which brings us back to that Gothic cathedral of a question: what is evil anyway? Is it the impulse only of tyrants? Of enemies alone? Or is it tied to the personal entitlement onto which America, too, hangs its bunting? Is evil the thing, perhaps, that forever inclines human beings to believe that they are themselves untouched by it? Moral maturity, mellowed across the distance of history, begins in the acknowledgment that evil, whatever its primal source, resides, like a virus in its niche, in the human self. There is no ridding the world of evil for the simple fact that, shy of history's end, there is no ridding the self of it.

But there's the problem with President Bush. It is not the moral immaturity of the texts he reads. Like his callow statement in the National Cathedral on September 14, 2001, they are written by someone else. When the president speaks, unscripted, from his own moral center, what shows itself is a bottomless void. To address concerns about the savage violence engulfing "postwar" Iraq with a cocksure "Bring 'em on!" (as he did last week) is to display an absence of imagination shocking in a man of such authority. It showed a lack of capacity to identify either with enraged Iraqis who must rise to such a taunt, or with young GIs who must now answer for it. Even in relationship to his own soldiers, there is nothing at the core of this man but visceral meanness.

No human being with a minimal self-knowledge could speak of evil as he does, but there is no self-knowledge without a self. Even this short "distance of history" shows George W. Bush to be, in that sense, the selfless president, which is not a compliment. It's a warning.

Unintelligence

July 15, 2003

So the intelligence community provided faulty information to policy makers, who then used it to justify disastrous decisions. When have I heard this story before?

- Was it in 1944 when a savage Allied air war against cities was based on British intelligence assessments (disputed by some Americans) that bombing would destroy enemy "morale"?
- Or was it in 1945 when Manhattan Project intelligence, overseen by Brigadier General Leslie Groves, provided estimates (disputed by scientists) that the Soviet Union would not have the atomic bomb for up to twenty years?
- Or was it in the 1950s when American intelligence so emphasized the monolithic character of world communism that it missed the obvious anti-Moscow nationalist fractures in Yugoslavia and China?
- Or was it in 1960 when U.S. Air Force intelligence, having seen a "bomber gap," then discovered a "missile gap," sparking major escalations in the arms race with the Soviet Union?
- Or was it in 1968 when military intelligence, obsessed with "body counts," had so exaggerated the progress of the war (counting dead women and old people as soldiers) that the Tet Offensive took Washington by complete surprise?
- Or was it in 1969 when Richard Nixon, to justify his Anti-Ballistic Missile proposal, cited intelligence reports (disputed by the director of the Defense Intelligence Agency) that the Soviet Union was preparing to launch a first strike?
- Or was it in the 1970s when U.S. intelligence, propping up the

shah of Iran, dismissed as irrelevant the tape-recorded rantings of an exiled mullah named Khomeini?

• Or was it in the 1980s when, emphasizing the "Evil Empire," American intelligence missed entirely both the internal collapse of the Soviet economy and the historic significance of the nonviolent democracy movements?

Failure of intelligence, leading Washington to make world-threatening policy mistakes, is not the exception but the rule. Analysts are conditioned to emphasize worst-case scenarios, but something else equally governs such instances. Notice what each involves: an information system that is at the service of the preexisting desires and assumptions of those in authority. Intelligence assessments moving up the chain of command have a way of confirming presuppositions at the top. Truman wanted to believe in a long-term American nuclear monopoly so that he could berate Moscow—and Groves assured him it would be so. Nixon wanted a justification for the ABM, and a slanted reading of Soviet missile deployments gave it to him. And so on. This is not to say that intelligence officials "lie," but that at each level of gathering and analysis—from the "body count" in the field through a dozen intermediate stages of reporting and refinement, to the National Intelligence Estimate provided to the president—contradictions are eliminated and ambiguities are shaded, perhaps unconsciously, to meet the expectations of superiors.

In 1960 U.S. reconnaissance photos showed many monuments in vast Soviet graveyards, upright granite obelisks honoring Red Army war dead. The first photoanalyst would have identified the structures as "almost certainly" grave markers; the second, "probably grave markers, but small chance they are missiles"; the third, "could well be missiles"; the fourth, "probably missiles, although maybe grave markers." By the time John F. Kennedy was warning of the missile gap, he would have been depending on a report that had seen "hard evidence" of missile deployments across the Soviet Union. Not incidentally, those reports, having supported air force budget requests, fueled Kennedy's criticism of the Republican administration.

One needn't believe George W. Bush "lied" about Iraqi weapons of mass destruction. Following the tradition, he simply relied on reports that gave him what he wanted—reports having filtered out the warnings, contradictions, and ambiguities that did not square with his oft-stated purpose. It was to such filtering that CIA director George Tenet recently pled guilty. No duh.

And lest one think of this as heinous, it should also be noted that this "filtering" is exactly what the vast majority of Americans, politicians, and "opinion makers" employed in their eager rush to war last fall and winter. Many of the Democrats and pundits now condemning an intelligence "deception" did exactly the same thing to support a war they were too cowardly to oppose—ignoring the much noted evidence (enough to sustain U.N. opposition) that contradicted patently ludicrous claims made by the Bush administration.

Not all intelligence officials willingly participate in this corruption, either today or in the past. Each of the instances outlined above involved officials who dissented from the top-down consensus, sometimes at their peril. I happen to know of one such case personally, and it is why I find this pattern of smug American self-deception so painful. The director of the Defense Intelligence Agency who defied the Nixon administration in 1969 by contradicting its claim about Soviet "first-strike" intentions was my father, Lieutenant General Joseph Carroll. Speaking that truth cost him his career.

Was the War Necessary?

July 22, 2003

Why does the apparent suicide of David Kelly strike such a chord? The British weapons expert found himself in the middle of the controversy over the Bush-Blair hyping of the Saddam Hussein threat. Unsourced BBC reports, an aggressive parliamentary interrogation, the stresses of weapons inspection, a government's credibility in jeopardy, a rat's nest of deceptions—all of this together could weigh too much on one man. Though the private demons of any suicide remain mysterious forever, it seems that being snagged into this dispute sparked an anguish in Dr. Kelly that he could not bear. "He told his wife he was taking a walk," an AP report said. "A local farmer said Kelly smiled as he passed." Some hours later, he was found near a woods, his left wrist slashed.

Dr. Kelly gives a name and a face to the fact that the dispute over intelligence manipulated to justify a "preventive war" is a matter of life and death. This is not a mere question of politics anymore, another argument between liberals and conservatives. When told of Kelly's death, Prime Minister Tony Blair called it "an absolutely terrible tragedy." But the burden that broke this man was, at bottom, the weight of the absolutely terrible question: was the British-American war against Iraq necessary?

Every person killed in that war—certainly including the young American soldiers still dying by the day—represents "an absolutely terrible tragedy." On *The News Hour with Jim Lehrer*, a daily honor roll is kept, with photographs of dead Americans shown in silence. It has become a poignant and depressing ritual, but in that silence, one also asks: and what of the Iraqi dead?

The coalition air war commander, Lieutenant General T. Michael Moseley, revealed this weekend that Secretary of Defense Donald

Rumsfeld had to personally sign off on any air strike "thought likely to result in deaths of more than 30 civilians," as the *New York Times* reported. "More than 50 such strikes were proposed, and all of them were approved." General Moseley also revealed that the much celebrated stealth attack on Hussein's bunker early in the war was a double miss. Not only was there no Hussein; there was no bunker. Sorry about that.

One sees the traditional just-war ethic at work: a necessary war can involve the "collateral damage" of civilian deaths—tragic, yet acceptable. But *was the war necessary?* That question defines the stakes in the dispute over the ways George Bush and Tony Blair misrepresented the prospect of Saddam Hussein with nuclear, biological, and chemical arms. When allied warplanes knowingly and repeatedly attacked targets that would kill significant numbers of civilians, only the urgent effort to prevent Hussein's mass-destructive and imminent aggression could have justified such carnage. But now the proffered rationale of necessity is being shown to have been false. The "preventive war," as it turns out, prevented nothing.

At a press conference in Japan the day after David Kelly's body was found, Tony Blair was asked, "Have you got blood on your hands, prime minister?" Alas, there is an ocean of blood on the hands of Tony Blair and George Bush. Whether shown to be "lying" or not, they shunted aside the ambiguities and uncertainties that characterized the prewar intelligence assessments of Hussein's threat. And though, as I argued last week, there is a long tradition of leaders manipulating intelligence estimates for their own preset purposes, the act of war is in a special category. When disputed intelligence is the basis of war, the leader's reading of that intelligence had better be proven true. Otherwise, the just-war argument from necessity fails.

No wonder the dispute won't die. The questions matter too much. No wonder polls are shifting away from Bush. Citizens of the United States do not like to think of themselves as wanton killers. No wonder American soldiers in Iraq are openly expressing doubts. A democracy's first requirement of military discipline is the army's belief in the moral necessity of its mission. No wonder, even, pressures of the dispute may have driven one man to kill himself. The issue is mortal: was George Bush's new-style "preventive" war just another war of aggression, after all?

Tony Blair was asked if he would resign, and at least one prominent Democrat hurled the word *impeachment* at the president. But the political consequences of this controversy begin to take second place to the moral, and even legal. The traditional ethic declares that a war of aggression is inherently unjust, and that every civilian death caused by such a war is murder. More than fifty air raids, each with more than thirty Iraqi civilian fatalities, each expressly approved by Rumsfeld. Absolutely terrible tragedies, every one. And also—more evident by the day—every one a war crime.

The Habit of Revenge

August 5, 2003

"Although the war did not make any immediate demands on me physically, while it lasted it put a complete stop to my artistic activity because it forced me into an agonizing reappraisal of my fundamental assumptions." These words were spoken by Thomas Mann in his Nobel laureate speech in 1929, a reflection of the broad psychological rupture inflicted on the European mind by World War I. But just as war can lead to the "reappraisal of fundamental assumptions," it can do the opposite, reinforcing assumptions to the point of shutting down debate. That seems a more American story.

Tomorrow marks the fifty-eighth anniversary of the atomic bombing of Hiroshima. Oceans of ink have been spilled on the questions whether Harry Truman's decision to use the bomb was justified; whether the Japanese would have surrendered without it; whether the bomb, therefore, was truly an alternative to a bloody invasion; whether the bomb was actually aimed at intimidating the Russians; whether, in fact, given the momentum of war, Truman's decision was really a decision. Such questions never go fully away because each has some claim on the truth, even if only partial. But the "fundamental assumption" underlying the bomb's use is rarely addressed.

"Having found the bomb, we have used it." These are words spoken by President Truman in a radio address to the American people on the evening of August 9, the day a second bomb fell on Nagasaki. "We have used it against those who attacked us without warning at Pearl Harbor, against those who have starved and beaten American prisoners of war, against those who have abandoned all pretense of obeying international laws of warfare." President Truman, and others who justified the bomb, would rarely speak this way again—a direct articulation of revenge as a main motivation for the overwhelming destruction of the Japanese cities. In his radio remarks, Truman went on then to add the other justifications: "We have used it in order to shorten the agony of war, in order to save the lives of thousands and thousands of young Americans. We shall continue to use it until we completely destroy Japan's power to make war. Only a Japanese surrender will stop us." But even the surrender, when it came, would prompt after-the-fact controversy, since, still insisting on the emperor's permanent authority, it wasn't unconditional. If we accepted their hedged surrender after the atomic bomb, why wouldn't we accept it before?

Every justification offered for the use of the atomic bomb would be clouded by ambiguity, except one: revenge. It was the first justification Truman offered, speaking the primal truth, and it was the only justification the American people needed by then. But soon enough, revenge would disappear from all official explanations, and even Truman's critics would rarely address it, except obliquely. Much better to debate the necessity of that invasion.

Americans do not like to acknowledge that a visceral lust for vengeance can be the main force behind national purpose, and that is why the August 6 anniversary always arrives beclouded. In 1995, when the Smithsonian attempted to mount a retrospective exhibit observing the fiftieth anniversary of Hiroshima and Nagasaki, a mainstream consensus slapped down any effort to "reappraise the fundamental assumptions" of the bomb's use. President Bill Clinton declined to second-guess Truman, and the Smithsonian exhibit was canceled. What terrifies Americans is the possibility that stated reasons are distant from, or even unrelated to, the real reasons for the nation's behavior. But Truman had it right the first time: to understand August 6, 1945, you must return to December 7, 1941, the score that had to be settled.

Pearl Harbor resurfaced in the American memory on September 11, 2001. Again and again, the Day of Infamy was invoked as the relevant precedent—the only other time the United States had suffered such a grievous blow. And just as before, there was never any doubt that the blow would be avenged. Moving quickly away from the unsatisfyingly abstract war on terrorism, and then from the frustration of Osama bin Laden's escape from Afghanistan, President Bush took America to war against Iraq to satisfy that primordial need. And it worked. The United States of America clenched its fist the day the Twin Towers came down. Against Iraq, the United States finally threw a punch. That is all that matters.

The controversy over the Bush administration's misleading "justifications" for the war in Iraq is a reprise of the endless debate over "justifications" offered for the atomic bomb. Neither set of questions grips the American conscience. There is no "agonizing reappraisal of fundamental assumptions" in this country. When we want our revenge, we take it. And, even as the flimsy rationales with which we cloak it are stripped away, we fervently deny that vengeance, not justice, defines our purpose.

The War Is Lost

September 2, 2003

The war is lost. By most measures of what the Bush administration forecast for its adventure in Iraq, it is already a failure. The war was going to make the Middle East a more peaceful place. It was going to undercut terrorism. It was going to show the evil dictators of the world that American power is not to be resisted. It was going to improve the lives of ordinary Iraqis. It was going to stabilize oil markets. The American army was going to be greeted with flowers.

None of that happened. The most radical elements of various fascist movements in the Arab world have been energized by the invasion of Iraq. The American occupation is a rallying point for terrorists. Instead of undermining extremism, Washington has sponsored its next phase, and now moderates in every Arab society are more on the defensive than ever. Before the war, the threat of America's overwhelming military dominance could intimidate, but now that force has been shown to be extremely limited in what it can actually accomplish. For the sake of regime change, the United States brought a sledgehammer down on Iraq, only to profess surprise that, even as Saddam Hussein remained at large, the structures of the nation's civil society were in ruins. The humanitarian agencies necessary to the rebuilding of those structures have been fleeing Iraq.

The question for Americans is: now what? Democrats and Republicans alike want to send in more U.S. soldiers. Some voices are raised in the hope that the occupation can be more fully "internationalized," which remains unlikely while Washington retains absolute control. But those who would rush belligerent reinforcements to Iraq are making the age-old mistake. When brutal force generates resistance, the first impulse is to increase force levels. But, as the history of conflicts like this shows, that will result only in increased resistance. Secretary of Defense Donald Rumsfeld has rejected the option of more troops for now, but, in the name of force protection, the pressures for escalation will build as U.S. casualties mount. The present heartbreak of one or two GI deaths a day will seem benign when suicide-bombers, mortar shells, or even heavier missile fire find their ways into barracks and mess halls.

Either reinforcements will be sent to the occupation, or present forces will loosen the restraints with which they reply to provocation. Both responses will generate more bloodshed and only postpone the day when the United States must face the truth of its situation. The Bush administration's hubristic foreign policy has been efficiently exposed as based on nothing more than hallucination. High-tech weaponry can kill unwilling human beings, but it cannot force them to embrace an unwanted idea. As rekindled North Korean and Iranian nuclear programs prove, Washington's rhetoric of "evil" is as self-defeating as it is self-delusional. No one could have predicted a year ago that the fall from the Bush high horse of American Empire would come so hard and so quickly. Where are the comparisons with Rome now? The rise and fall of imperial Washington took not hundreds of years but a few hundred days.

Sooner or later, the United States must admit that it has made a terrible mistake in Iraq, and it must move quickly to undo it. That means the United States must yield not only command of the occupation force but participation in it. The United States must renounce any claim to power or even influence over Iraq, including Iraqi oil. The United States must accept the humiliation that would surely accompany its being replaced in Iraq by the very nations it denigrated in the buildup to the war. With the United States thus removed from the Iraqi crucible, those who have rallied to oppose the great Satan will lose their raison d'être, and the Iraqi people themselves can take responsibility for rebuilding their wrecked nation.

All of this might seem terribly unlikely today, but something like it is inevitable. The only question is whether it happens over the short term, as the result of responsible decision making by politicians in Washington, or over the long term, as the result of a bloody and unending horror. The so-called lessons of Vietnam are often invoked by hawks and doves alike, but here is one that applies across the political spectrum. The American people saw that that war was lost in January 1968, even as the Tet Offensive was heralded as a victory by the Pentagon and the White House. But for five more years, Washington refused to face the truth of its situation, until at last it had no choice. Because American leaders could not admit the nation's mistake, and move to undo it, hundreds of thousands of people died, or was it millions?

The war in Iraq is lost. What will it take to face that truth this time?

14

WAR SPREADS

At the beginning of September 2003, a tape likely containing the voice of Saddam Hussein was aired on Arabic television. Its message: "O great heroes, intensify your brave blows against the foreign aggressors." Resistance to the American occupation of Iraq—six major bomb blasts in July and August—began to spread in the fall. Targets were expanded from GIs to the U.N. to the Red Cross, and to Japanese, South Korean, Italian, Bulgarian, Thai, and Spanish personnel, as well as to the U.S-picked Iraqi Governing Council and others cooperating with the occupation. Where before attacks had come mainly from Baathist diehards and in Sunni areas more likely to be supportive of Saddam, now Shi'ite fighters joined the fray, some with the express goal of a Tehran-style Islamic state. Shi'ites, a sizable majority of Iraq, hated Saddam, but what chance was there that they would accommodate themselves to the American occupation when President Bush, at the outset of the war on terrorism, had demonized the Shi'ite regime in Iran as part of the Axis of Evil?

In the United States, there were signs that relatively marginal objections to the war were becoming more broadly shared. The expressly antiwar presidential campaign of Howard Dean, for example, began to pick up steam. Months after that "Mission Accomplished" banner flew over the USS *Abraham Lincoln*, American soldiers were still dying. Yet the misbegotten character of the "coalition" war went deeper than its refusal to end. Whether Americans knew it or not, Osama bin Laden's civilizational "clash" was well under way. Islamist jihadis from Syria, Pakistan, Saudi Arabia, and other Arab countries were reported to have joined the struggle in Iraq, as the impression in the House of Islam of anti-Muslim religious war took firmer hold than ever.

But as the depth of the nation-splitting fissures in Iraq became more evident, the United States showed signs of hastening its retreat from responsibility. The handoff to some kind of Iraqi sovereign body had to happen well before Americans cast ballots for president. (The only thing that matters more to George W. Bush than his wars is his reelection.) At the same time, leaders of the Shi'ite majority began to openly question the U.S.-imposed procedures for returning sovereignty to Iraq. A new Washington nightmare began to take form: Iraq under an Islamist Shi'ite regime. The last thing the Bush administration had intended by going to war in Iraq was to create a radical Shi'ite power bloc in the area—Iraq in firm alliance at last with Iran. The oldest martial law of all—the rule of unintended consequences—was once again proving to be self-enforcing.

The Other 9-11

September 11, 2003

The coincidence of dates is precious to human beings because it creates the impression that underlying the chaos of normality is a structure of order. The passage of time is not a mere matter of chance, and even things that seem unrelated are tied together, if not by links of causality, by meaning. In casting an eye back across the terrain of the past, a human being with a feeling for history looks for the juxtaposition of seemingly disparate events that will illuminate the hidden connection that alone explains their full significance.

September 11 will live in the American memory. But as what? In memory, so we saw citing Auster in the introduction, things happen again and again. On September 11, 1941, at almost exactly the moment in which the Pentagon would be hit by American Airlines Flight 77 sixty years later, ground was broken for that building in a solemn ceremony. On September 11, 1944, Allied soldiers arrived at the German border, sealing Hitler's fate. But also on September 11, 1944, as I read in W. G. Sebald's *On the Natural History of Destruction*, Germans watched the night sky above the city of Darmstadt: "The light grew and grew until the whole of the southern sky was glowing, shot through with red and yellow." It was a night of Allied terror bombing. On September 11, 1973, terrorists launched the violent overthrow of a democratic government in Chile. In that case, the result was the murder of the head of state, Salvador Allende, and the terrorists were sponsored not by an ad hoc nihilist group but by the United States. On September 11, 1990, as we saw, President George H. W. Bush gave his most noted speech, declaring a "New World Order" as a prelude to the first Gulf War.

September 11 as an anniversary of savage violence pushes the mind also to September 11, 1945, the date that marks Secretary of War Henry L. Stimson's post-Hiroshima proposal to President Truman that the United States immediately share the secrets of the atomic bomb with the Soviet Union in order to head off an arms race "of a rather desperate character," as Stimson put it. "The chief lesson I have learned in a long life," Stimson said, anticipating his critics, "is that the only way you can make a man trustworthy is to trust him." As I noted a year ago, Stimson's proposal marks the great American road not taken.

On September 11, 1906, more than three thousand men of Indian origin gathered at the Empire Theater in Johannesburg, South Africa, to denounce the just-passed Asiatic Law Amendment Ordinance—a new set of racial laws condemning them to second-class citizenship. As I learned from Jonathan Schell's recent masterwork *The Unconquerable World*, one of those who stood and took a God-invoking oath against obedience to such laws was Mohandas Karamchand Gandhi. He recognized this joint commitment to a radically individual act—"a new principle," he later said of that day, "had come into being"—as the generating spark of *satyagraha*, the truth-force. Gandhi said, "The foundation of the first civil resistance under the then-known name of passive resistance was laid by accident. . . . I had gone to the meeting with no preconceived resolution. It was born at the meeting. The creation is still expanding." What began on that September 11 would generate the great counterstory of nonviolence running through the most violent century in history.

At the dawn of the new century, what story do we tell? Does September 11 represent only the experience of American grief, victimhood, justification for revenge? Does September 11 live on only as the engine driving America's shocking new belligerence? Or, in recalling the nobility of those selfless New Yorkers and Pentagon workers who reentered the wounded buildings, who remained behind to usher others out, or who simply maintained calm as worlds collapsed around them—can we carry this date forward as an image of the possibility of public love? It may help to see September 11, 2001, in the context of those other days in other years. How, when the ground was first broken for the Pentagon, its builders assumed one day it would be a hospital. How the leader of America's greatest war sought in its aftermath to end war forever. How knowing that Washington, too, can sponsor terrorism must lead to humility. How the age-old dream of nonviolence became actual.

Ordinarily, we think of such incidents in isolation, but there can be an archaeology of the calendar that uncovers harmonies in the layers of time. September 11 is an anniversary of the future, a day enshrining the worst of human impulses—and the best. A day, therefore, that puts the choice before us. How are we going to live now? We are on the earth for the briefest of interludes. Thinking in particular of all those who died in New York, Washington, and

Pennsylvania, let us honor them by building the earth, instead of destroying it. Let us make peace, instead of war.

From Politics to Resistance

September 16, 2003

The catastrophe in Fallujah—ten Iraqi policemen killed by U.S. forces, acting, as one Iraqi said, "just like Saddam"—can be the occasion of new recognitions. The normal ecology of war is chaos and confusion. But once in a while something occurs to snap the ambiguities into focus, and the real character of what is happening becomes apparent. Indeed, that is the meaning Aristotle gave to the word *catastrophe* in his analysis of the tragic form. Ten of the very men Iraqi recovery needs most—dead by the hands of our soldiers? Pro-American police at risk from Americans? A tragedy for sure, but here is what the incident reveals:

- This "accident" was not, in fact, an aberration. The killing of allies, and of innocents, is part and parcel of what the American occupation involves now. Death has overtaken strategy.
- Whether the soldiers who killed the Iraqi policemen "intended" the act or not is irrelevant. American pietism excuses dastardly outcomes when they are committed with good intentions, but morality is measured more by consequences than by purposes. No U.S. soldier is "innocent" in this enterprise.
- But every U.S. soldier in Iraq has been taken hostage. The hostage takers are not the terrorists but the small clique of Bush administration officials who have violated U.S. tradition, international agreements, and the sacred trust that commanders owe their soldiers.

- Those who fault the Bush administration for the failed details of this operation (too few troops, poor planning, not enough foreign support, etc.) miss the larger point that there was no "right" way to invade Iraq, and there is no "right" way to occupy it. Iraq belongs to Iraqis.
- The corruptions of Bush policies in Iraq are infecting the entire American nation. Such aggressive violence requires deceit, and lies are more welcome in Washington than at any time since Vietnam. The Justice Department is increasingly an instrument of repression. On the eve of elections, the American people are in the grip of a vast ennui.

So what is to be done? Such recognitions change the context of what is required now. Instead of politics, it is time for resistance. One needn't assert a facile moral equivalence to know that the relevant precedents for the present circumstance in the United States are the broad-based citizen resistance movements that mobilized against Hitler in the 1940s; against the Vietnam War in the 1960s; against the Kremlin in the 1980s. This means:

- Hope shifts away from the Democratic politicians vying to replace Bush. By timidly giving the vague appearance of opposition while assuming the broad necessity of America's ongoing military presence in Iraq, the candidates are Bush's effective collaborators.
- "Supporting the troops" gets redefined. Instead of muting criticism out of fear of undermining military morale, declare that U.S. soldiers have been conscripted into an unnecessary and therefore immoral war. The troops must simply be removed from Iraq.
- The cutting edge of the political debate becomes the money. All funding for the American occupation, including the $87 billion Bush requested last week, must be opposed. Military appropriations must be cut off.
- Patriotism is asserted more by opposition than by affirmation.

The Bush administration has cagily turned large-hearted American expressions of love for the nation into license for a criminal foreign policy. Just as Bush has kidnapped our young people in uniform, he has captured the flag. For now, the way to take the flag back is to take it down.

- Americans refuse to be deceived, even while being lied to. There is no way for an American president to engage in such an unprecedented act of aggression without trying to disguise its true character. The very audacity of Bush's manipulations stimulates a cooperative self-deception in the population. That, above all, must be resisted.

- Mortal danger becomes apparent. Bush policies have reinvigorated suicide-bombers across the world, while simultaneously igniting a new round of nuclear proliferation. The prospect of that combination—nuclear weapons in the hands of suicidal fanatics—poses the greatest risk in human history. Bush himself has thus become the ultimate suicide-bomber.

Hence resistance. Public life in America must take its energy now from the word *No*. Such opposition does two things. As happened especially in the Soviet empire, it can transform politics, moving even the Democratic candidates from timid calls for adjustments at the margins to demands for substantial change of policy. And, meanwhile, a life lived in resistance remains a human life. In a time of rampant public immorality, it is the only way to live humanly.

The catastrophe at Fallujah can be the occasion of such recognition. But catastrophe, as Aristotle also taught, is the occasion of reversal. The time to turn the momentum of Bush's war back upon itself has come.

Antiterrorism Creed

September 23, 2003

Everyone knows what threatens the United States: *terrorism*. But what, exactly, is terrorism? The suffix *ism* is a clue. The dictionary defines it as "a distinctive doctrine, system, or theory." Thus, what we fear are not merely uncoordinated and unrelated acts of nihilist violence—mailed anthrax, airliners-turned-into-missiles, malicious computer hackers—but a coherent "system of principles" that sponsors such acts. Terrorism so conceived can threaten even a powerful nation like America because it is understood to possess global reach, apocalyptic ambition, an entangled network of hostile alliances abroad, and a capacity to exploit vulnerabilities of our democracy at home. Thus America's response is the war on terrorism, as if the enemy is one thing.

But is this way of evaluating the danger a mistake? The suffix *ism* was key to defining a mortal threat once before, and in that case the result was a disastrous misreading of what the United States confronted—both abroad and at home. To evaluate the present danger, it can help to cast the mind back to another time, another danger.

On March 12, 1947, President Truman delivered a speech outlining the "Truman Doctrine," an explicit definition of the threat from the Soviet Union. Instead of seeing the ambitions of the men in the Kremlin in traditional terms of nationalistic self-interest, or even of imperialist purposes like the czars before them, Truman saw a Manichaean struggle between "freedom" and the "ism" of communism. The threat from Moscow was not the normal challenge of a nation competing for power or territory. The Kremlin wanted to be not only a transnational capital but a transhistorical one. Russia was seen to be driven by a cosmic, apocalyptic, evangelical determination to overturn not just borders and economies but whole systems of belief—especially ours.

Navy Secretary James Forrestal, chief among those who saw the Soviet threat in such terms, said, "Nothing about Russia can be understood without understanding the implacable and unchanging direction of Lenin's religion-philosophy."

The Truman speech, in defining the threat in transcendent terms, proposed a response of such ideological sweep—"doctrine" indeed—that it too could be described, as it was by one senior American statesman, as "a declaration of religious war." Such rhetorical extremity served a political purpose, shoring up support in Congress and among Americans for the administration's program. But by seeing Moscow exclusively through the lens of the "ism" of communism, the United States missed the significance of nationalist differences among the various Communist movements and soon found itself embroiled in a futile worldwide effort to "contain" not Russia, however imperialist, but every insurgency around the globe that raised the banner of Karl Marx.

And because the threat was taken to be apocalyptic, Moscow's capacity to inflict actual harm on the "Free World" was consistently overestimated, which also helped shore up domestic political support. Mystical dread replaced analysis. However the conflict was defined in Moscow, in Washington it took on theological significance that pointed politics toward the afterlife ("Better dead than Red"), which alone explains how the United States could so enthusiastically pursue an arms race that put everything this side of the afterlife at risk.

Not only that. The "ism" threatened inside America, too, which is why the search for Communists required, beginning within days of the Truman Doctrine speech, the suspension of traditional guarantees of American citizenship. Anti-Communist dread redefined the purposes of the American government, which then exploited that dread to solidify support for those purposes among the American people. Perceptions of the "ism" that threatened the United States introduced a climate of suspicion inside the country and overturned the traditional understanding of relations among nations. "The Soviet Union, unlike previous aspirants to hegemony," the 1950 policy statement NSC-68 said, "is animated by a new fanatic faith, antithetical to our own, and seeks to impose its absolute authority over the rest of the world."

It may be true that Moscow under Stalin aimed at world dominance, but, if so, the goal was Moscow's dominance—not communism's. Traditional imperial politics, not theology. Washington's failure to grasp this distinction prompted a quasi-religious American response, which gave Russians the motive to adopt the cosmic rhetoric Washington expected, and then drove both nations toward the brink of nuclear Armageddon. Washington imagined a holy-war fanaticism and set about to match it.

Is it happening again? A sure sign that a theology of "terrorism" has come into its own is that wildly dispersed mischief makers are elevated to mystical status. Xenophobic tribal leaders, local insurgent groups, mafia chieftains, freedom fighters, malevolent anarchists, and "rogue regimes" are all now branded as "terrorists," and their dangerous but hardly equivalent purposes are labeled "terrorism." This "ism" justifies America's aggressive war abroad and Patriot Act assaults on rights at home. But the cold war teaches that such transcendent aggrandizing of antagonists is the thing that makes them really dangerous.

Boykin's Bigger God

October 21, 2003

"I knew that my God was bigger than his," Lieutenant General William G. Boykin said of his Muslim opponent. "I knew that my

God was a real God, and his was an idol." That and other remarks derogatory of Islam caused a stir last week, especially because the general holds a key position in the war on terrorism. Awkward memories surfaced of President Bush's inadvertent use of the term *crusade* to define that war, and fears broke into the open that the war was, despite disclaimers, a religious war after all.

Boykin's Pentagon superiors did not seem to take offense, but Muslim leaders did, and so did members of Congress. One imagines how the story played in the Arab media. On October 17 the general offered a sort of apology. "I am neither a zealot, nor an extremist," he said, "only a soldier who has an abiding faith."

The general's critics are right to deplore the denigration of the faith of Muslims, but the problem goes deeper than a crudely expressed religious chauvinism. In point of fact, the general's remarks do not make him an extremist. It was unfashionable of him to speak aloud the implications of his "abiding faith," but exclusivist claims made for Jesus Christ by most Christians, from Vatican corridors to evangelical revival tents, implicitly insult the religion of others. When Catholics speak of "salvation" only through Jesus, or when Protestants limit "justification" to faith in Jesus, aspersions are cast on the entire non-Christian world. In the past, the step from such exclusivist theology to contempt for those excluded has been small indeed, and the step from such contempt to open violence has been even smaller. Especially in relation to Islam.

Last week's response to General Boykin, however, suggests a new sensitivity to the links between intolerant theology and intolerant behavior. The danger of religious war is real. And religious war follows less from conscious intentions of warriors than from the beliefs that inspire them. Boykin makes the question urgent: what kind of God does this general—and the nation he serves—believe in?

General Boykin describes a "bigger" God in conflict with smaller gods, vanquishing them. Idols get smashed. The soldier's faith is braced by the assumption that God, too, can have recourse to violence, and foundational texts of Judaism, Christianity, Islam, and other religions posit just that. "The Lord is a man of war," Exodus says (15:3). As violence is one of the notes of the human condition, religions often attribute it to God, and then divine violence cycles back to justify the human propensity to act violently. The omnipotent warrior God is so firmly entrenched in the human imagination that even atheists affirm it in the very act of denying that such a God exists.

The ethical dilemma facing all religions today, but perhaps especially religions of revelation, is laid bare here: how to affirm one's own faith without denigrating the faith of others. The problem can seem unsolvable if religion is understood as inherently dialectic—reality defined as oppositions between earth and heaven, the natural and the supernatural, knowledge and revelation, atheism and theism, secularism and faith, evil and good. If the religious imagination is necessarily structured on such polarities, religion is inevitably a source of conflict, contempt, violence. My faith is true; yours is idolatry. My God is bigger than your god. My God is a warrior, and so am I.

But there can be such a thing as an inclusivist religious faith, which rejects this way of thinking. Instead of polarity, this other way of being religious assumes unity—unity between God and God's creation, which serves in turn as a source of unity among God's creatures. This reconciling truth is what all the great religions—certainly the three Abrahamic religions—assert when they identify God, most basically, not with conflict but with love. General Boykin says that his God is "real" because his God brings him victory in battle. But the first standard against which the reality of God is measured, even in Boykin's own Christian tradition, is not "bigness" or power but empathetic love. God is love, and the only way to honor God is by loving the neighbor. This is not a minor theme but the essential affirmation.

Therefore, Boykin has it wrong—but so do legions of his fellow believers, from the Vatican, to those revival tents, to the Oval Office. The general's offense was to speak aloud the implication of a still broadly held theology. But that theology is dangerous now. A respectful religious pluralism is no longer just a liberal hope but an urgent precondition of justice and peace. In the twenty-first century, exclusivist religion, no matter how "mainstream," and no matter how muted the anathemas that follow from its absolutes, is a sure way to religious war.

Full-Spectrum Dominance

October 28, 2003

The Iraq war may not be the worst of what President Bush is doing. Last month, the United Nations Conference on Disarmament in Geneva adjourned, completely deadlocked. This is the body that, since 1959, has hammered out the great arms control and reduction treaties—the regime of cooperation and "verified trust" that enabled the cold war to end without nuclear holocaust. The last agreement to come out of Geneva was the Comprehensive Test Ban Treaty in 1996, and the incoming Bush administration's attitude toward the whole enterprise was signaled by its explicit approval of the U.S. Senate's rejection of that treaty.

Now the issue is the grave question of weapons in space, and for several years, while China and other nations have pushed for an agreement aimed at Preventing an Arms Race in Outer Space (PAROS), the United States has insisted no such treaty is necessary. Last August, China offered a compromise in its demands, hoping for a U.S. moderation of its adamant refusal, but no progress was made. As of now, the 1967 Outer Space Treaty governs the military uses of space, but China argues that strategic plans openly discussed in the Pentagon, including the Missile Defense Program, involve deployments that will violate that treaty. In the words of John Steinbruner and Jeffrey Lewis, writing in *Daedalus*, "The Chinese were particularly alarmed by a 1998 long-range planning document released by the then United States Space Command. That document outlined a concept called *global engagement*—a combination of global surveillance, missile defense, and space-based strike capabilities that would enable the United States to undertake effective preemption anywhere in the world and would deny similar capability to any other country."

If the Chinese were alarmed in 1998 by such "full-spectrum dominance," as U.S. planners call it, imagine how much more threatened they feel now that Pentagon fantasies of preemption and permanent global supremacy have become official Bush policies. For decades, "deterrence" and "balance" were the main notes of Pentagon planning, but now "prevention" and "dominance" define the U.S. posture. Such assertions can be made in Washington with only good intentions, but they fall on foreign ears as expressions of aggression. When it comes to space, the Chinese have good reason for thinking of themselves as the main object of such planning, which is why they are desperate for a set of rules governing military uses of space. (At the American Academy of Arts and Sciences, a study of what such rules should be is under way, codirected by Steinbruner and the academy's Martin Malin.)

Two weeks ago, China put a man in space, a signal of China's arrival—and of the arrival of this grave question. Beijing has invested heavily in commercial development of space and will become a significant economic competitor in that sphere. But such peaceful competition presumes a framework of stability, and it is inconceivable that China can pursue a mainly nonmilitary space program while feeling vulnerable to American military dominance. China has constructed a minimal deterrent force with a few dozen nuclear-armed ICBMs, but U.S. "global engagement," based on missile defense, will quickly undercut the deterrent value of such a force. The Chinese nuclear arsenal will have to be hugely expanded.

Meanwhile, America's "high frontier" weapons capacity will put Chinese commercial space investments at risk. No nation with the ability to alter it would tolerate such imbalance, and over the coming decades there is no doubt that China will have that capacity.

Washington's refusal to negotiate rules, while seeking permanent dominance and asserting the right of preemption, is forcing China into an arms race it does not want. Here, potentially, is the beginning of a next cold war, with a nightmare repeat of open-ended nuclear escalation.

Today, on the surface, U.S.-Chinese relations seem good. Partly in response to Beijing, President Bush, while in Asia, moderated his refusal to offer North Korea nonaggression assurances. Bush met with China's president, Hu Jintao, and reiterated America's congratulations on China's man in space. This week, Chinese defense minister Cao Gangchuan is meeting in Washington with Secretary of Defense Donald Rumsfeld. But a dark undercurrent runs between the two nations, and it is fraught with danger. The problem, as manifest in Geneva, is America's refusal to discuss the problem.

What makes this situation so ominous is that the Pentagon's aggressive strategic planning for space and the Bush administration's rejection of treaty restraints not only are unchallenged in the American political discourse but are largely unnoted. Was the issue even hinted at in the Democrats' recent debate in Detroit? What Democrat has raised the question of the sabotaged Conference on Disarmament? Who is warning of the Bush-sponsored resumption of the arms race? And where is the defense of the idea, once sacred to Americans, that outer space marks a threshold across which human beings must not drag the ancient perversion of war?

15

EVERY OCCUPATION ENDS BADLY

In November of 2003, U.S. combat deaths totaled eighty-one just for those few weeks. Six months after the end of "major combat," the month of President Bush's drive-by visit to Iraq, at Thanksgiving, had been America's worst month yet. Indeed, the radical insecurity of the besieged U.S. force in Iraq could not have been more fully dramatized than by the stealth required for the president's holiday adventure: lies to his parents, an air traffic blackout, fighter escorts, a lights-off landing, wheels-up in less than three hours. If the most fortified enclave in the world is so vulnerable, what of the men, women, and children outside it, whose well-being this war was supposed to restore?

By the time of his visit, it was commonly said that in Iraq George Bush had given America its own West Bank, and increasingly, the U.S. occupation army began to imitate the profoundly failed tactics of the Israeli Defense Force. The demolition of buildings, the jailing of family members of guerrilla fighters, the encircling of whole villages in razor wire, the imposition of identity cards, the ubiquity of checkpoints, the mistreatment of prisoners, targeted assassinations—the brute force of something called Operation Iron Hammer. The humanitarian organization Human Rights Watch would document some of these abuses, but, as is true in the Israeli military, so would critics within the U.S. Army itself.

Such tactics in Israel are no doubt a response to Palestinian terror, but their result has nevertheless been to turn the Jewish state into a fenced-off garrison land. In Iraq, American forces, far from triumphant, are effectively building their own "security barrier." Razor wire as relief. The Iraqi population, once defined as the object of U.S. liberation, has now been redefined as the enemy. And that was where the vaunted Thanksgiving drop-in was so revealing. The world's last and unchallenged military superpower had beaten a retreat behind a brutally maintained barrier, its every sentry as twitchy at the trigger as a Secret Service agent guarding the president.

"I was just looking for a warm meal somewhere," Bush told the three hundred corralled troops at Baghdad International Airport with casual bluster. "Thanks for inviting me to dinner." The president joined the chow line to dish out some food, but, in fact, he did not stay long enough to eat. There was nothing relaxed about it. As an image, his entrance into the hangar-fort of an airport had the feeling of the warden coming down from his tower into the cavernous dining hall to catch an anxious word with the prison guards. Riots brewing? Breakout? Electricity in the air—a warning of trouble.

The visit illuminated a conundrum at the heart of America's Iraq: Arabs are humiliated by this war, but so are the GIs. The latter's very insecurity contradicted every claim of victory they had heard, and the ubiquity of enemies violated the compact under which they were sent to war. So it should come as no surprise that they were fighting it with increasing—and self-defeating—mercilessness. Morally, if not literally, the war was in the process of becoming America's prison.

The Solution Is the Problem

November 4, 2003

It is a fool who defines a problem in such a way that it cannot be solved. That was a watchword of arms-limitation negotiators during the cold war but seems a forgotten lesson now. When President Bush defines the problem of terrorism by decreeing simplistically, "If you're not with us, you're against us," he makes solution of this complex problem impossible. By driving allies away, demonizing the non-aligned, and forcing an either-or choice on people who reject it, he is playing into the hands of the terrorists. In Iraq, more and more average people, including many who hated Saddam Hussein, see America as the enemy. The sixteen U.S. soldiers killed in a helicopter two days ago are the latest to pay the tragic price for Bush's foolishness.

And so in Israel. Ariel Sharon is George Bush's junior partner, but when it comes to defining problems in ways that make solution impossible, Sharon is past master. Israel is traumatized by the despicable suicide-bomber assaults, and a people made to fear even the most mundane of transactions—on a bus, in a café—are given to extreme reactions. Once a struggle is experienced as a fight for survival, public virtues of restraint, moderation, and even compassion for innocents on the other side can go out the window. It's either us or them. Those so ruthless in judgment of Israelis now are failing to grasp the single most important fact of their experience—which is radical fear, not only for themselves and their children personally but for the very survival of their nation. No Palestinian leader has yet emerged who seems willing to say aloud that such Israeli fear is the Palestinian problem, not the Palestinian solution.

If Palestinians, including those who have no use for the suicide killers among them, seem to take satisfaction in this Israeli fear, it is as a match for their own fear. Frightened Palestinians, too, are at the mercy of "us or them." The broad population may reject suicide-murder in theory, but their mostly mute resignation before the fact undergirds the unwillingness of the Palestinian Authority to challenge the militant extremists. Trouble is, to define the problem as the Palestinian nihilists have is to make solution impossible. A national resistance movement that depends on the suicides of individuals can only end in the suicide of the nation.

Meanwhile the Sharon government's policies have recruited many more suicide terrorists to act against Israel than they have deterred. Sharon has made Israel a far more dangerous place today and an extraordinarily burdened one tomorrow. As with Bush, Sharon's definition of the problem has come back to bite him. Now comes news of a new Israeli war machine—a bulldozer that is operated by remote control. The bulldozer, used to destroy the homes of Palestinians linked to terror, however ambiguously, was already a symbol of the troubling policy of general retribution. With such bulldozers unmanned, the Israeli soldiers who were their operators will no longer face the jeopardy of retaliation for demolition. But to what problem is such a bulldozer the solution?

How can Palestinian villagers experience such a machine as anything but a terrifying monster? As if war were not bad enough, this further depersonalization makes it worse—and it must escalate the very fear that fuels violence. Depersonalized war becomes its own justification. Palestinians, confronting faceless demolition, will be more at the mercy of group-think hatred than ever. Israelis, at a distance from the actual work of a machine designed to destroy homes and olive groves, will increasingly avoid the disturbing questions this tactic must give rise to. And so with Israel's new "security fence," aiming to keep terrorists out, but also keeping Israelis detached from the ever worsening Palestinian suffering, to which such a fence can only add.

If the problem between Israelis and Palestinians is defined by each side as the mere existence of the other—there is no solution. Similarly, if America defines its enemy as anyone who is not, as President Bush put it, "with us," we are embarked on a lonely road to nowhere. (Curiously, the president here negatively reverses the position of his favorite political philosopher, Jesus of Nazareth, who said, positively, "Anyone who is not against us is for us" [Mark 9:40].) Now that, with Iraq, Bush has a West Bank of his own, Jerusalem and Washington find themselves on the same dead-end street, mapless.

Among Israelis and Palestinians, remarkably, hope for a new way persists. That is the significance of the so-called Geneva Accords, which build on the near agreement of the Clinton years, and about which Israeli leader Amram Mitzna has recently written. The peace movement in Israel is not dead, and Palestinian voices can be heard denouncing terror and reaching for compromise. Now both sides must redefine the problem in such a way that it can be solved.

Day of Remembrance

November 11, 2003

Veterans Day, in Canada, is called Remembrance Day. On this day, in 1918, World War I ended, and the date was set aside, first, to honor that decimated generation of men who fell into the abyss of the trenches. Eventually, in the United States, Veterans Day became a time to remember all Americans who lost their lives in war, as well as those who served in defense of their country. Today, properly, the prayers of the nation go to the national cemeteries, and its thoughts to those in uniform. We carry in our hearts, especially, the young men and women serving in Iraq. Whatever the moral and political burdens of the war, and however much in dispute remain the decisions of the country's leadership, the people of the armed services deserve to feel the gratitude of their fellow citizens. Today we remember our soldiers, above all.

But the act of memory can be larger. We can recall, equally, what the searing experience of World War I did to the conscience of humanity. That war's unprecedented scale of mechanized death forced a new awareness on men and women that war is no longer tolerable. In their desperation to avoid future wars, they made a first stab at constructing a new social order. Old empires disappeared, new political arrangements were adopted, and finding alternatives to violence became an international priority.

After the "appeasement" of Munich, that idealistic impulse was regarded as a mistake. Hitler and Stalin exploited the soft legacy of November 11, 1918. The urgent requirement of stopping each of them has been taken ever since as proof that the post–World War I dream of peace was not only unrealistic but irresponsible.

And yet, on Remembrance Day, perhaps we can revisit the question. The post–World War I generation was determined never again to send the flower of youth into the maw of destruction. After World War II, in which urban devastation and gas chambers replaced the trenches as signals of evil, the defeated nations reinvented themselves as pacifist peoples, and even the victors resolved to leave war behind. "The weapons of war must be abolished," President Kennedy told the United Nations, "before they abolish us."

But again the vision fell short of being realized. In America, an open-ended embrace of those weapons, justified by the threat from Stalin's children, not only defined a main national purpose but changed the meaning of politics, tied universities to war theory and defense grants, and created an unbreakable economic dependence on military manufacturing. Then the cold war ended, and the whole world seemed ready, at last, for the establishment of a realistic and dependable peace. An ultimate "peace dividend" seemed about to be paid out.

Washington alone, of the great powers, still regarded war as meaningful and war preparation as a priority. The now enemy-less Pentagon insisted on maintaining forever the "hedge" of its nuclear arsenal, and the White House, especially under George W. Bush, replaced the dream of an international order based on diplomatic agreement with the idea of a Pax Americana based on "full-spectrum dominance."

On Remembrance Day, look at what has been forgotten. Washington's view of the world, replicating imperial Prussia's of a hundred years ago, treats the main epiphany of the twentieth century as if it did not happen. As if no lessons were learned in the trenches of Flanders, the fires of Dresden and Tokyo, the fallout of Hiroshima, the countless peasant wars that threw back the great powers, the genocides that sacrificed whole peoples to ferocious versions of the truth.

The much derided human impulse to find another way in fact succeeded, with the nonviolent overthrow of the Soviet empire from within, but that, too, is forgotten in a Washington that prefers to think of itself as the cold-war victor. The rituals of remembrance are all military, and the ethos of war is still made to seem ennobling. Alas, a new generation of the young are being fed with this lie—and into it. That the roster of America's war dead is being added to on this Veterans Day should outrage the nation's conscience.

We began by thinking of Iraq, and we end there, too. Reports come back that many GIs have inadequate equipment and faulty protective gear, but their vulnerability is worse than that. They lack the protection of a clear and just cause. Their enemies multiply in the poison cloud of Bush's callow taunts. Bush has put this country's soldiers in an impossible position, for no good reason. This betrayal of the young is a betrayal of the old, too. Bush's war defiles what the heroes of the last century saw when they saw through war, and betrays the memory of their bravely imagined alternative future—peace—which is the only future there can be.

JFK'S November

November 18, 2003

The chill wind from the north has come. The days fall into darkness with premature finality. Now begins the season that first made human beings afraid of the year. The rotations and revolutions of the earth define the very limits of existence, the controls of light and warmth, yet no direct perception of these movements is possible. Indeed, your daily perception—that the sun is the thing that moves from dawn to dusk—is unreliable, or so science tells you. And now the seasonal evidence is equally perplexing. In the northern climes, this is the time of what seems the sun's retreat. Yet it is only the arc of earth's rotation. Never mind. As the sharp green leaves once turned to follow the sun's course in the sky (the leaves believe it moves), so the winter soul adjusts itself for dark.

So, too, with what the calendar evokes. In America, you prepare to observe the fortieth anniversary of the death of John F. Kennedy, which violated every law of nature except this season's. He had a certain mythic air but was no deity. Yet an illumination failed when he did. The hopes associated with him could have been extinguished, so it felt, only in the desolations of November.

What was it about Kennedy that made him seem a source of light? You know now what chill winds cut through his bones, making him brittle with self-protecting pretense. He seemed an icon of masculine maturity yet secretly raced to the ever ticking clock of an adolescent sexuality. He knew the risks of war from his own experience yet infinitely exacerbated them by unleashing an ungodly missile race. He was sick, while seeming the most fit of men. A wit, with an ever-ready smile, he was never more himself than when brooding alone. You picture him always on that overcast Cape Cod beach, photographed from behind, head bent, trudging through the sand, khakis rolled—and only now it hits you that that, too, was probably November. Grim complacencies of some Thanksgiving weekend.

The odd thing is, the more the air of myth has been dispelled, the more irresistibly human he is made to seem. The more ambiguous his legacy appears, the firmer his grip on your affection. And loyalty. On the cusp of senior discounts yourself, you remain one of Kennedy's children. In him you saw far more than you knew you were seeing at the time. The possibility of public—and private—style, yes. But also, as it turned out, of enduring commitment. Militant cold-war resolution, yes—those missiles—but also an impulse for another way. When that other way showed itself so unexpectedly through the likes of Lech Walesa and Václav Havel, didn't they, by their own accounts, embody something glimpsed long before in Kennedy, too?

His hold on the imagination of a global generation could be, as some say, only that you lost him young. But you say no, it's more than that. Even in the fullness of his own life, which was the first flower of yours, he pointed to the relevance of a realm of experience from which politicians are conditioned to turn away. He made his argument for peace and against the arms race not primarily in geopolitical terms but in human ones. "For in the final analysis, our most basic common link is that we all inhabit this small planet. We all breathe the same air. We all cherish our children's future. And we are all mortal."

In uttering such words at American University a few months before he—and you—were so untimely confronted with his own mortality, Kennedy was expressly addressing the enemy of the United States, and in Moscow his words were taken as unprecedented. For the first time, an American leader was connecting with that frightened, if belligerent, nation—belligerent *because* frightened—as a group of fellow human beings. All mortal. All afraid. All looking for transcending bonds. You thought even at the time that what Kennedy had said might help, because it was the way he had connected all along with you. As events showed—the Partial Test Ban Treaty came soon after, and other similar treaties would save the world—Kennedy had moved the tiller across the wind and changed the course of history. Kennedy gave Lech Walesa his chance.

What happened in November forty years ago sealed forever what you already knew. The chill wind. The fading light. Infinite danger of contingent life on earth. Universal mortality, which is the unexpected source of hope. Grief, oddly, as a source of peace. Death is not proud. When the weather turns, you go inside in search of those you love. These are the notes of the world as it is. Notes of the world, therefore, exactly as you want it.

Of Thanks and Mercy

November 25, 2003

At Thanksgiving time more than thirty years ago—when I was Catholic chaplain at Boston University—I preached yet another sermon on the evils of the American war in Vietnam. I probably took off on U.S. consumerism, too, with a swipe at the Pilgrims of "Plimouth Plantation" for their eventual betrayal of Massasoit, the Wampanoag chief who taught the Europeans how to catch those turkeys. After Mass, a professor whom I admired rebuked me. Speaking of the students who made up the bulk of my congregation, she said, "These beleaguered kids don't need another guilt trip from you. They need to be reminded their lives are filled with good things for which they can be grateful."

I think of that professor now, and of those students. Preaching is not the purpose of this column, but I am aware of its obsessive drumbeat on the subject of President Bush's war. More dead GIs over the weekend, now mutilated. More global terror as the blowback spreads. More opposition in the streets abroad. But at Thanksgiving, can't the columnist let up? War, war, war. What about all the things for which we Americans can be grateful?

As Thanksgiving approaches this year, how can we square our proper impulse to celebrate the bounty of life with a citizen's solemn responsibility to measure the course our government has set, and to reckon with warnings of even rougher water ahead? On Thanksgiving, yes, we pause to reflect on what we have been given, but we also measure what we are making of our abundance. It is a time, therefore, of moral reckoning.

Can we be thankful for our national plenitude without reinforcing the virulent idea that we Americans are somehow destined to be blessed above others? From the Pilgrims forward, Thanksgiving has all too easily been a celebration of American election, and it is not grim sermonizing to sense the danger in that. Massasoit's people *were*, in the name of that election, eventually exterminated.

We prize Thanksgiving because, unlike other holidays, this one does not separate us from one another. A spirit of generalized gratefulness unites a diverse people in the mystery of what lies beyond every creed and doctrine, and no one rushes to put an excluding name on the one to whom thanks are offered. Yet exclusivist religious assumptions undergird the holiday, as they undergird the nation, and it behooves us to be aware of what those assumptions imply. When "God" is routinely thanked for "blessing" America—for making the nation special, for "choosing" us—can we simultaneously affirm that the greatest bounty lies in what we share with the human family, not in what sets us apart? Is it possible to feel grateful, that is, without feeling triumphal? Or to put it religiously, can we thank God without making a possessive claim on God, as if our good fortune is defined by disasters that befall the unelected?

Perhaps what I meant to say to the BU students all those years ago is that we must do two things, instead of one. Yes, we do have so much to be grateful for. Our lives. Our world. Each other. The very day. Thanksgiving is the abundant feast of our rejoicing. And why shouldn't our hearts be full?

And yes, admit it. Our hearts, equally, are sorely pressed with worry. The Bush administration wants us to ignore the human cost of the war. The government barely acknowledges the fallen GIs and carries on as if Iraqi and Afghan dead count for even less. Indeed the Pentagon proudly keeps no count of them. Yet Americans know that there are empty places at Thanksgiving tables this week, and the end of Ramadan for untold Muslim families in two nations is equally a time of grief. And for what? Last week, George W. Bush and Tony Blair offered justifications for their war—"democracy"—that had nothing to do with justifications offered last March—"prevention." Are we not supposed to notice that? And what of months from now, when the purpose of democracy, too, will have failed and faded? What then? We went to war for the fun of it?

Whether democracy ever comes to Iraq and Afghanistan, it defines what America is most grateful for on Thanksgiving. But democracy means citizens are responsible for the actions of government. Bush's war belongs to all of us. There are guilt trips, in other words, but there are also necessary examinations of conscience. Moral second thoughts force themselves upon us. If we are beloved of God, so is our hated enemy. That we human beings, all in the name of virtue, have fallen to killing one another again shows that prayers of thanks must equally be prayers for mercy. And always—pace Massasoit, pace today's war dead—of repentance.

Why Peace Won't Come

December 9, 2003

Why is it so difficult to make peace? In Northern Ireland, die-hard Ian Paisley is back, once more empowered to throw up obstacles to the longed-for resolution of the Protestant-Catholic conflict. Despite overwhelming Irish readiness for reconciliation, the bitter fringe can still poison the future. When Israeli and Palestinian private citizens demonstrate the possibility of agreement by coming to the so-called Geneva Accords, they are treated as mischief makers by many from both sides. When hardened Israeli military figures— an army chief, three former heads of the security service, air force pilots—label Ariel Sharon's approach as self-defeating, they are dismissed as "soft," or even denounced as traitors, as if loyalty to Israel requires devotion to the unbearable status quo. Meanwhile, Palestinians who seek accommodation with Israel are made by some among their own to fear for their lives.

In America, the difficulties of peacemaking exist in a different order. At the end of the cold war, when the enemy against which the United States had defined itself disappeared, this nation's military establishment proved unwilling or unable to change. Because the Pentagon continued to perceive a world of mortal threats, levels of investment in weapons systems—including nuclear—remained extraordinarily high, with the result that American military capabilities have become literally unrivaled. The simple possession of such might, when unmatched, carries with it an irresistible momentum toward use, which in large part explains why the United States now goes to war even when it is unnecessary to do so.

Iraq, of course, is showing two things that are wrong with this situation. First, the perception of threats that justify such military assumptions is rooted not in the actuality of the threat (there are no Iraqi weapons of mass destruction) but in the a priori need to vindicate those assumptions, since they consume so much treasure and are a source of so much national meaning. And second, even unparalleled military supremacy is irrelevant to winning hearts and minds—which is always the endgame of war. The more we smash those who hate us, the more they hate us, and the more of them there are. Iraq is showing that American firepower is precisely what creates America's enemies.

A curtain was lifted last week on the fundamental cause of this destructive situation. Clearly exposed, if only briefly, was the real reason that the Pentagon clung to cold-war thinking even after the Soviet threat was gone, as well as the root source of George W. Bush's own hair-trigger war policy. A week ago yesterday, Philip M. Condit shamefully resigned as CEO of Boeing, the giant aircraft manufacturer. In the days preceding that disgrace, Boeing had acknowledged that other senior executives had committed ethical violations—if not violations of the law—in pursuit of a $20 billion contract with the U.S. Air Force for the construction of a new fleet of tanker aircraft. The chief financial officer and a vice president were fired, causing Secretary of Defense Donald Rumsfeld to begin his own inquiry.

But the scandal was not just Boeing's. The hugely expensive tanker project had been nursed along by, among others, Richard Perle, an intimate of Secretary Rumsfeld and President Bush—and a beneficiary last year, as the *New York Times* reported, of a $20 million Boeing investment in the financial company he heads. Furthermore, the aircraft project had advanced with Capitol Hill support that had been secured by Boeing lobbyists and campaign contributions. In 2002, Boeing received almost $20 billion in federal contracts, while spending almost $4 million on lobbyists and almost $2 million to help friendly legislators win elections.

Critics like Senator John McCain (R-Arizona) had argued that the air force did not need the new planes at all, but hard-pressed Boeing needed the business, and the air force depends on such endless rounds of gross expenditure. If there is a brand-new fleet of tanker aircraft, can a brand-new fleet of the bombers they service be far behind? Whether there is an actual, real-world need for any of this is simply not the question. America's global military posture is defined not by authentic requirements of national security but by the profit-driven collusion of contractors, Pentagon officials, politicians, and defense-friendly pundits. The obvious waste inherent in this corruption is one outrage, but the more grievous problem is what it leads to in the world. What it has led to in the broken cities of Iraq.

Why is it so difficult to make peace? In places like Northern Ireland and the Middle East, the answer is all about the passions of grief, unforgiven wounds, fears that won't yield. But in the United States, the answer is far more coarse. Not grief, hurt, or fear. Alas, the answer is money. War remains the turbine that drives America's economy—therefore, its politics, its shallow pride.

Captives: Hussein and Hiroshima

December 16, 2003

The news stopped America: Saddam Hussein captured—not in some kind of command bunker, running the guerrilla war, but in a "spider hole," with mice and rats. For the last two days, interruption was the motif as the report upended assumptions about the war in Iraq, the war on terrorism, the Israeli-Palestinian conflict, the U.S. presidential election, the financial markets, even the shopping season. Good news all around, if you can believe the first reactions. December 13, 2003, was being described as a historic day because of the bedraggled man found cowering in the dark.

Thinking especially of Saddam's history as a longtime murderer of Kurds and Shi'ites, a range of people declared a day of celebration—from Baghdad passersby, to U.S. soldiers, to Howard Dean, to television anchors, to editorial writers. I might have said so, too, except for the meeting I was coming from when the news came to me.

I had spent December 13 in Washington at a conference organized to protest the Smithsonian's new National Air and Space Museum exhibit that opened yesterday. The centerpiece is the *Enola Gay*, the B-29 bomber that dropped the atomic bomb on Hiroshima. In 1995, a previous exhibit drew fire from veterans' groups and the Air Force Association because curators had provided "context" which suggested that President Truman's decision to use the weapon was not uncontroversial, even at the time. (Eisenhower's opposition was noted.) That exhibit was abruptly canceled.

The exhibit that opened yesterday provides no context for the display of the *Enola Gay*. Not even the casualties it caused (more than 140,000 deaths) are noted. The bomber is being displayed, the current museum director said, "in all of its glory as a magnificent technological achievement." A group of historians protested "such a celebratory exhibit" with a statement that drew hundreds of supporting signatures from scholars, and on December 13 more than a dozen of them, together with numerous Japanese survivors of the atomic bombings, came together. The issue is the construction and reconstruction of history, a question not only of the past but of the present and the future. If America remembers its first use of nuclear weapons as morally uncomplicated—or worse, as an event to be celebrated—its present commitment to a huge nuclear arsenal and its future readiness, under Bush policies, to build "usable" nukes will seem acceptable.

At issue in how the capture of Saddam Hussein is understood, also, is the construction and reconstruction of history. The melodrama of the seizure should not be allowed to obscure the fact that Saddam Hussein, by this point in the war, had long since stopped being the crucial issue. Hussein was a bloody tyrant whose crimes should be adjudicated, but to assess the meaning of America's war in Iraq with that as the key justification would be like remembering August 6, 1945, only with reference to the atrocities committed by the Japanese imperial army. The United States did not attack Iraq because of Hussein's wickedness. (The world is rife with wicked tyrants.) It did so because Hussein posed an imminent threat to his neighbors, and America, and there was no other way to stop that threat. Additionally, Washington tied Hussein to 9-11 (an al Qaeda–Iraq meeting in Prague), making the war against Iraq necessary to the war on terrorism.

It is already clear that these justifications were false. Even if Hussein now revealed a stock of chemical or biological agents, the question of "imminence" would remain, because postinvasion investigations have established that no weaponized agents were ready to be used. And as for the Hussein connection with 9-11 (what meeting in Prague?), that has been exposed as fantasy.

The war in Iraq is more the result of America's agenda than Hussein's. The violence in Iraq (multiple bombings since Hussein's capture) is a result of Washington's terrible miscalculations. The threat from terrorism (Pakistan's leader nearly assassinated) has been made worse by Bush policies. The structure of American alliances has been needlessly undermined (hence James Baker's mission to world capitals). America's extreme belligerence is imitated elsewhere (Israeli prime minister Ariel Sharon's faith in "overwhelming force"), making the world far more dangerous. These issues must not be blotted out in the glare of the media celebration of Saddam Hussein's capture. That he was caught in a hole, obviously unrelated to the guerrilla resistance, is a turning point in nothing that matters now: not in restoring order to Iraq; not in rebuilding structures of international law; not in thwarting terrorism; not in stemming the proliferation of weapons of mass destruction; not in reconciling the West and the world of Islam.

Such is the damage following from Bush's war. For what? The question about the Bush war and the Truman decision to use the bomb is the same: was it necessary? Even if Bush hopes we won't ask that question, history will.

A Year in America

December 30, 2003

This has been the year of American democracy. The values of this nation have never been more dramatically on display before the world. *Freedom* has been the watchword, from Operation Iraqi

Freedom to the coming Freedom Tower at ground zero in New York. In a period of enormous stress, America has pulled itself together, freshly defined its beliefs, and begun to press them on others. Washington aims at nothing less than the propagation of U.S. notions of civil order and social justice everywhere. And why shouldn't citizens be proud?

But this vision throws a shadow. Contradictions of American idealism have also been manifest with rare clarity this year—and not only in wars abroad. A signal event took place in Massachusetts as the year approached its end. A jury made up of citizens of one of the relatively few states that outlaws the death penalty nevertheless imposed it in the federal murder case against Gary Lee Sampson, the brutal killer of Jonathan Rizzo and Philip McCloskey. As advocates of the death penalty hoped, this decision in the heart of a community that has long rejected capital punishment—the last execution in Massachusetts was in 1947—speeds America's complete return to frontier justice.

Even in a period when the fallibility of the death penalty has been repeatedly exposed, roughly two out of three Americans still support it. I note regularly how George W. Bush, as governor of Texas, saw to the execution of 152 people—and is proud of it. That the blood of this slow-motion massacre on the president's hands is a political asset says everything about current American values. Where once leading Democrats opposed capital punishment, now, as the *Boston Globe*'s Brian C. Mooney reports, they (i.e., the Clintons, Gore, Dean, Kerry, Lieberman, Edwards, Gephardt, Clark) support it. As the world's democracies go in one direction on this question, the United States goes in another.

This grisly embrace of death is only part of the year's story of crime and punishment, American style. In August, the rapist of children, John J. Geoghan, was murdered by a fellow inmate at a prison in Massachusetts. As Geoghan's crimes had led to the exposure of the abusive secrets of the Catholic Church, his punishment led to revelations of what America's "criminal justice system" actually involves. Sadistic treatment by guards and a lawless culture in which prisoners are allowed to prey on each other—are these exceptions or the rule? In America, there is no question of an outright acceptance of torture, and U.S. sponsorship of democracy abroad insists on that (or did before the war on terrorism). Yet the U.S. prison system, with many abusive guards and unchecked sadist-inmates, effectively assumes torture as part of punishment. If Geoghan were not notorious, his fate would have gone unnoted.

But the year just ending marked other milestones toward a reckoning with the real meaning of American democracy. In late October, in a speech in Fall River, the Honorable Robert A. Mulligan, chief administrative judge of Massachusetts, noted current characteristics of U.S. criminal justice. The American prison population recently went over 2 million for the first time, putting the United States ahead of Russia as the world capital of incarceration. Add to that number those on parole or probation, and the total under "correctional" control grows to 7 million. Thirty years ago, one in a thousand Americans was locked up; today, almost five in a thousand are. In famously liberal Massachusetts, the prison population has grown, since 1980, from under six thousand to almost twenty-three thousand. In 2003, for the first time, the amount of money Massachusetts spent on prisons was more than what it spent on higher education.

These statistics accumulate a punishing weight falling more on African-American males than anyone else, and from that springs the year's fundamental epiphany. Justice? Democracy? In the United States, according to Judge Mulligan, one in three African-American males between the ages of twenty and thirty is "under correctional control." In places like Baltimore and Washington, more than half are. The number of African-American men in college is less than the number of those under supervision of the courts. And why? Such facts reveal far more about the way justice is administered in America than about the moral character of any group. Judge Mulligan, for one, points to the "war on drugs" as key, a war that has seen the rate of imprisonment of drug offenders jump by 700 percent since 1980; a war that depends on narrowly targeted law enforcement and on mandatory prison sentences. In 2002, 80 percent of those receiving

such sentences were minorities. The war on drugs has been dispro-
portionately a war on young black men.

The year 2003: The death penalty set loose. Prison populations
setting records. Effective torture as part of punishment. A system of
racial injustice that rivals slavery. American values across the world.
Please.

16

THE PASSIONS OF WAR

The day that John Kerry effectively won the Democratic nomination for president, in early March, was the most violent day in Iraq since the end of the invasion. At least 185 Shi'ite Muslims were killed in suicide-bomb attacks in Baghdad and Karbala, bringing to more than four hundred the total number of Iraqi civilians killed by terrorist bombings in a month. Another forty-five Shi'ites were killed by unknown gunmen in Pakistan. The attacks were assumed to have been carried out by Sunni militants, yet Shi'ite leaders immediately placed part of the blame for the new violence on the United States. "Down, down America!" cried mourners in Karbala.

In Russia, military forces had just come off the first large-scale combat maneuvers in years, including a simulated nuclear attack against an unnamed enemy that could only have been the United States. Under Vladimir V. Putin, Russia's defense expenditures had tripled, even though its conventional forces were still in a state of near collapse. Russian military power had become almost entirely defined by nuclear weapons, yet there, too, Moscow's strategic capacity seemed uncertain. In the exercises, with Putin looking on, two missile launches from submarines failed. Once the thing to fear was Soviet superiority. Now humiliatingly evident Russian decline seemed hardly less dangerous.

In the United States, the political discussion suddenly seemed re-focused on domestic matters, from job losses to trade policy to the question of marriage rights for homosexuals. Under George W. Bush, defense spending had grown by 50 percent, and while the Bush deficits were regularly decried by Democrats, this—one of their main sources—was not to be discussed. Democrats had fallen into a routine of criticizing the Bush administration's war policies, but offered little in the way of different policies of their own.

As Senator John Kerry closed in on the primary victories that would clinch his nomination, he found himself competing with Mel Gibson's *The Passion of the Christ* as an item of conversation. In its first week, the film played to larger audiences than any R-rated movie in history. Why did this film so resonate with Americans? Many believers saw the film in a spirit of devotion, but hidden chords also seemed to have been struck. The role of Jews became a flashpoint, and while Iraqis were crying, after the Karbala bombings, "No, no America! No, no Israel!" Americans found themselves confronted anew with the oldest question of antisemitism. The oldest question, that is, of how a society defines itself positively by defining "the other" negatively.

The Passion of the Christ emphatically portrayed Jesus as a victim. Were Americans consoled by a film which perhaps played on some of their own unarticulated feelings of victimhood? Was the film's hyper-violence tied to the Age of Terrorism's subliminal conviction that purification comes through mayhem? It was hard to dismiss the sense that free-floating, as yet unnamed anxieties in a broad population were being displaced onto a special-effects story of the extreme suffering and destruction of the Christ and the extreme evil of swarthy ones. On the day after Kerry won his Super Tuesday primaries, George W. Bush unveiled his first campaign advertisement. It showed the ruined hulk of the Twin Towers, and firemen carrying a flag-draped corpse out of the rubble. It had no title, but might have been called "The Passion of Americans," or even "The Passion of George W. Bush."

But McGovern Was Right

January 6, 2004

The Democrats see a hobgoblin under the bed, and his name is George McGovern. Low-grade panic is beginning to set in as pundits forecast a repeat of 1972: "As Massachusetts goes, so goes the District of Columbia." The prospect of "another McGovern" whets the appetite of Bush partisans, while generating gloom and shame among Democrats. Howard Dean, for one, flees the association, while other candidates tar him with it.

Here's the problem: in 1972, George McGovern was right. If there is shame attached to that election, it is America's for having so dramatically elected the wrong man. Apart from the rank dishonesty of Richard Nixon and his administration (a pattern of lies that would soon be exposed in Watergate), there were two world-historic issues that defined that election, and on both Nixon was wrong. Nineteen seventy-two was a fork in the road, and history shows that the United States made a turn into a moral wilderness from which it has yet to emerge.

Obviously, the first issue was the Vietnam War. Having been elected in 1968 promising "peace with honor," Nixon was well on the way to neither. Ground forces had been "Vietnamized" (the last U.S. combat units would be withdrawn a few months after the election), but a savage air war was under way throughout Vietnam (Nixon had spread it into Cambodia, too, disastrously). After the traumas of 1968, Americans had willfully accepted Nixon's sleight of hand on Vietnam, and the news media cooperated. As one NBC television producer recalled, news executives decided that, after 1969, the "story" would be peace negotiations, not combat.

By 1972, Americans did not want to hear about Vietnam. They

pretended that Nixon had ended the war. "And he *has* ended the war," the NBC producer said that year, "because you don't see the war on the tube any more. So the war has ended, though we are bombing the hell out of those poor people, more than ever." (On the media's failure, see Godfrey Hodgson's *In Our Time.*) Five weeks after the election, Nixon would order the Christmas bombing of Hanoi, the most ferocious air attack since the firebombing of Japan. Instead of peace with honor, there would be defeat with disgrace— after two more years of carnage. George McGovern faced the American people with the unwanted truth of what their government was doing. That is a source of shame?

But there was an even larger issue separating the two candidates in 1972. Nixon was the avatar of America's tragic cold-war mistake. His entire career was informed by a paranoid assessment of the Soviet threat. "It's a we/they world," Paul Nitze said when he served in the Nixon administration. "It's us against the Soviets. Either we get them first, or they get us first." This apocalyptic way of perceiving the enemy was already outmoded in the early 1970s, but it would take American statesmen another two decades to see it. Nitze, Richard Perle, Donald Rumsfeld, Paul Wolfowitz, Richard Cheney— such apostles of the "we/they world" were empowered in 1972, and if their bipolar vision had not been undercut (by Mikhail Gorbachev), the cold war would still be on. Indeed, these men of 1972 are back, aiming to create another.

George McGovern was an opponent of the "we/they" vision. A prophet of détente, he was vindicated by history. He offered America a way out of the trap that opposes "realist" and "idealist" perspectives. McGovern understood not only that the Vietnam War was wrong but that, in the nuclear age, the realist is the one who sees that structures of war itself must be systematically dismantled. One hears the complaint from today's Democrats that McGovern, a decorated World War II bomber pilot, did not tout his war hero's record, but that entirely misses his most important point—that fear of war and glorification of war are simply not to be exploited for political purposes, whether at the personal or the national level. What

McGovern the candidate refused to do was what American presidents should refuse to do.

George W. Bush obscenely exploits war for his own purposes. He sponsors a paranoid assessment of what threatens America now, and draws political advantage from the resulting fear. The news media propagate that fear. Pundits continue the false opposition between "realist" and "idealist" visions, marginalizing anyone who dares question Garrison-America. Meanwhile, the unnecessary Bush war rages, and not even the steady death toll of young GIs makes much news anymore. If a Democrat running for president of the United States dares to speak the truth about these things, it is no shame. And before feeling gloom about next November, ask what it means if the Democrat, to win, must do what Nixon did.

State of the Union

January 20, 2004

In his State of the Union address tonight, President Bush will speak of the nightmare he has created in Iraq as if it is a dream come true. Yet the contrary facts of the American misadventure have begun to speak for themselves. When the awful story of the Iraq war is written, the two weeks just past may be recognized as a time when the deception and disarray of Bush's policy were made clearer than ever. These are events to which the president will not refer tonight, yet taken together, they reveal the true state of his disunion:

- On January 4, the tape of a belligerent voice claiming to be Osama bin Laden was broadcast on Al Jazeera television. The next day the CIA confirmed that it was bin Laden, and that, made recently, the tape showed he is still alive.

- On January 8, the Carnegie Endowment for International Peace rebutted major Bush claims on Iraq, concluding that "administration officials systematically misrepresented the threat from Iraq WMD and ballistic missile programs."
- On January 11, on television, former treasury secretary Paul O'Neill confirmed reports in Ron Suskind's book *The Price of Loyalty* that the Bush administration planned war against Iraq before 9-11, "from the very beginning."
- On January 12, a paper published at the Army War College described the war on terrorism as "strategically unfocused." The assessment from within the military itself blasted the Bush-led effort because it "promises more than it can deliver, and threatens to dissipate U.S. military resources in an endless and hopeless search for absolute security."
- On January 13, the Bush administration reversed itself to announce that Canada could participate in contracts for the rebuilding of Iraq. Washington's punitive rejection of countries that had opposed the war was not working.
- On January 14, Human Rights Watch issued a report that held some U.S. tactics in Iraq to be in violation of the Geneva Convention, including home demolitions that "did not meet the test of military necessity." The report accused the army of arresting and holding Iraqi civilians simply because they were relatives of fugitives.
- On January 14, it was reported that the captured Saddam Hussein was in possession of a letter he had written instructing his followers not to throw in with foreign fighters, further puncturing the myth that Hussein was in active alliance with al Qaeda.
- On January 14, a secret study conducted by the U.S. Army Command in Baghdad was published. It faulted the army's tactics in Iraq as needlessly confrontational, and it asserted—against the claims of the Bush administration—that "the capture of Saddam will have nominal effect within Iraqi borders."

- On January 15, responding to Shi'ite leader Ayatollah Ali Sistani, thirty thousand Iraqis took to the streets to protest American plans for transition to Iraqi rule, making even more unlikely Washington's fantasy that Iraq will not join Iran as a Shi'ite-dominated state. Will that put Iraq back on the Axis of Evil?
- On January 15, the Bush administration was reported to be considering opening Iraq reconstruction contracts to France, Germany, and Russia, as it had to Canada. Washington is scrambling.
- By January 19, yesterday, the Bush administration had reversed itself to press at the United Nations for urgent help with the transition to Iraqi self-government, the clearest sign yet that Washington's go-it-alone policy had failed.

In the days before the State of the Union address one year ago, the Bush administration denigrated U.N. weapons inspector Hans Blix, dismissing the inspections and containment strategy favored at the United Nations. Secretary of Defense Donald Rumsfeld mocked what he called "old Europe." Secretary of State Colin Powell promised to provide compelling evidence of Saddam Hussein's imminent threat. The State Department published an indictment of Saddam titled *Apparatus of Lies.*

In the State of the Union address itself, President Bush bragged that he had "liberated" Afghanistan—a country which today, except for a small zone around Kabul, belongs to warlords. He boasted that "one by one terrorists are learning the meaning of American justice"—thinking, perhaps, of the concentration camp at Guantánamo Bay, where American justice is mocked. Bush detailed a long list of Saddam Hussein's weapons of mass destruction. He said that Iraq had obtained "uranium from Africa," and he referred to certain metal tubes to suggest a nuclear weapons program. He said that Saddam Hussein "aids and protects" al Qaeda, and, projecting into the future, he linked the 9-11 hijackers with Saddam. He promised that

Colin Powell would provide evidence of the link between Saddam and the terrorists.

The president set a rigorous standard last year, constructing an apparatus of lies it will be hard to match tonight. One bald falsehood not even he will dare repeat: "We seek peace," Bush said a year ago. "We strive for peace."

Dying for a Mistake

February 3, 2004

Since chief weapons inspector David A. Kay's testimony before a Senate committee last week, the public focus has fixed upon mistaken intelligence that led to the American invasion of Iraq. Democrats are pounding the issue, which may actually be fine with President Bush. Events of a year ago are not the urgent question. Democrats should be asking: what about Iraq right now?

No one misses Saddam Hussein, but the unjustified method of his removal has set in motion a train of terrible consequences. Politicians, including the leading Democratic presidential candidates, would rather talk about past American "mistakes" than present policies or future decisions for the simple reason that the present and the future of Iraq involve certain tragedy for which the United States is responsible. Such is the climate of chaos that the Bush aggression has created that there is no clear way forward, and bad things are going to happen in Iraq—no matter what Washington does now. Such unhappy news can sink the politician who dares admit it. Better to advance the conventional wisdom that, however mistaken the origins of this conflict, there is no choice now but to "see it through"—if only to "support the troops." Bush critics suggest that the coalition forces need to be more fully "internationalized," but otherwise most seem to accept an open-ended U.S. occupation of Iraq. We broke it; we have to fix it. For the sake of "credibility," or even "honor," we must "stay the course"—even if the American presence itself causes the chaos.

In counterpoint testimony to David Kay's from thirty-three years ago, young John Kerry famously asked a difficult question: "How do you ask a man to be the last man to die for a mistake?" After Kay's revelations, even the Bush administration seems ready to admit that the *past* justifications of the war in Iraq were "a mistake" (if only the CIA's), but what will it take for the U.S. government to admit that the *present* course of policy is, equally, a mistake? If the war was a mistake in its very origins, it is a mistake in its prosecution. As the young Kerry was surely loath to apply the word *mistake* to a conflict that had killed and maimed some of his friends, an American leader must be loath to make such an admission to the families of more than five hundred dead U.S. soldiers. Yet what they died for was clearly not the noble cause as defined by Colin Powell a year ago, nor the "freedom" of which President Bush blithely speaks. Some American leader, in profound repentance, must acknowledge the awful truth to those families: *"Your sons and daughters died for a mistake."*

Only such truth telling at home will make possible what must be done immediately in Iraq. If our getting into the unnecessary war was wrong, our carrying it on is wrong. The U.S. military presence in Iraq, no matter how intended, has itself become the affront around which opposition fighters are organizing themselves. GIs in their Humvees, U.S. convoys bristling with rifles, well-armed coalition checkpoints, heavily fortified compounds flying the American flag— all of this fuels resentment among an ever broader population, including Saddam's enemies. It justifies the growing number of jihadis whose readiness to kill through suicide has become the real proliferation problem. The occupation is its source and must end. "The day I take office as president of the United States," a true American leader would declare, "I will order the immediate withdrawal of the entire American combat force in Iraq."

And so with American commercial interests in Iraq. Certainly, the United States has the obligation to enable the efficient repair of the social and civic structures destroyed in the war, but not in the mode of Halliburton. Such infuriating corruption also fuels the war. Therefore, even while the U.S. Treasury funds an international reconstruction effort through the United Nations, American companies—especially oil companies—should be barred from making profits off this "mistake." No president has the authority to forbid the commercial initiatives of corporations acting abroad, but powerful inhibitions can be put in place through regulation and licensing. "When I am president," a true American leader would declare, "I will do all in my power to fight the fact and perception that we have in any way profited from our invasion of Iraq."

Ending occupation and preventing exploitation are, of course, corollary to the far more difficult acknowledgment a new president must make—to grief-struck American families, to the Iraqi people, and to the world: "What we did in Iraq was a mistake. Innocent people died. The fabric of international order was torn. We see that and have moved to undo it. But there is no undoing the unnecessary suffering we caused. And for that we are sorry."

The Real Passions of Christ

February 10, 2004

Can a pious Christian make *too* much of the passion of the Christ? Can the suffering of Jesus be remembered as *too* bloody? Or *too* unique, for that matter? Can the crucifixion be made *too* central to Christian faith? Indeed, can that faith be distorted by an overemphasis on blood and cruelty, into a perversion of the message Jesus preached—or even into a source of new cruelty?

These are questions in my mind as I sit outside the small chapel in Jerusalem that marks the very place where Jesus died. Sensational news stories and a clever publicity campaign lead me to associate Golgotha with Mel Gibson's *The Passion of the Christ*. I am aware of the danger of prejudgment, having not seen the film, yet Gibson's many comments and selective screenings of excerpts, which I have seen, are enough to have me thinking of it here. The possibility that the film levels the old "Christ-killer" charge against Jews prompted my first concern.

But an afternoon's meditation at the place where Christians have remembered the death of Jesus for sixteen hundred years raises the question of whether we have more broadly misused that memory. This shrine memorializing Golgotha is, in fact, a kind of side chapel in a much larger church which gives overwhelming emphasis to the memory of Jesus being raised from the dead. One sees this in the fact that the church is called the Holy Sepulcher by Latin Christians, indicating the tomb, not the execution place, and even more in the fact that Eastern Orthodox Christians call it the Church of the Resurrection. A celebration of the joy of resurrection trumps the grief of crucifixion in every way here.

In the first centuries of the church, the bloody crucifixion had little hold on the religious imagination of Christians. Scratched on the walls of the ancient catacombs, for example, one finds drawings of the communion cup, the loaf of bread, the fish—but rarely if ever the cross. Early Christians revered the death of Jesus, of course, but they evoked it metaphorically, not literally, more with the image of going down into the waters of baptism than with nails and blood. The cross comes into the center of Christian symbolism only in the fourth century, with Constantine and his mother, Helena, who is remembered as having discovered it here, only yards from where I sit. But even then, the cross was taken more as a token of resurrection than of brutal death.

It was only in the medieval period that the Latin church began to put the violent death of Jesus at the center of faith, but that theology was tied to a broader cultural obsession with death, related to plagues, millennialism, and the carnage of the Crusades. Grotesquely literal renditions of the crucifixion came into art only as self-flagellation and other "mortifications" came into devotion. Good Friday began to replace Easter as the high point of the liturgical year. And God came to be understood as cruel enough to will the Son's agonizing death as the only way to "atone" for the sins of fallen humanity.

Such is the piety into which many Christians, including Catholics of my generation, were born. From all reports, it is the piety on display in Mel Gibson's movie. But in nothing have the reforms of the Second Vatican Council been more significant than in a rejection of that piety and the return of the Resurrection to the center of faith. That is why, in the Catholic Church, white vestments replaced black at funeral services, why Easter rites have been reemphasized, why the cross itself, in church architecture, is downplayed. All of this is to say that death was not the purpose of Jesus' life, but only one part of a story that stretches from incarnation at Bethlehem, to life as a Jew in Nazareth, to preaching in Galilee, to a courageous challenge to Roman imperialism in Jerusalem, to permanent faith in the God of Israel whose promise is fulfilled in resurrection. In this full context, the death of Jesus can be seen as a full signal of his humanity—and more. In being crucified, Jesus was not uniquely singled out for the most extreme suffering ever inflicted, but was joined to thousands of his fellow Jews who said no to Rome—and who suffered similarly for it.

Leaving aside questions of taste, or even of prurience in displays of graphic violence, any rendition of the death of Jesus that attributes sacred meaning to suffering, or cruelty to "God's will," not to mention special guilt to Jews, is a betrayal of the real passions of Christ—which were for truth, for love, and for life. Life, as he put it, to the full.

A Wall Across the World

February 17, 2004

A fence, by definition, looks different from its opposite sides. Here in Israel the Sharon government is constructing what it calls a "terrorism prevention fence," an uncrossable barrier that will run hundreds of miles along a circuitous route dividing Israeli and Palestinian areas. In populated places, it is a high cement wall. From the side of Israel, the dull gray construction glimpsed mostly from a distance can appear as an affront on the landscape, and as an unpleasant reminder of the garrison character of a state under siege, but it is seen also as a remedy to Israeli borderlessness and a necessary bulwark against suicide-murder. The problem the fence aims to solve is real, but it causes new problems. Israel's Supreme Court will hear arguments against the fence soon, and in the Israeli press it is fiercely debated. The government is now considering adjustments to its route. But even many Israelis who regret the paralysis of the peace process can see the fence as a signal of security.

From the Palestinian side, the construction is a wall pure and simple, and objections have been registered with the International Court of Justice. Seen up close, as the barrier is by the villagers upon whose territory it intrudes, it is a looming monstrosity that offends in numerous ways. First, it is a running monument of destruction, as bulldozers obliterate property, olive groves, farmland, wells, and playing fields. The wall interrupts roads and bisects towns and cities. Members of families are separated, workers are impeded from getting to jobs, pregnant women and other patients find themselves cut off from doctors and hospitals. Because the fence-and-wall meanders along a serpentine path designed to protect as many Israelis as possible, its loops isolate dozens of Arab villages and create numerous Palestinian enclaves, effective cages. Most disturbingly, the obstruction veers far from the 1967 Green Line border in numerous places, and thus represents a unilateral Israeli appropriation of disputed land, a repudiation of the hope for a negotiated resolution to the conflict over territory. The barrier can kill the peace process once and for all.

The 1.5 million Palestinians who live in the West Bank already endure unprecedented levels of impoverishment and social collapse, with rampant unemployment among adults and shocking malnourishment among children. The wall promises to make all this worse— and perhaps permanent. The Palestinian people have been grotesquely betrayed by a corrupt leadership. In despair, Palestinians have broadly tolerated the nihilist violence of their most extreme elements. But the Palestinian people did not create the disaster within which they live, and the wall is a further symbol of that powerlessness. They can see it only as a new source of rage and despair, which are the root causes of the very terror the Israeli "security fence" intends to protect against.

There is a certain kind of American narcissism that sees every world problem as originating in Washington, but still a visitor here sees connections. George W. Bush has thrown up a wall across the world, exacerbating an "us versus them" bipolarity that grips this and other places. Bush sponsors the illusion that deep sources of terror can be ignored in favor of a civilizational "clash" that efficiently feeds those sources. The failure of this approach is on full display in Iraq, which is quickly becoming the rallying point for whole new jihadist belligerence as Islamic extremists take up Bush's challenge.

As for the crisis here in Israel, there is deep significance in the fact that it did not merit even a mention in the president's recent State of the Union address. Washington has done nothing real to support the emergence of moderate Palestinian leadership, and Palestinian Muslims as a whole, perceiving a rising tide of hatred of Islam in the West, are understandably inclined to regard America as the enemy. The Sharon government, meanwhile, sees itself as waging the frontline battle of the war on terrorism, but that war's futile

strategies were drawn up in Washington. Bush's example has reinforced the most self-defeating impulses of the Israeli government.

But there is a big difference between Israel and America. Israelis,
unlike Americans, confront mortal danger on a daily basis, with
buses and cafés as occasions of threat, children as targets. No American has the right to judge Israeli responses glibly. But even less
should Americans ignore how Washington's abdication makes things
worse for both sides here. Having walked away from this conflict,
Bush betrays a long-standing American commitment to advance a
negotiated peace. He leaves Israelis and Palestinians both to their increasing desperation, an indifference that betrays America's ideal of
justice and its foundational friendship with Israel. The wall rises in
Palestinian towns and villages because Israelis and Palestinians cannot resolve their conflict alone. But Israelis and Palestinians, alas, are
together on the wrong side of the wall that George W. Bush has
built.

An Obscene Portrayal of Christ's Passion

February 24, 2004

The Passion of the Christ, by Mel Gibson, is an obscene movie. It will
incite contempt for Jews. It is a blasphemous insult to the memory
of Jesus Christ. It is an icon of religious violence.

Like many others, I anticipated the Gibson film warily, especially
because an uncritical rendition of problematic Gospel texts that un-
fairly blame "the Jews" for the death of Jesus threatened to resuscitate the old "Christ-killer" myth. But seeing Gibson's film convinces
me that it does far worse than that. His highly literal representation
of the Passion narratives, his visual presentation of material that, in

the tradition, is meant to be read and heard, together with his preju-
diced selection of details and his invention of dialogue and incidents
cause one serious problem, very much at the expense of Jews. But
the impact of his perverse imagination on a sacred story, coming at a
time when the world is newly riven with primal violence in the
name of God, threatens an even more grievous problem. The subject
of this film, despite its title, is not the Passion of the Christ but the
sick love of physical abuse, engaged in for power.

Jews as presented in this movie are overwhelmingly negative. Roman soldiers brutally execute Jesus, but Pontius Pilate is a good man,
who stands in dramatic contrast to Caiaphas, the Jewish High Priest.
Going well beyond anything in the Gospels, Gibson's film emphasizes Roman virtue and Jewish venality by inventions like these:

- Pilate's wife, Claudia, is an actual heroine, who aligns herself
  with Mary. Mary, terrified for her son, appeals to benign Romans against the hostile Jewish crowd.
- Claudia is the woman behind the Romans. Her dramatic coun-
  terpart, the woman behind the Jews, is none other than a fe-
  male Satan.
- Pilate kindly offers Jesus a cup of water. Pilate orders Jesus
  flogged, but only to satisfy the Jewish bloodthirst.
- The Jews are expressly indicted by the Good Thief, who, after
  the crucified Jesus says, "Father, forgive them . . . ," tells Caiaphas that "He prays for you." Jews are indicted by Jesus, who
  consoles Pilate by telling him, "It is he who has delivered me to
  you who has the greater sin."

The centerpiece of the film is a long sequence constructed
around the flogging of Jesus. It is the most brutal film episode I have
ever seen, approaching the pornographic. Just when the viewer
thinks the flaying of the skin of Jesus can get no crueler, it does.
Blood, flesh, bone, teeth, eyes, eye sockets, ribs, limbs—the man is
skinned alive, taken apart. In these endless moments, with the tor-
turers escalating instruments and vehemence both, the film puts

Gibson's decadent *Braveheart* imagination on full display. On-screen and in the theater, there is nothing to do but look away. Long after the filmgoer has had enough, even the Romans stop. And here is the anti-Semitic use to which this grotesque scene is put: *Then* Jesus is returned to the crowd of "the Jews," and *then*, as if they are indifferent to what the filmgoer has just been physically revolted by, "the Jews" demand the crucifixion of Jesus. Not even the most savage carnage a filmgoer has ever seen is enough for these monsters. This scene, with the Jewish crowd overriding tender Pilate, is the most lethal in the Scriptures, but in Gibson's twist, "the Jews" are made to seem more evil than ever.

There is no resurrection in this film. A stone is rolled back, a zombie-Jesus is seen in profile for a second or two, and that's it. But there is a reason for this. In Gibson's theology, the resurrection has been rendered unnecessary by the infinite capacity of Jesus to withstand pain. Not the Risen Jesus but the Survivor Jesus. Gibson's violence fantasies, as ingenious as perverse, are, at bottom, a fantasy of infinite male toughness. The inflicting of suffering is the action of the film, and the dramatic question is, How much pain can Jesus take? The religious miracle of this Passion is that he can take it all. Jesus Christ Superstoic. His wondrous capacity to suffer is what converts bystander soldiers, and it is what saves the world.

In an act of perverse editing, Gibson has Jesus say "I make all things new" as his torment approaches climax, as if cruel mayhem brings renewal. When Jesus cries out near the end, "My God, why have you forsaken me?" the film conveys not his despair but his numb gratification. There's the film's inadvertent reversal, the crucifixion as a triumph of sadomasochistic exploitation. That triumph seems to be what Gibson's Jesus salutes when he says finally, "It is accomplished."

It is a lie. It is sick. Jews have every reason to be offended by *The Passion of the Christ*. Even more so, if possible, do Christians.

274 | JAMES CARROLL

One Year Later

March 16, 2004

"It must be considered that there is nothing more difficult to carry out, nor more doubtful of success, nor more dangerous to handle, than to initiate a new order of things." This warning is from Niccolò Machiavelli, yet it has never had sharper resonance. More than a decade ago, after Saddam Hussein's invasion of Kuwait, George H. W. Bush explicitly sought to initiate, as he put it to Congress, a "new world order." As we noted earlier, he made that momentous declaration on September 11, 1990. Eleven years later, the suddenly mystical date of 9-11 motivated his son to finish what the father began. A year ago this week, Bush the younger launched a war against the man who tried to kill his dad, initiating the opposite of order.

The situation hardly needs rehearsing. In Iraq, many thousands are dead, including 564 Americans. Civil war threatens. Afghanistan, meanwhile, is choked by drug-running warlords. Islamic jihadists have been empowered. The nuclear profiteering of Pakistan has been exposed but not necessarily stopped. Al Qaeda's elusiveness has reinforced its mythic malevolence. The Atlantic alliance is in ruins. The United States has never been more isolated. A pattern of deception has destroyed its credibility abroad and at home. Disorder spreads from Washington to Israel to Haiti to Spain. Whether the concern is subduing resistance fighters far away or making Americans feel safer, the Pentagon's unprecedented military dominance, the costs of which stifle the U.S. economy, is shown to be essentially impotent.

In America, the new order of things is defined mainly by the sour taste of moral hangover, how the emotional intensity of the 9-11 trauma—anguished but pure—dissolved into a feeling of being trapped in a cage of our own making. As the carnage in Madrid makes clear, the threats in the world are real and dangerous to handle, but one U.S. initiative after another has escalated rather than diffused such threats. Instead of replacing chaos with new order, our nation's responses inflict new wounds that increase the chaos. We strike at those whom we perceive as aiming to do us harm, but without actually defending ourselves. And, most unsettling of all, in our attempt to get the bad people to stop threatening us, we have begun to imitate them.

The most important revelation of the Iraq war has been of the Bush administration's blatant contempt for fact. Whether defined as "lying" or not, the clear manipulation of intelligence ahead of last year's invasion has been completely exposed. The phrase "weapons of mass destruction" has been transformed. Where once it evoked the grave danger of a repeat of the 9-11 trauma, now it evokes an apparently calculated American fear. The government laid out explicit evidence defining a threat that required the launching of preventive war, and the U.S. media trumpeted that evidence without hesitation. The result, since there were no weapons of mass destruction, as the government and a pliant press had ample reason to know, was an institutionalized deceit, maintained to this day. At the United Nations, America misled the world. In speech after speech, President Bush misled the Congress and the nation. And note that the word *misled* means both to have falsified and to have failed in leadership. To mislead, as the tautological George Bush might put it, is to mislead.

The repetition of falsehoods tied to the war on terrorism and the war against Iraq has eroded the American capacity, if not to tell the difference between what is true and what is a lie, then to think the difference matters much. The administration distorted fact ahead of the invasion, when the American people could not refute what had not happened yet. And the administration distorts fact now, when the American people do not remember clearly what they were told a year ago. That President Bush retains the confidence of a sizable proportion of the electorate suggests that Americans don't particularly worry anymore about truth as a guiding principle of government.

In that lies the irony. The Bush dynasty has in fact initiated a new order of things. The United States of America has become its own opposite, a nation of triumphant freedom that claims the right to restrain the freedom of others; a nation of a structured balance of power that destroys the balance of power abroad; a nation of creative enterprise that exports a smothering banality; and, above all, a nation of forcefully direct expression that disrespects the truth. Whatever happens from this week forward in Iraq, the main outcome of the war, for the United States, is clear. We have defeated ourselves.

EPILOGUE

"This crusade, this war on terrorism." We began this two-and-a-half-year chronicle of the war on terrorism by noting its connection to the crusade launched by Pope Urban II in 1095. We end by observing that two and a half years after Pope Urban's "God Wills It!" sermon, that campaign of political violence was given its sacred justification by the most influential Christian theological treatise ever written, *Cur Deus Homo?*, published by St. Anselm in 1098. *Why Did God Become a Man?* Anselm answers the question by promulgating what came to be known as "atonement" theology, the idea, as subsequently interpreted by many Catholics and Protestants both, that the infinite offense God took at the sin of human beings could be atoned for only by an infinite act of punishment. In this understanding, God became a man, in the person of Jesus, not to preach a message of love, nor to reveal the goodness of creation, nor even to offer hope through resurrection—but expressly to die a brutal death on the cross. Jesus underwent the blood-soaked fate of the scapegoat. In this theology, it was the violence of Golgotha that saved humankind—an idea that soon became enshrined in a Christian religious imagination fixated on the crucifix, and in a piety built on "mortifications" like self-flagellation. Suffering was no longer seen as the opposite of life but the purpose of it. If a vindictive God could inflict infinite agony on God's own son, and—by their identification with him—on God's people, then crusaders could inflict it on Muslims (and on Jews, who were the ones identified by then as having crucified the Lord in the first place). With St. Anselm, the Crusades had their theological justification, and the Latin West had its ideology of sacred violence.

The St. Anselm of George W. Bush's war on terrorism, coming in an exactly equivalent period of two and a half years after the September 11 assaults, is Mel Gibson, whose film *The Passion of the Christ* is this brand of atonement theology in slow motion and with special effects. There are numerous ways to account for the movie's astounding mass appeal, not all of them edifying: the film dramatized the "us-versus-them" spirit of the Bush era, simplified complicated questions of good and evil, and put the traumatic at the center of experience. The ultimate trauma of contemporary time had been widely considered to have been the Holocaust, but *The Passion of the Christ*, in its extraordinary reach, seemed to want to remove the Holocaust as a defining point of moral reference, which is the relevance of the film's over-the-top portrayal of the Jews as villains. (That Mel Gibson's father is an outright Holocaust denier is less relevant than Gibson's own self-proclaimed status as a Holocaust minimizer.) Gibson's answer to the Holocaust is simple: *Enough already, get over it. If you want to see what real suffering is like, check out the battered, flayed Christ. And, by the way, look who caused his misery.*

At the time of the film's release, it was widely noted that Gibson had rejected the renewed Catholicism of Vatican II, especially its renunciation of the anti-Jewish "Christ-killer" myth that his film did so much to resuscitate. The subtler point is that Vatican II had decisively moved "Christology," the theology of Christ, away from Anselm's atonement schema, away from death and suffering, away from the oedipal antagonism that sets father against son in mortal conflict. We saw earlier in this chronicle how, with Vatican II, the Catholic Church deemphasized Good Friday in favor of Easter Sunday, and put the resurrection back in the center of faith, but perhaps its most relevant change was in the way the church embraced a skepticism toward war and violence that returned the religion to its earliest roots. This began with Pope John XXIII's 1963 encyclical *Pacem in Terris*, which shook American assumptions by rejecting nuclear weapons as an instrument of justice, and then in 1965 with Pope Paul VI's stirring address at the United Nations, where he explicitly denounced the nascent U.S. war in Vietnam by declaring, "No more war! War never again!"

Such a direct repudiation of the "God wills it!" tradition put the Roman Catholic Church firmly on the side of the then burgeoning peace movement, where it remains. Pope John Paul II vigorously denounced the abandonment of diplomacy and the use of violent force in the 1991 Gulf War; he opposed the NATO air war in Kosovo; and he firmly decried George W. Bush's war against Iraq. And the thing to emphasize is that these developments in Catholicism were directly tied to a moral reckoning, however overdue or incomplete, with the Holocaust.

All of this suggests how theology and politics are intermingled in what the anti–Vatican II Catholic Mel Gibson rejects. That is why his film must be discussed in the context of the contemporary resurgence of religious conflict and antisemitism both. Gibson's bloody film celebrates the violence of the Crusades then and now, making it a big-screen-icon version of George W. Bush's war. Its celebration of contempt for Jews is not incidental here, since for every victim there has to be a victimizer, and Jews have long played that role in the Western imagination. Gibson wants them back there.

But the issue goes even deeper. The United States of America, with its new doctrine of "preventive war," and its unprecedented moves to enforce a Washington-centered vision of globalism, is embarked on unprecedented military adventures. Fundamental violations of traditional American restraints, the dishonor of treaty violations, the palpably unnecessary bloodshed inevitably provoke in U.S. citizens unwanted feelings of ambivalence, fear, and, in some, even shame. That is doubly so because of the way in which our experience of the new American enterprise comes to us—through images broadcast on television. Increasingly, since Vietnam, the spectacle of the horrors of war has been part of the mundane routine of life in the United States. Americans have become spectators to the pain and suffering of victims. The experience of such witness, at a distance, in the living room, inevitably provokes feelings of disgrace in spectators—the shame of the voyeur—but there is an additional remorse if one acknowledges some responsibility for the horror one is watching.

The unrelenting, if simultaneously detached, confrontation with the anguish of strangers took on a new meaning when the spectacle of misery finally involved our nation, too. The trauma was twofold. There were those airplanes smashing into the Twin Towers, and then there were the endlessly repeated television images of mass destruction. *Our* destruction. It was horrible, yes. But wasn't there also some secret element of relief, finally to be a victim as well as a voyeur? Why else were we hypnotized by that replay?

The American feeling of victimhood, tied to 9-11 and dramatized now for voyeurs and spectators in Mel Gibson's Jesus, in some strange way perhaps restored an American sense of virtue. Instead of feeling guilty about the still unadjudicated American terror bombing of German, Japanese, and Vietnamese cities, we feel some kind of absolution in having been terror-bombed ourselves. Instead of worrying about "enemy combatants" being held against Geneva norms and routinely mistreated by GIs in Guantánamo Bay—or, by extension, worrying about the globe's impoverished throng of nobodies being mistreated by a made-in-America market economy— this nation's moviegoers, whether Christian or not, can at last identify with the mistreated Jesus. By becoming spectators at the spectacle of Jesus' agony, we are purged of the shame that we might otherwise feel at our nation's problematic new status as the superpower that claims the right to remake the world. We are voyeurs, perhaps, but we are not villains.

Bush and Gibson share a psychological horizon as well. Both are self-described "recoverers," whose victories over youthful debaucheries were enabled by Jesus Christ, but these are not men, apparently, who underwent such transformation in the company of others, as is true of participants in the various twelve-step programs. Instead of their acknowledged flaws putting them in touch with the human condition shared by all—the roomful of broken strangers meeting in the church basement—Bush and Gibson have been converted as solitary individuals in direct communion with their savior.

A profoundly American strain of individualism is on display here, and it celebrates not "grace" mediated by a community, but willpower exercised alone. Jesus Christ is George W. Bush's favorite political philosopher because, as he said, "Christ changed my heart." The president and the moviemaker understand themselves as having been rescued from a nether zone of decadence, and now nothing less than moral purification will do—for themselves and for the world. And if purification comes through a stoic exercise of will—well, that's how it was with them. And with Jesus. This is the mindset that sees evil outside the self. In the devil. In the hated other. The destruction of such evil is the end that justifies the means.

A book of essays about war might not have been expected to conclude with such overtly religious reflections, but one of the conclusions to which these essays inexorably point is that the war on which America has embarked is essentially religious. A year after the war in Iraq began, that had become all too evident. There is no understanding the phenomenal American response to *The Passion of the Christ* apart from an unarticulated but broad cultural anguish tied to the war into which George W. Bush had taken the nation.

Wars, that is, do not unfold apart from underlying social assumptions, and while the United States traditionally understands itself in secular terms, as a polity arising from an Enlightenment-era rejection of the irrationalities that led to sectarian strife, George W. Bush has tapped a deeply religious vein in the American psyche. The Manichaeism of the Puritans, the murderous self-righteousness of Indian killers, the Truman Doctrine's assumption of a bipolar division between global forces of light and dark, Ronald Reagan's easy characterization of an "evil empire"—again and again a simplistic vision imposes itself on a complex world. What makes the Bush era different is that, owing to America's overwhelming military preeminence, the complex world can do little directly to temper the power of such imposition, or to challenge its hubris. And when such military dominance is combined with a near mystical conviction of moral license, you have to ask: where will this lead?

In order to more fully understand the implications of the Bush crusade, one might consider what followed from the Crusades themselves. Those religious wars—recall that seven or eight of them were launched from the late eleventh to the early thirteenth centuries—established the first central political authority in Europe since the Roman empire, only now that authority belonged to the one who sponsored the wars—the pope. The absolute spiritual and even political claims of the papacy—"No salvation outside the Church"—came directly out of the Crusades. As George W. Bush declared, "You're either with us or against us," the first warrior pope, Gregory VII, said, "Anyone who is not in accord with the Roman Church should not be regarded as a Catholic."

At a more mundane level, the Crusades, mobilizing huge populations throughout Europe, required new and overarching systems of social control, like effective conscription and a tightening of the lines of feudal authority. These innovations involved burdens to which all classes submitted in large part because of the public psychosis of crusading fervor. But fervor was not enough. Privileges were extended to crusaders, ranging from promised spiritual "indulgences" in the afterlife to worldly rewards like canceled debts and freedom from taxes and tolls.

Bush's crusade proved to be the occasion for equivalent extensions of claims to power, from the USA Patriot Act at home to the further militarization of America's global reach abroad, even into what the Pentagon dubbed the "high frontier" of space. "Indulgence" is just the word to define the Bush administration's system of rewards for its partners, whether war profiteers like Halliburton or the culture warriors of the religious right. Meanwhile, the better term for the Bush illusion that the extraordinary expenditures of war required no new taxes might be *self*-indulgence.

The Crusades are remembered in Europe and America as episodes of high romance, and historians emphasize all the good that the Crusades brought to "Christendom"—the new structures of economy, the jelling of political systems, the seeding of the West with technologies of the East, and innovative cultural ideals from martial monasticism to courtly love. But in actuality the Crusades both sparked and reflected two hundred years of social disorder, and one need not be a Muslim to see it that way. As the twenty-first century picks up steam, great forces of religiously inspired violence have been loosed upon the world, not all of them Islamic. From the point of view of a nation whose leader has, even if inadvertently, embraced "crusade" as a defining metaphor, perhaps the most relevant fact about the Crusades is that, on their own terms and notwithstanding the romance of history, they were, in the end, an overwhelming failure. The 1096 campaign, the "First Crusade," finally "succeeded" in 1099, when a remnant army fell upon Jerusalem, slaughtering much of its population. But armies under Saladin reasserted Islamic control in 1187, and subsequent Crusades never succeeded in reestablishing Latin dominance in the Holy Land. The *reconquista* Crusades reclaimed Spain and Portugal for Christian Europe, but in the process destroyed the glorious Iberian *convivencia*, a high civilization never to be matched below the Pyrenees again.

Meanwhile, intra-Christian Crusades, wars against heresy, only made permanent the East-West split between Latin Catholicism and "schismatic" Eastern Orthodoxy, and made inevitable the eventual break, in the Reformation, between a Protestant north and a Catholic south. The Crusades, one could argue, established basic structures of Western civilization, while undermining the possibility that its grandest ideals would ever be realized.

Will such consequences—new global structures of an American *imperium*, hollowed-out hopes for a humane and just internationalism—follow in the train of George W. Bush's crusade? This question will be answered in smaller part by anonymous, ad hoc armies of on-the-ground human beings in foreign lands, many of whom will resist Washington to the death. In larger part, the question will be answered by those privileged to be citizens of the United States. To us falls the ultimate power over the American moral and political agenda. As has never been true of any empire before, because this one is still a democracy, such power belongs to citizens absolutely. If the power is ours, so is the responsibility.

ACKNOWLEDGMENTS

These essays appeared as columns in the *Boston Globe*. I gratefully acknowledge my editors there, Renée Loth, Robert Turner, Marjorie Pritchard, Steve Morgan, Robert Hardman, Peter Accardi, and Glenda Buell. With their support, I discovered what I wanted to say. For much of the period covered in this chronicle, I was chair of the Visiting Scholars Center at the American Academy of Arts and Sciences, and colleagues there helped me in many ways. Thanks to Leslie Berlowitz, Martin Malin, Leigh Nolan, Sheri Landry, Alexandra Oleson, Deborah Bender, Beth McLean, James Miller, Phyllis Bendell, Mark Kagen, Elaine Potter, and Brendan Lewis. Thanks also to the visiting scholars: Joseph Entin, Jay Grossman, Andrew Jewett, David Greenberg, Page Fortna, Eric Bettinger, Ann Mikkelsen, Eileen Babbit, Robert Chodat, Crystal Feimster, Jonathan Hansen, Matthew Lindsay, Jerrold Meinwald, Charlotte Greenspan, and Adam Webb.

Tom Engelhardt first proposed the idea of gathering these essays into a book. He enabled that to happen, and offered sharp editorial guidance along the way. It was he who helped me see the value of this commentary as a chronicle of an important period in America's life. Through his own work as writer and editor of the influential Internet site www.tomdispatch.com, Tom provides inspiration and prophetic insight, and I am proud to have this work of mine stand with his.

I am grateful to Sara Bershtel of Metropolitan Books, and to John Sterling of Holt, each of whom has brought her and his publishing power to bear on the important questions raised in this book. And I acknowledge the Metropolitan Books editors and staff who brought it to readers.

And thanks always to my colleagues Wendy Strothman and Don Cutler, and, especially, to my beloved wife, Alexandra Marshall, and to our daughter, Elizabeth, and son, Patrick.

I have dedicated this book, in love, to William Sloane Coffin Jr., who taught me the first lessons of peace.

ABOUT THE AUTHOR

JAMES CARROLL, a columnist for the *Boston Globe*, is the best-selling author of the National Book Award–winning memoir *An American Requiem* and *Constantine's Sword*, a history of Christian antisemitism. He has also written ten novels, most recently *Secret Father*. He lectures widely on war and peace and on Jewish-Christian-Muslim reconciliation.

The American Empire Project

In an era of unprecedented military strength, leaders of the United States, the global hyperpower, have increasingly embraced imperial ambitions. How did this significant shift in purpose and policy come about? And what lies down the road?

The American Empire Project is a response to the changes that have occurred in America's strategic thinking as well as in its military and economic posture. Empire, long considered an offense against America's democratic heritage, now threatens to define the relationship between our country and the rest of the world. The American Empire Project publishes books that question this development, examine the origins of U.S. imperial aspirations, analyze their ramifications at home and abroad, and discuss alternatives to this dangerous trend.

The project was conceived by Tom Engelhardt and Steve Fraser, editors who are themselves historians and writers. Published by Metropolitan Books, an imprint of Henry Holt and Company, its debut volumes were *Hegemony or Survival* by Noam Chomsky, *The Sorrows of Empire* by Chalmers Johnson, and *How to Succeed at Globalization* by El Fisgón.

For more information about the American Empire Project and for a list of forthcoming titles, please visit www.americanempireproject.com.

ERIC CARLE
The Tiny Seed

LITTLE SIMON

New York London Toronto Sydney New Delhi

It is Autumn.

A strong wind is blowing. It blows flower seeds high in the air and carries them far across the land. One of the seeds is tiny, smaller than any of the others. Will it be able to keep up with the others? And where are they all going?

One of the seeds flies higher than the others. Up, up it goes! It flies too high and the sun's hot rays burn it up. But the tiny seed sails on with the others.

Another seed lands on a tall and icy mountain. The ice never melts, and the seed cannot grow. The rest of the seeds fly on. But the tiny seed does not go as fast as the others.

Now they fly over the ocean. One seed falls into the water and drowns. The others sail on with the wind. But the tiny seed does not go as high as the others.

One seed drifts down onto the desert.
It is hot and dry, and the seed cannot grow.
Now the tiny seed is flying very low,
but the wind pushes it on with the others.

Finally the wind stops and the seeds fall gently down on the ground. A bird comes by and eats one seed. The tiny seed is not eaten. It is so small that the bird does not see it.

Now it is Winter.
After their long trip the seeds settle down.
They look just as if they are going to sleep in
the earth. Snow falls and covers them like a
soft white blanket. A hungry mouse that also
lives in the ground eats a seed for his lunch.
But the tiny seed lies very still and the mouse
does not see it.

Now it is Spring.
After a few months the snow has melted. It is
really spring! Birds fly by. The sun shines. Rain fall
The seeds grow so round and full they start to
burst open a little. Now they are not seeds any
more. They are plants. First they send roots down
into the earth. Then their little stems and leaves
begin to grow up toward the sun and air. There is
another plant that grows much faster than the
new little plants. It is a big fat weed. And it takes
all the sunlight and the rain away from one of
the small new plants. And that little plant dies.

The tiny seed hasn't begun to grow yet.
It will be too late! Hurry! But finally it too
starts to grow into a plant.

The warm weather also brings the children out to play. They too have been waiting for the sun and spring time. One child doesn't see the plants as he runs along and —Oh! He breaks one! Now it cannot grow any more.

The tiny plant that grew from the tiny seed is growing fast, but its neighbor grows even faster. Before the tiny plant has three leaves the other plant has seven! And look! A bud! And now even a flower!

But what is happening? First there are footsteps.
Then a shadow looms over them. Then a
hand reaches down and breaks off the flower.

A boy has picked the flower to give to a friend.

It is Summer.
Now the tiny plant from the tiny seed is all alone
It grows on and on. It doesn't stop. The sun shin
on it and the rain waters it. It has many leaves.
It grows taller and taller. It is taller than the peo
It is taller than the trees. It is taller than the
houses. And now a flower grows on it. People
come from far and near to look at this
flower. It is the tallest flower they have
ever seen. It is a giant flower.

All summer long the birds and bees and butterfli
come visiting. They have never seen such a big a
beautiful flower.

Now it is Autumn again.
The days grow shorter. The nights grow cooler.
And the wind carries yellow and red leaves past
the flower. Some petals drop from the giant
flower and they sail along with the bright leaves
over the land and down to the ground.

The wind blows harder. The flower has lost almost all of its petals. It sways and bends away from the wind. But the wind grows stronger and shakes the flower. Once more the wind shakes the flower, and this time the flower's seed pod opens. Out come many tiny seeds that quickly sail far away on the wind.

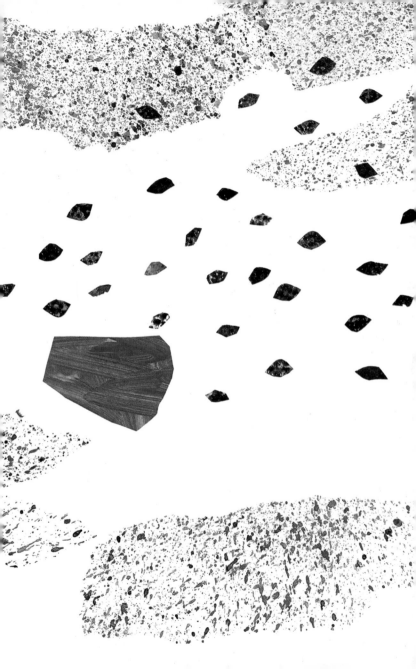